Morning Star Dawn

Campaigns and Commanders

Morning Star Dawn

*The Powder River Expedition
and the
Northern Cheyennes, 1876*

Jerome A. Greene

University of Oklahoma Press : Norman

Also by Jerome A. Greene

Evidence and the Custer Enigma: A Reconstruction of Indian-Military History (Kansas City, 1973)

Slim Buttes, 1876: An Episode of the Great Sioux War (Norman, 1982)

Yellowstone Command: Colonel Nelson A. Miles and the Great Sioux War, 1876–1877 (Lincoln, 1991)

Battles and Skirmishes of the Great Sioux War, 1876–1877: The Military View (Norman, 1993)

Lakota and Cheyenne: Indian Views of the Great Sioux War, 1876–1877 (Norman, 1994)

Frontier Soldier: An Enlisted Man's Journal of the Sioux and Nez Perce Campaigns, 1877 (Helena, 1998)

Nez Perce Summer, 1877: The U.S. Army and the Nee-Me-Poo Crisis (Helena, 2000)

Morning Star Dawn: The Powder River Expedition and the Northern Cheyennes, 1876 is volume 2 in the Campaigns and Commanders series.

Published with the assistance of the National Endowment for the Humanities, a federal agency which supports the study of such fields as history, philosophy, literature, and language.

Library of Congress Cataloging-in-Publication Data

Greene, Jerome A.
    Morning Star dawn : the Powder River expedition and the Northern Cheyennes, 1876 / Jerome A. Greene.
        p.   cm. — (Campaigns and commanders ; 2)
    Includes bibliographical references and index.
    ISBN 0-8061-3548-4 (hc : alk. paper)
        1. Dull Knife Battle, Wyo., 1876.   2. Cheyenne Indians—Wars, 1876.
3. Mackenzie, Ranald Slidell, 1840–1889.   4. United States. Army.
Cavalry, 4th.   I. Title.   II. Series.

E83.866.G74 2003
973.8'2—dc21

                                                                        2002045598

1   2   3   4   5   6   7   8   9   10

To the Crazy Dogs,
and to the Memory of
Last Bear (Luke John Brady), 1963–2002

Contents

Illustrations

Maps

Preface and Acknowledgments

THE DULL KNIFE BATTLEFIELD lies on private land about eighteen miles west of the modern community of Kaycee, Wyoming. The expanse traces a high-walled canyon containing part of the Red Fork of Powder River. It encompasses the site of a major encounter during the U.S. Army's campaign against the Teton Sioux (Lakota) and Northern Cheyenne Indians in 1876 that was key in forcing events culminating in the tribesmen's surrender at the agencies in Dakota Territory and Nebraska in the spring of 1877. (These tribes had participated in the destruction of Lieutenant Colonel George A. Custer's Seventh Cavalry command at the Little Bighorn River in Montana the preceding June.) Operating under orders from Brigadier General George Crook, commanding the Department of the Platte, Colonel Ranald S. Mackenzie struck the large Cheyenne village of Chiefs Morning Star (Dull Knife) and Little Wolf on the canyon floor at dawn in late November, charging in from the east with eleven hundred men (including Indian scouts) and driving the occupants from their lodges as they sought refuge behind ridges and hills. Most of the rest of the engagement consisted of a fight for control of the village and its contents as well as a large pony herd. The attack on the encampment and its subsequent destruction not only compelled the Cheyennes' eventual surrender but also influenced many of their Lakota compatriots, including the war leader Crazy Horse, to do likewise.

Almost seventy-two years later, on a summer day in 1948, area residents gathered on the windswept tract to dedicate a simple monument sponsored by the local chapter of the Daughters of the American Revolution. T. J. Gatchell, a prominent Buffalo, Wyoming, entrepreneur with deep ties to the history of the area, spoke about the Dull Knife engagement, one of several retaliatory strikes by the army that followed Custer's defeat. The weathered stone, still in its original location, reads:

> *Here Nov. 25, 1876*
> *Gen. R. S. Mackenzie*
> *With U.S. forces*
> *Composed of*
> *Detachments of the*
> *2nd, 3rd, 4th, 5th*
> *Cavalry, 4th and 9th*
> *Artillery, 9th, 23d*
> *Infantry defeated*
> *The Cheyennes under*
> *Dull Knife.*
> *Lieut. McKinney and*
> *Six soldiers were*
> *Killed in battle.*

The marker is not altogether correct with respect to the units that were present; it was purely a cavalry operation (although the Second Cavalry was not present), with no infantry or artillery taking part (the Ninth Artillery did not exist in 1876). The foot troops, including those of the Fourth Artillery, who were campaigning as infantrymen, were miles away when Mackenzie attacked the Cheyennes. And there is no mention of the more than three hundred Indian scouts who fought alongside the troops. But the gist of the message is accurate. The Cheyennes were defeated and their village destroyed.

The marker overlooks a historical scene that is largely undisturbed in its principal elements—the bluffs, ridges, hillocks, ravines, and draws that played important roles in the progress of the conflict. These include the area of Mackenzie's advance through the east end of the canyon; the deep ravine running north-south from which the Cheyenne warriors stopped a critical cavalry charge; the bluff tops on the south of the field from which the army's Shoshone scouts leveled devastating gunfire into the village; the red butte at the edge of the field behind which the troops established their field hospital; the Red Fork stream itself, along which stood the imposing village of 173 buffalo hide lodges; and the recesses in the western part of the canyon where rock breastworks were raised by the Cheyennes to help cover the withdrawal of noncombatants. Modern development consists of the landowner's ranch and outbuildings along with dirt roads, fence lines, and irrigation ditches, most of which are located in the western part of the site and scarcely detract from its largely pristine appearance. The Red Fork land encloses the scene of one of the most significant encounters of the Great Sioux War of 1876–77 as well as one of the most important in the annals of all the western army–Indian conflicts. It is a compelling story in itself as well as in its significance for both the army and the Northern Cheyennes. As such, it deserves attention.

Mackenzie's attack on the Cheyennes was the most consequential aspect of the army's Powder River Expedition, headed by General Crook. Herein, the story of the expedition and the assault is played out against a thematic backdrop of national expansion grounded in economic and political objectives. National expansion embraced colonization, necessitating the conquest, control, subordination, consolidation, and relocation of Indian tribes whose presence barred the way—an elementary part of the country's attempt to advance and control its boundaries and internal resources. The treaty system, in which tribes were viewed as domestic entities within the boundaries of the United States, afforded means of removing Indians from lands that white people wanted to use. Army campaigns—such as Crook's in 1876—provided the punitive means to fulfill the process of conquest. Tribal resistance was based in concepts of homeland that reflected spiritual relationships with the land, a conviction white Americans of the day could not comprehend. The resulting warfare wrought destruction of material resources in homes and property. Even more damaging was the trauma inflicted within tribal social and political patterns, reaching deep into band and family units and ripping at cultural fabric to threaten tribal existence. As a result of the campaigns, many Indian tribes were changed forever. What the Northern Cheyennes experienced in November 1876 as a result of their involvement in the Great Sioux War proved only the beginning of a series of ramifications that would permeate their society for all time.

Various people and institutions have aided in this work, and I extend my appreciation to the following persons for their contributions. I especially want to thank Ken and Cheri Graves, Red Fork Ranch, Barnum, Wyoming, who own much of the historic site and who graciously supported my visitations and furnished information about the landscape. Others who contributed by providing documentary information or good counsel include Thomas R. Buecker, Fort Robinson Museum, Crawford, Nebraska; Paul Fees, Cody, Wyoming; Douglas C. McChristian, National Park Service, Sierra Vista, Arizona; John D. McDermott, Rapid City, South Dakota; the late Don G. Rickey, Evergreen, Colorado; R. Eli Paul, Overland Park, Kansas; Paul A. Hutton, University of New Mexico, Albuquerque; James Potter, Nebraska State Historical Society, Lincoln; Douglas D. Scott, National Park Service, Lincoln, Nebraska; Neil C. Mangum,

Chiricahua National Monument, Arizona; John A. Doerner and Kitty B. Deernose, Little Bighorn Battlefield National Monument, Crow Agency, Montana; B. J. Earle, Bureau of Land Management, Buffalo, Wyoming; Wayne R. Kime, Fairmount State College, Fairmount, West Virginia; Gene Galloway, Council Bluffs, Iowa; L. Clifford Soubier, Charles Town, West Virginia; Michael T. Meier, Michael P. Musick, and Michael E. Pilgrim, National Archives, Washington, D.C.; Richard J. Sommers, David Keough, Pamela Cheney, and John Slonaker, U.S. Army Military History Institute, Carlisle, Pennsylvania; Ben F. ("Colonel Absaraka Ben") Irvin, Pocatello, Idaho; Scott Forsyth, Great Lakes Branch, National Archives, Chicago; Robert Wooster, Corpus Christi State University, Texas; Richard W. Dorst, Atherton, California; Gary L. Roberts, Tipton, Georgia; David Hays, Western History Collection, University of Colorado at Boulder Libraries; David F. Halaas, Museum of Western Pennsylvania, Pittsburgh; Michael Wagner, Braun Research Library, Southwest Museum, Los Angeles; Robert M. Utley, Georgetown, Texas; William Y. Chalfant, Hutchinson, Kansas; Robert Pilk, National Park Service, Denver; Lisa R. Hinzman, Wisconsin Historical Society, Madison; Margot Liberty, Sheridan, Wyoming; Ken R. Stewart, South Dakota State Historical Society, Pierre; Gordon S. Chappell, National Park Service, Oakland, California; and Dick Harmon, Lincoln, Nebraska. Special thanks go to Father Peter J. Powell, St. Augustine's Center for American Indians, Inc., Chicago, for his help in the final preparation of the manuscript.

I must also thank the staffs of the following repositories and institutions who provided information on my behalf: Wyoming State Archives and Historical Department, Cheyenne; National Archives, Washington, D.C.; Library of Congress, Washington, D.C.; Western History Department, Denver Public Library; Archives and Manuscripts Division, Harold B. Lee Library,

Brigham Young University, Provo, Utah; Dull Knife Memorial College, Lame Deer, Montana; the Nebraska State Historical Society, Lincoln; the State Historical Society of North Dakota, Bismarck; U.S. Army Military History Institute, Carlisle, Pennsylvania; the Newberry Library, Chicago; the Great Lakes Branch, National Archives, Chicago; Arizona Historical Society, Tucson; The Gilcrease Institute, Tulsa, Oklahoma; and the U.S. Military Academy Library, West Point, New York.

Last, I warmly thank my battlefield compadre Paul L. Hedren for his help and encouragement during the many years that this study has been under way. Paul's sage advice and sound conclusions infuse the work, and for that it is a better book, indeed.

Morning Star Dawn

Region of closing operations of the Great Sioux War, late 1876

Chapter 1
Preliminaries

ON A MID-SEPTEMBER DAY IN 1876, a column of more than two thousand battle-weary U.S. soldiers pulled up along the banks of the Belle Fourche River in what is now western South Dakota. There they were met by a civilian-operated wagon train bearing foodstuffs from the nearby Black Hills mining communities of Deadwood and Crook City. The nearly starved soldiers, who had subsisted over recent days on the flesh of their own cavalry horses, killed after rations ran out, now fought over such prized niceties as bread, butter, and fresh potatoes brought by the caravan. This impromptu celebratory feast served as a reward for the men's hard labor during the centennial summer's Great Sioux War, a wide-ranging conflict between the army and the Lakota Sioux and Northern Cheyenne Indians that until recently had proved an abject embarrassment for the army. Only days before at Slim Buttes, seventy miles north of the Belle Fourche, these troops had registered the first substantive victory over the Indians, thereby reversing a string of previous defeats that had sapped them psychologically and physically.

The Great Sioux War was the largest military operation to that time since the close of the Civil War in 1865. It involved the federal government's prosecution of the Lakotas, a large tribe of around thirty-five thousand people, of whom perhaps a third had long refused to subscribe to provisions of the treaties negotiated between their relatives and federal representatives by placing themselves under government control on a reserve

3

in western Dakota Territory. The Lakota tribe consisted of seven bands, or subtribes, embracing the Hunkpapas, Oglalas, Minneconjous, Brulés, Two Kettles, Blackfeet Sioux, and Sans Arcs. Decades earlier, they along with the Cheyennes had migrated west into the areas of the Black Hills and lower Yellowstone River, where they competed for game resources, primarily the immense moving buffalo herds, and conflicted with native groups already established there. More recently, they posed a threat for settlers and entrepreneurs, notably those with railroad interests, who were in the process of making commercial inroads into the Yellowstone Valley. Gold discoveries in the Black Hills, on the very reservation lands assigned to the Sioux in the Fort Laramie Treaty of 1868, ultimately provoked a rush by white miners into that region in 1874 and promoted efforts by the government to purchase the coveted property. Determined to finally clear the Yellowstone country of those Indians who threatened this regional enterprise while simultaneously pressuring those on the reservation to give up the Black Hills, federal authorities laid the basis for a military campaign designed to at once compel and intimidate all of the Lakotas and their allies.[1]

The northern plains region inhabited by the tribes and thus targeted by civilian and military authorities late in 1875 encompassed parts of Wyoming, Montana, and Dakota Territories. Administratively, this country composed part of the broad Military Division of the Missouri, headquartered at Chicago under command of Lieutenant General Philip H. Sheridan, former cavalry mastermind of the Army of the Potomac during the Civil War. Bureaucratic subdivisions under Sheridan included the Department of Dakota, commanded at St. Paul, Minnesota, by Brigadier General Alfred H. Terry, and the Department of the Platte, under Brigadier General George Crook, headquartered at Omaha, Nebraska. Of the six agencies established to supervise the Indians on the Great Sioux Reservation east and southeast

of the war zone, four—Standing Rock, Cheyenne River, Crow
Creek, and Lower Brulé—stood along the Missouri River and
two—Red Cloud and Spotted Tail Agencies—lay in northwestern Nebraska, actually outside the reservation boundary.[2]

The soldiers initially sent to prosecute the Indians—mostly
followers of the Hunkpapa Lakota leader Sitting Bull, of the
Oglala Lakota leader Crazy Horse, and of lesser-known chiefs of
smaller bands—belonged to Crook, one of the army's premier
Indian-fighting officers. Crook's offensive had begun in March
1876 when a column of troops under his command struck a
wintering band of Indians along the Powder River in southeastern Montana Territory. The soldiers routed the camp,
believed to contain Teton Sioux, and captured large numbers
of their ponies, but the officer in direct charge, Colonel Joseph
J. Reynolds, allowed the warriors to regain the offensive and
retake most of the animals. Reynolds, subsequently court-
martialed for his performance, also destroyed the provisions in
the camp on which Crook had planned to subsist his force,
necessitating the column's early return to its base at Fort Fetterman, Wyoming. Moreover, and significant for the course of
future events, Reynolds's men had charged a village of Northern Cheyennes, cultural relatives of the Lakotas, the effect of
which was to enhance the Sioux-Cheyenne military alliance, a
development that would complicate the work of the army in the
months ahead.[3]

Crook's failed initiative had the result of further solidify-
ing the so-called renegade elements of the Sioux and Northern
Cheyennes in their intent to avoid going to, or returning to, the
reservation agencies. In May 1876 the army redoubled its efforts,
sending three large columns of soldiers into the eastern Montana lands occupied by the Indians. The plan called for loosely
coordinated movements that would bring about the tribesmen's
subjection. On June 17 Crook's column, again moving north from

Fort Fetterman, was boldly attacked by Sioux and Cheyenne warriors, and following a day-long battle in southeastern Montana along the headwaters of Rosebud Creek, the general withdrew his command to await reinforcements. Meantime, the other two columns, one from Fort Abraham Lincoln, Dakota, and the other from Forts Ellis and Shaw, Montana, headed respectively by General Terry and Colonel John Gibbon, commander of the District of Western Montana in Terry's department, proceeded to meet. Unaware of Crook's defeat, Terry and Gibbon developed plans to surround a village reported to be located below the Yellowstone along the Little Bighorn River. On June 25 a command of the Seventh Cavalry under Lieutenant Colonel George A. Custer found and attacked this village, estimated to contain as many as eight thousand people, including perhaps as many as fifteen hundred warriors. Over the course of several hours, the warriors destroyed Custer's battalion and forced the remainder of his regiment to seek refuge on bluffs above the river until the Indians finally withdrew because of the advance of Terry and Gibbon.[4]

The Battle of the Little Bighorn was the climactic event of the Great Sioux War; thereafter the army directed its efforts to catch and punish the tribesmen who had participated in that action. Over subsequent weeks Crook, Terry, and Gibbon, bolstered by reinforcements, fruitlessly combed the country of the Powder, Tongue, and Yellowstone Rivers trying to find the now-scattered elements of the immense Sioux-Cheyenne coalition. Only one skirmish of consequence occurred, far removed from the war zone, when a cavalry command under Colonel Wesley Merritt, en route to join Crook, encountered a band of Northern Cheyennes in northwestern Nebraska bound for the north country and drove them back to their agency. Finally, Terry and Gibbon withdrew their forces from the field. Crook, however, continued his pursuit east into Dakota Territory. After marching his weakened troops through enervating rain and lightning storms that turned the earth into a quagmire—and directing them to eat cavalry horseflesh after rations ran out—Crook sent an advance force south to gather food from the Black Hills mining settlements. On September 9 this column of 150 men of the Third Cavalry headed by Captain Anson Mills found and charged a mixed Sioux-Cheyenne encampment at Slim Buttes, driving out the occupants and securing the village until the main column arrived in time to help repel an aggressive counterattack by the warriors. Of all the fighting to date in 1876, only the Slim Buttes contest, which coincidently occurred within the boundaries of the Great Sioux Reservation, afforded the army a clear victory over a body of tribesmen suspected of having taken part in Custer's defeat. As was typical in such encounters, the troops burned the village and its contents both to ensure that they would never be used again and to deliver a strong message to the Indians respecting their long-term prospects for survival in choosing to remain away from the agencies.[5]

The Battle of Slim Buttes thus marked a turning point in army fortunes during the Great Sioux War. It also coincided with a marked change in strategy among the army hierarchy for dealing with the Lakotas and Northern Cheyennes. With congressional approval, Lieutenant General Sheridan, who oversaw direction of the field operations, pressed a long-advocated course of action that was readily endorsed by General William T. Sherman, the U.S. Army's commander. To that end, in late July the Interior Department yielded its civilian administration of the affected agencies to military authorities. Averse to further wide-scale army campaigning to curb the tribesmen, and in order to prevent further elements of the agency Indians from arbitrarily leaving the reservation to augment their kin yet afield, Sheridan directed that troops in Dakota and Nebraska enter the agencies and disarm and dismount all warriors. Under the plan army officers would replace civilian authorities at the affected agencies.[6] Concurrently, to notify the followers of Sitting Bull and Crazy Horse that their further free movement through the Yellowstone-Powder River hinterland would not be tolerated, Sheridan directed that a contingent of troops be stationed permanently in their midst through the winter of 1876–77. Colonel Nelson A. Miles and troops of the Fifth and Twenty-second Infantry Regiments in response occupied a point at the confluence of Tongue River with the Yellowstone and began building a large cantonment from which they would monitor the activities of the Sioux and Cheyennes.[7]

So critical did Sheridan regard the newly implemented policy for subjugating the Indians that in September he ventured west from his Chicago headquarters to meet with Crook and relate his views of how matters should proceed. Arriving at Fort Laramie on September 16, just one week after the Slim Buttes encounter, the general and his staff had to wait five days for Crook and his retinue en route from the Black Hills. Also greeting Crook on September 21 at the post was Colonel Ranald S. Mackenzie, Fourth Cavalry, whose regiment had been summoned from Texas and the Indian Territory (modern Oklahoma) in the wake of the Little Bighorn disaster to help effect the dismounting and disarmament at the Red Cloud and Spotted Tail Agencies. The meeting of Sheridan, Crook, and Mackenzie at Fort Laramie on September 21–22 set the course of future operations to end the Sioux war. It was the first face-to-face meeting between Crook and Sheridan since before campaigning had begun in March, and it allowed Crook to learn firsthand the specifics of Sheridan's disarming and dismounting policy as it affected the agency Indians. He learned that men of the reconstituted Seventh Cavalry would begin the program at the agencies along the Missouri River and that Mackenzie would undertake to do the same at the Red Cloud and Spotted

Tail Agencies in Nebraska. Furthermore, warriors coming into the agencies after traveling with the "hostiles" through the summer were to be immediately disarmed and dismounted. With hope for instilling rudiments of husbandry among the Indians, all ponies taken in the operation were to be sold, with the proceeds used to purchase cattle for them.

Crook also learned further particulars of the general's plan to place strong garrisons of troops in the heart of the country occupied by the nonagency people of Sitting Bull and Crazy Horse. Notably, besides the cantonment underway for the Yellowstone country in Montana, another was specified for the area between the Black Hills and the Big Horn Mountains in Wyoming. Regarding future field operations, it was Sheridan's belief that a focused and tightly managed fall campaign, occurring in conjunction with Colonel Miles's occupation of the Yellowstone region, would finally promote disintegration of the Sioux-Cheyenne coalition and yield large-scale surrenders at the agencies. Crook would organize such a movement, which would include the major involvement of Mackenzie and his command. Soon after the council concluded, Crook directed Captain Edwin Pollock of Company E, Ninth Infantry, to prepare to move to the site of Old Fort Reno, near Powder River in east-central Wyoming Territory and abandoned since 1868, and to begin work establishing the cantonment Sheridan had called for west of the Black Hills. The lieutenant general departed Fort Laramie for Chicago on September 23, leaving Crook and Mackenzie to devise a course of action in the southern zone of operations that would implement his design.[8]

Meantime, as the Sheridan-Crook meeting proceeded at Fort Laramie, civilian authorities labored elsewhere to complement the military movements by stripping the Indians of the gold-rich Black Hills and the so-called unceded lands in the Yellowstone country. In August, as the army commands still reeled from the successive losses at the hands of the Sioux and Northern Cheyennes, Congress, determined now to open the disputed country while punishing the tribesmen for their transgressions, passed legislation withholding funds for feeding the agency people until they yielded the tracts and permitted roads through the reservation lands to the Black Hills. In addition to signing this measure, President Ulysses S. Grant suggested that the Indians be moved south to Indian Territory; he appointed a seven-man commission to deliver this news to the Indians and to solicit their approval.

Headed by former Commissioner of Indian Affairs George W. Manypenny, the party reached Red Cloud Agency, the first stop on their tour of coercion, on September 7, just two days before Crook's troops scored the army's first major victory at Slim Buttes. Whether or not that encounter influenced the successful outcome of the commissioners' solicitation of signatures of concurrence from the Red Cloud people, the threat of starvation succeeded, and on September 20 twenty-nine Oglalas, five Cheyennes, and six Arapahoes touched pen to the agreement giving up the treaty land. Although they swore they would never move south, the Sioux leaders agreed to send a delegation to examine the country. The specter of starving families had similar effects at the other agencies, and by late October the chiefs at Spotted Tail, Standing Rock, Cheyenne River, Crow Creek, and Lower Brulé had succumbed to the pressure. At each agency the commissioners heard complaints about earlier government promises that had gone unfulfilled. "At times they told their story of wrongs with such impassioned earnestness that our cheeks crimsoned with shame," wrote Manypenny.[9] Despite this, the commissioners repeatedly warranted the Indians' rights to their individual property, presumably including their ponies. The agreement also ignored the proviso of the Fort Laramie Treaty of 1868 stipulating that future changes in that accord be approved by three-fourths of the adult males residing on the reservation. In this manner the Indians lost forever the Black Hills and the unceded hunting grounds in the Powder River–Yellowstone River hinterland.[10]

The Sioux commissioners had been at the Red Cloud Agency, near Camp Robinson, when Crook and his entourage passed through the post en route to his meeting with Sheridan. In Crook's absence Colonel Wesley Merritt led the troops of the Big Horn and Yellowstone Expedition at a leisurely pace through the Black Hills, a movement designed not only to ease the rigors of the campaign for the men but also to gain intelligence of the presence of Indians in the vicinity and of their passage to the agencies. On September 19 the soldiers departed Crook City in the northern hills. In the course of the next four days, they passed through Deadwood to Box Elder Creek, where supplies from Red Cloud reached them; on to Rapid City, where beef cattle and forage from Fort Laramie met them; and on next to Custer City in the southern Black Hills, where more supplies from Camp Robinson greeted them. Although desertions increased while in the vicinity of the gold fields, Merritt kept the command bivouacked to allow them to regain their strength. Several hundred recruits arrived, even though active campaigning for the present was over. From October 13 to 20, the colonel led a scouting force to the south fork of the Cheyenne River but reported only old trails, all headed toward Red Cloud and Spotted Tail Agencies. "If Indians have left the Agencies for the north in the last month," Merritt concluded, "it must be by trails to the westward of the Black Hills." The command continued south to Camp Robinson, where on October 24 Crook met them and formally concluded his summer campaign.[11]

Because of its proximity to the Red Cloud and Spotted Tail Agencies (reservation seats, respectively, for the Oglala and Brulé Lakotas who resided on the Great Sioux Reservation),

Camp Robinson had assumed a major presence as events unfolded during the Great Sioux War and would continue to do so as the conflict wore down and more and more tribesmen returned from the Yellowstone country. The post, founded in 1874 on the north bank of White River for the purpose of monitoring activities at Red Cloud Agency, stood 25 miles below the south boundary of Dakota Territory and some 35 miles east of Wyoming Territory. Postured in the wooded Pine Ridge country of the Nebraska Panhandle, Camp Robinson lay 125 miles north of the Union Pacific Railroad and 82 miles northeast of the large army installation at Fort Laramie. In 1876 the post, constructed mainly of logs and adobe around a 165-square-yard perimeter, boasted quarters for four companies of infantry and one of cavalry and contained seven double sets of officer quarters, an administrative office, quartermaster and commissary offices, and appurtenant corrals, stables, and warehouses.[12]

From an administrative and operational standpoint, Camp Robinson's role had broadened in August with the arrival of Colonel Mackenzie and six companies of the Fourth Cavalry from the Indian Territory. Mackenzie had been appointed commander of the District of the Black Hills, a regional military subdivision formerly commanded by Colonel Merritt and established within the Department of the Platte to track the high incidence of Indian activity in a concentrated zone embracing parts of Dakota, Wyoming, and Nebraska. Mackenzie located his headquarters at Camp Robinson and called on the post commanders there and at Camp Sheridan and Fort Laramie to report monthly on the disposition of troops at those garrisons as well as to monitor and report on the activities of Indians in their vicinities. Besides the Fourth Cavalry companies, the garrison at Camp Robinson was augmented throughout August by the arrival of troops from the Fifth Cavalry, Fourteenth Infantry, and Fourth Artillery, all expected to help implement Sheridan's "rule of 1876" dictum for dismounting and disarming the agency people. By month's end, no fewer than 650 soldiers had set up temporary encampments between the post and the Red Cloud Agency, the steady military accretion prompting among anxious agency tribesmen several minor outbursts that were quelled by the troops.[13]

In the wake of the summer's fighting, the military situation regarding the Lakotas and Northern Cheyennes remained unresolved both in the field and at the Dakota agencies. To the north and west, large numbers of tribesmen with Sitting Bull and Crazy Horse still occupied the Yellowstone and Powder River country, having returned to the region to hunt buffalo after the columns of Crook and Terry departed. Although some of those people were turning up at the agencies (reports at Red Cloud indicated that warriors wounded in the Rosebud battle were convalescing there), the implementation of Sheridan's military takeover and its perceived threat of force in fact influenced other tribesmen to leave. Whereas in the spring of 1876 some thirteen thousand Indian people occupied Red Cloud Agency, by August less than five thousand were accounted for there, numbers that continued to decline into the fall. The military agent at Spotted Tail reported a similar trend. Significantly, many defectors from Red Cloud through the summer consisted of Northern Cheyenne families, including that of the revered old man chief Morning Star (Dull Knife), who had left the agency in July. And as summer passed into autumn, indications that the Indians intended to continue fighting became increasingly clear, with a spate of attacks on civilians and livestock north and west of Fort Laramie by isolated parties of Sioux and Cheyenne raiders. On October 14, troops from Fort Laramie engaged some of these warriors in a brief exchange along Richard Creek, in which one soldier was killed.[14]

For both the Indians and the army, the provision of the recent agreement stipulating the tribesmen's removal to Indian Territory produced considerable angst. Locally, Colonel Mackenzie resisted the departure of any headmen to examine the southern tracts because they were harboring in their camps at Red Cloud and Spotted Tail parties "who have been absent engaged in war." Also Sheridan feared that compliance would be manifest in renewed warfare in the spring, for which "every Sioux Indian capable of bearing arms is now getting ready to take the field." Furthermore, the provision could only encourage their brethren yet afield to stay out and await the arrival of these new reinforcements. General Sherman agreed, stating his belief that the "older men and families" could move to a point near the Missouri River where they might receive their annuities more cheaply, thereby paving the way for mining enterprise and settlement in eastern Wyoming. The Indians likewise resisted the stated move south, although to appease the government Spotted Tail of the Brules agreed to lead a delegation to Indian Territory and examine the country.[15]

These lingering uncertainties over the results of the summer's campaign, together with ongoing concerns about the fluctuating status of the agency tribesmen, influenced Sheridan's decision to resurrect a page from past successes. In August, from his Chicago headquarters, the general summoned Frank North, an erstwhile frontiersman who had organized and commanded a battalion of Pawnee Indian scouts in years past. North was serving as a guide and interpreter at Sidney Barracks, Nebraska, and Sheridan directed him to visit the Pawnees in Indian Territory to solicit their help in the ongoing confrontation with the Sioux and Northern Cheyennes. The Pawnees, who had been removed from their Nebraska homeland earlier in 1876, had served the government intermittently between 1864 and 1870 in its campaigns against the Indians' traditional enemies. North, commissioned a major for the purpose, and his younger brother, Luther, who served as Frank's subaltern, had raised and trained a battalion of four companies of scouts. With the Norths in command, the Pawnees had variously ranged through Kansas and Nebraska and through Wyoming, Montana, and Colorado Territories, tracking and fighting the Sioux, Cheyennes, and Arapahos as a component of pursuing military columns. In Brigadier General Patrick E. Connor's Powder River Expedition of 1864, the scouts had shown their mettle in locating and joining in the attack upon an Arapaho camp north of the Big Horn Mountains. Five years later Major North's Pawnees participated in the Battle of Summit Springs, Colorado Territory, where the famed Cheyenne Dog Soldier leader Tall Bull was killed. As dedicated allies and fierce fighters, the Pawnees promised to introduce yet a new element into the equation for subduing the Lakotas and Cheyennes on the northern plains.[16]

On Sheridan's authority, the North brothers traveled to the Pawnee agency in north-central Indian Territory to select and enroll one hundred scouts. The potentially explosive consequences of drawing these men from a tribe hated by the Sioux, and near whom the Sioux tentatively might reside following their own removal south, evidently did not influence Sheridan's thinking.[17] The enterprising brothers had no trouble recruiting the specified number. While many of the Pawnees were sick with malaria, all were nostalgic for Nebraska and desirous of once more combating the Sioux. But the Indians were horseless, and instead of marching them overland as originally planned, Frank North entrained them at Coffeyville, Kansas, for the trip to Omaha, then west over the Union Pacific Railroad to Sidney Barracks. On September 18 at that post, the Pawnees were formally mustered into the service of the United States. According to Sheridan's stipulation, Frank North would serve as captain of the Pawnee company. North selected his brother, Luther, as his first lieutenant and Sylvanus E. Cushing, who had similarly served the Norths in earlier times, as second lieutenant. At Sidney Barracks, the Pawnees drew uniform clothing, rations, and tentage. Each man also received the standard-issue Springfield carbine and revolver, while ponies left over from area cattle drives served as mounts. In the ensuing days the scouts prepared for their duties and accustomed their animals to themselves and the country.[18] Their role in the final drive against the Sioux and Cheyennes was to be significant, and their moment of first involvement was nigh.[19]

Chapter 2
Camp Robinson to Fort Fetterman

IMPLEMENTATION OF GENERAL SHERIDAN'S edict respecting the Sioux agencies got underway after the land commissioners had garnered their needed signatures and departed. Of the six agencies scattered about the Great Sioux Reservation, the ones of most concern in terms of numbers of warriors returning from the field were Red Cloud, Spotted Tail, Standing Rock, and Cheyenne River. The military takeover began in earnest at the latter two stations in August and September, when units of the Eleventh, Fourteenth, and Twentieth Infantry arrived to support the move. Indian unrest at Standing Rock and Cheyenne River prompted Sheridan to direct the companies of the Seventh Cavalry, then returning from the Sioux campaign, to bolster the troops at those agencies. In October, on Sheridan's orders, General Terry readied soldiers from Custer's old outfit and detachments of the Seventeenth and Twentieth Infantry to move out and to dismount and disarm the Lakotas at the two northernmost Missouri River agencies.

On October 20, with Terry accompanying, Colonel Samuel D. Sturgis and Major Marcus A. Reno led contingents of these units south from Fort Abraham Lincoln along either side of the Missouri. Two days later Reno's men reached Standing Rock, where Terry threatened the Sioux with ration cuts if they refused to comply with the dismounting and disarmament procedure. In a day's time the troops confiscated arms, ammunition, and more than twelve hundred ponies from Hunkpapa, Blackfeet

Sioux, and Yanktonai camps on either side of the stream. While Reno consolidated matters at Standing Rock, Sturgis moved on to the Cheyenne River Agency, his force supported by additional infantry from Fort Sully. The Sioux there remained intractable for a time, but threats to withhold their provisions caused them finally to relent and to surrender arms and nearly one thousand mounts. Driven overland to St. Paul, Minnesota, fewer than one-fourth of the animals taken from the northern agencies actually reached that destination to be sold at public auction; many died from disease and exposure, while others drowned crossing the Missouri River, were stolen or bartered away en route, or otherwise became lost.[1]

While enforcement of Sheridan's dictum proceeded in the northern area of the Great Sioux Reservation, similar measures got underway at the southernmost agencies. Attention there shortly centered on the Oglala camp of Red Cloud and the Wazaza Brulé camp of Red Leaf, which were determined to spurn what they regarded as further government interference into their tribal affairs. Red Cloud, then fifty-four years old, was venerated among the Oglalas for his early resistance to the army during the Bozeman Trail War of 1866–68. Thereafter recognized by federal authorities as chief of the Sioux, he had remained on the reservation ever since, drawing on wily diplomatic skills and obstructionist tactics to better his people's standing with the government and its agents, as well as with the other Lakota bands. Red Leaf was the brother of Conquering Bear, the Brulé leader killed in the Grattan fight near Fort Laramie in 1854. A peace advocate, Red Leaf had nonetheless rejected the government's overtures in 1866 and had cast his lot with Red Cloud in the Bozeman Trail War.[2] Now in 1876, following the meetings with the Sioux commission, anger and divisiveness had arisen among the Indians at Red Cloud Agency, causing concern for Colonel Ranald Mackenzie at Camp Robinson. Finally, in early October the camps under Red Cloud, Red Leaf, and Oglalas Little Wound and Blue Horse, in protest of the removal schemes, abruptly broke away from the agency, the former two moving their people to Chadron Creek, some thirty miles northeast. Crook believed that these people not only remained in close communication with the Indians in the Powder River country and might therefore encourage them in their ways, but also that their own defiance effectively flew in the face of the prevailing philosophy of strictly controlling the agency tribesmen, and he soon settled on a course of military action to return the recalcitrants. Accordingly, Mackenzie sent word directing them to return to the agency or have their rations stopped and be forced back. In compliance, Little Wound and Blue Horse moved their people to Crow Butte, near the agency. Red Cloud, however, through a spokesman notified Mackenzie that henceforth any rations should be sent out to their camps. After ration day passed and the Red Cloud and Red Leaf people still refused to budge, Mackenzie dispatched another message that again strongly warned of the colonel's intention to use force to gain their compliance.[3]

Fearing that the Red Cloud and Red Leaf groups might flee north, Crook initially relied on Merritt's troops, then marching south toward Camp Robinson from the Black Hills, to counter the Indians' movement. He had planned to await the proper time to advance a contingent of soldiers to quickly surround the two camps and prevent their escape, then force them back to Red Cloud Agency. But realization that the Sioux could bolt at any time prompted the general to order an immediate advance on Sunday night, October 22.[4] Anticipating possible action, a week earlier orders had gone to Frank North to start his Pawnee scouts from Sidney Barracks. Their march proceeded in stages; the scouts forded the North Platte River near present Bridgeport and pushed on to the Niobrara River, about one hundred miles north of Sidney, where they went into camp and awaited further instructions. As the Pawnees ate dinner on October 22, couriers arrived with orders urgently directing them to march for Camp Robinson. En route, an officer from Mackenzie arrived, whereupon North, his brother, and forty-two of the Indians pressed forward on an all-night ride to overtake the colonel on the way to the Chadron camps. Lieutenant Cushing with the remaining fifty-eight scouts and wagons kept on to Camp Robinson, reaching the post at 3:00 A.M. on the twenty-third.[5]

In their forced march of some seventy miles through the night of October 22–23, the Norths and their Pawnees diverged from the road and rode diagonally northeast, eventually over-taking Mackenzie and momentarily startling his rearguard, which believed they were under attack from hostile Indians. Mackenzie's force, which had departed Camp Robinson at 9:00 P.M., skirting Red Cloud Agency so as not to draw attention, consisted of six companies (B, D, E, F, I, and M) of his Fourth Cavalry plus two companies (H and L) of the Fifth Cavalry, detached from Merritt's force since July, the whole divided into two equal battalions commanded by Major George A. Gordon, Fifth Cavalry, and Captain Clarence Mauck of the Fourth. The troops carried no baggage and but one day's rations.[6] An officer of the Fourth Cavalry described the advance:

The night was pitch-dark and very cold. The country was intersected by a series of ravines and washouts; but the most positive orders hav-ing been issued by Mackenzie . . . for the whole column to keep closed up, at all hazards, the trot and gallop were continued throughout the night. Occasionally a troop would be brought down to a walk, at the bottom of some gully or dry creek, and then, on emerging, would be compelled to go at a gallop to overtake the preceding troops, which had already disappeared in the blackness ahead. The only sounds to be heard were the thunder of the column as it tore along over the

frozen ground; the rattle of the harness of the horses (the men's sabres
being thrust between their knees and saddles) and the muttered excla-
mation of some trooper as his steed stumbled or fell in the darkness.[7]

The action that followed significantly exemplified Sheridan's
disarm-and-dismount policy among the Sioux that eventually
contributed to ending the warfare.

The two camps stood on Chadron Creek, Red Cloud's
approximately two miles southwest of the present community of
Chadron and beginning about five miles from the confluence of
that stream with White River. That of Red Leaf, which also
included another Brulé headman, Swift Bear, stood near a bluff
on the west side in a bend of the creek about three miles above,
or south, of Red Cloud's camp. That night the members of the
Red Leaf village had gone to the Red Cloud camp to enjoy a
game of handball, following which they had walked back to their
own lodges; some, apparently suspecting imminent military
action, moved their families from the village during the night.[8]
Meantime, riding ahead in the darkness for about twenty miles,
Mackenzie's command reached a fork in the trail, the two
branches leading to the respective villages. There the cavalry
force divided into its two battalions with each accompanied by
one North brother and twenty-four Pawnees. One, under Major
Gordon, veered right in the direction of Red Leaf's camp, while
Mackenzie and the balance of the troopers swung off to the left
toward Red Cloud's lodges.[9]

The night was cloud-covered with gusting winds. Riding
well in advance of Mackenzie's column, Captain North and his
scouts had gone several miles when they heard a rooster crow.
It was near 3:00 A.M. on the twenty-third, and North took the
news to the colonel. After a discussion in which it was clear to
all that the village was close by, Mackenzie's advance resumed
as the troops followed the sound. Officers cautioned their men

against talking loudly or lighting matches for fear the column would be discovered. Presently, they came to the edge of a cut bank leading to Chadron Creek; beyond, stretched along the east side of the stream, they discerned a darkened cluster comprising about forty tipis of Red Cloud's people. Through some confusion, however, Mackenzie's troops found Major Gordon's men already there, mistakenly having been led to that point by a man who the colonel had earlier engaged to keep track of the camps. Mackenzie sent Gordon's command off toward the other village, and for the next two hours readied his own battalion for a dawn attack, taking measures to invest the camp completely so that no one could escape, much in the manner of a conventional army strike. At around 5:00 A.M. Mackenzie directed an interpreter to go to the cut bank and call out in Lakota that the village was surrounded. For a time there was no response beyond barking dogs, but soon some women and children appeared and took cover in the nearby brush. Then, on command, the Pawnees raced through the camp from the north, capturing the Oglala ponies and corralling them in the rear, whereupon Mauck's soldiers, approaching from the northwest, dismounted and filed into the village. The action was a total surprise; the only noise, remembered the Sioux, was "the clattering of the horses and the commands from the soldiers." Red Cloud's warriors were quickly disarmed and placed under guard.[10] Mackenzie directed the women to select ponies from the captured herd on which to mount their baggage and to break camp preparatory to moving out. When the women initially demurred, the colonel warned them that he would burn the lodges if they did not comply, and some tipis were torched before the women realized that the threat was sincere.[11]

Meantime, at the Red Leaf–Swift Bear camp—which was bigger than Red Cloud's—events unfolded in similar fashion. Arriving at the village at dawn following his miscue, Major

Gordon issued instructions that there should be no gunfire unless initiated by the Indians. Apparently, no weapons were fired.[12] From a hill west of the camp, a solitary Indian boy reportedly watched the soldiers approach up Chadron Creek and shouted a warning to his people. But Gordon's troopers surrounded the tipis, and the Pawnees dashed through yelling war whoops and driving the ponies before them. None of the Red Leaf people came out until the ponies had been secured by the scouts. They then eventually appeared and talked at length to Major Gordon, who explained that they now must return to Camp Robinson. During the conference, Gordon learned that Red Leaf was not present, having gone earlier to spend the night with friends closer to the agency. His subordinate, Swift Bear, helped arrest a villager who had aimed a gun at the major, then the tribesmen delivered up their arms. As in the case of Red Cloud's camp, the women selected the stock to carry themselves, the children and elderly, and associated dunnage. Then Gordon started them off, meeting Mackenzie's troops after a short distance. By 8:00 A.M. all was secured, and Mackenzie penciled a brief report to Crook. In all, his operation resulted in the confiscation of arms from more than 150 warriors plus the capture of more than seven hundred ponies.[13]

The men and women moved separately in the formation, and on gaining Ash Creek, the latter went into camp near Crow Butte under guard of soldiers, while the men proceeded afoot to Camp Robinson with the remaining troops and the captured ponies, gaining the post at around 2:00 A.M. on the twenty-fourth. Hoping to stem alarm elsewhere among the tribesmen, Mackenzie had sent word of the capture to the agency camps of Chiefs Young-Man-Afraid-of-His-Horses and Little Wound.[14] Nonetheless, these people, having otherwise anticipated or learned of the troops' action and fearful for their own situation, began streaming into Camp Robinson and the agency ahead of the returning troops. Perhaps not altogether coincidentally, Colonel Merritt's command, which had been toiling through the Black Hills for more than a month, entered the post almost simultaneously. A witness recorded the scene late on the twenty-third:

As far as the eye with a good field glass could discern the bright light tipped ridges of prairie, the moving Sioux could be seen winding their way in towards the agency from every point of the compass, most of them disarmed and dis-spirited; and the balance having heard . . . of the grand success of the army the night before, badly frightened, came pouring in for dear life . . . ; and in this deeply interesting spectacle, most conspicuous of all, were the long lines of our troops, Crook's old command from Custer City taking the advance, while the 13 companies of cavalry from here seemed divided into two columns almost surrounding the . . . bands of Sioux that had been disarmed. . . . The vast hordes of squaws, children, ponies and dogs, that were being driven in towards this common centre, the Agency, could not half reach there that night.[15]

Once arrived at the post, the Red Cloud and Red Leaf people erected their tipis and soldiers searched their baggage for ammunition. Then the tipis were dismantled and moved over to the agency to be finally raised once more. As reward for their service, Mackenzie gave each of the Pawnee scouts a pony from the captured camps, an action that affronted the Sioux.[16]

Following the capture of the two villages, Crook wired the news to General Sheridan, terming the event, "the first gleam of daylight we have had in this business."[17] He did not disarm or dismount the other Indians at the Red Cloud and Spotted Tail Agencies, despite Sheridan's injunction, because he believed that they had been loyal to the government. Moreover, he hoped to enlist those Sioux warriors as scouts for his forthcoming campaign. Crook tried to make Sheridan see that his recruitment of scouts would provide "the entering wedge by which the tribal organization is broken up," but to little avail.[18] "There must be no halfway work in this matter," replied Sheridan. "All Indians out there must be on our side without question, or else on the side of the hostiles."[19] A major result of the army action was the demotion of Red Cloud from his status as supreme chief. At a grand council and ceremony on October 24, Crook designated the Brulé leader, Spotted Tail, as chief of all the Sioux at both Red Cloud and Spotted Tail Agencies and the true friend of the whites. "The line of the hostile and peaceably disposed is now plainly drawn and we shall have our enemies in the front only in the future."[20]

That same day Crook proclaimed the end of the Big Horn and Yellowstone Expedition, then resumed preparations for his new campaign.[21] On rumor that the agency tribesmen planned to stampede the ponies captured from the Red Cloud and Red Leaf camps, the general at once detailed Captain North to conduct the herd to Fort Laramie, where sufficient corral facilities awaited. North and fifty of his Pawnees, not having slept since before leaving the Niobrara at dusk on October 22, started away after 5:00 P.M. with 722 ponies on an all-night trek, during which, after midnight, the scouts surprised a wagon train and its cavalry escort en route to Camp Robinson with winter clothing for Crook's men. "Almost everyone . . . rushed behind the wagons for protection from the bullets expected to be flying about our heads in a few seconds," wrote a newsman accompanying the train. After stopping to eat and to warm themselves, North and his Pawnees pushed on and reached Fort Laramie at 8:00 P.M. on October 25.[22] On Crook's authority North selected a pony for himself and one for his brother. From those that remained, he chose some 350 more to serve as extra saddle horses for the other scouts and guides in the upcoming operation. The remaining animals were sold at auction at Fort Laramie, Cheyenne Depot,

and at Sidney Barracks, Nebraska. Luther North and Sylvanus
Cushing, with the other Pawnees, reached Fort Laramie three
days later.[23]

Having thus challenged and intimidated the agency Indians, Crook proceeded with arrangements for his next expedition, expected to specifically target Sioux located in the areas of
Rosebud Creek and Powder River in Montana. Those people,
who Crook believed composed the major elements of Sitting
Bull's and Crazy Horse's bands, were reported to be hunting
buffalo below the Yellowstone.[24] He had earlier indicated his
views: "Our next objective point is Crazy Horse. He should be
followed up and struck as soon as possible. There should be no
stopping for this or that thing, [as] the Indians cannot stand a
continuous campaign. . . . The best time . . . is in the winter."[25]
Crook planned to advance north into that region from Fort Fetterman, and he asked Sheridan for authorization to supply his
command from provisions on hand at the Tongue River Cantonment. Granting it, the divisional commander informed Crook
on October 30 that Indians had recently attacked an army supply train as it advanced from the cantonment at Glendive Creek,
Montana, to Colonel Miles's Tongue River station. Sheridan
pointedly told Crook that he needed to more precisely specify
his campaign plans, admonishing him that "complaints are made
that your reports are not sufficiently detailed."[26]

Sheridan's criticism of his department commander reflected
something of a schism between the two that went back to the
Civil War and seemed omnipresent in 1876. George Crook was
already famous for his exploits as an Indian campaigner. He had
graduated from West Point with Sheridan in 1852 and had gone
immediately to fight Indians in the Pacific Northwest, where in
an 1857 combat he received an arrow wound. During the Civil
War, Crook fought at Antietam, Winchester, and Cedar Creek,
among other places, rising to major general of volunteers and

command of the Army of West Virginia. Captured by the Confederates early in 1865, he was exchanged in time to participate in the closing operations leading to Appomattox. His friendship with Sheridan soured when that officer denied Crook credit for his performance at Winchester; their relationship scarcely improved thereafter and remained an issue through most of Crook's postwar career in the West.

Following Appomattox, Crook, reduced in grade to lieutenant colonel with the postwar reorganization of the Army, returned west, where he led campaigns in Idaho, Oregon, and northern California before being reassigned to Arizona Territory to deal with the Apache Indians. There he employed innovative techniques that he had learned in the Northwest—employment of native scouts, utilization of pack mules over conventional supply wagons, selection of officers possessed of sound tactical judgment and ability, and, most important, unrelenting pursuit—and prosecuted his campaigns with similar enthusiasm. After eighteen months his command forced the Apaches to yield and agree to reservation status, further boosting Crook's stock and winning for him promotion to brigadier general. Moving to Omaha in 1875 as commander of the Department of the Platte, he took the field the following year against the Sioux and Northern Cheyennes, tribes new to him, determined to prosecute them using the same methods that had brought him success elsewhere.

In appearance, the forty-eight-year-old Crook stood slightly over six feet tall. He was broad-shouldered with squinting blue eyes, aquiline nose, firm mouth, and sandy blond whiskers that he often wore braided on either side of his face. In the field he was most comfortable in flannel shirt and civilian canvas hunting garb usually devoid of insignia of rank. Beyond an easygoing appearance, however, Crook was quiet and taciturn in demeanor, keeping his own counsel to the point that ranking subordinates—as well as news correspondents—often speculated over his preparedness and intentions during the earlier operations of 1876. These traits would continue to vex some of the officers of his new command. Some of these criticisms had evidently made their way back to Sheridan and prompted him to voice his displeasure over elements of Crook's performance.[27]

The troops that Crook readied to field for the Powder River Expedition consisted of an assemblage of some seventeen hundred officers and men, guides, and scouts. His command did not include soldiers from the recently disbanded Big Horn and Yellowstone Expedition, who, worn and exhausted from their summer service, started for their home stations. Many of the new troops had been at Camp Robinson since August overseeing developments there while raising temporary winter camps along White River between the post and the Red Cloud Agency. So great had been the impetus to enlist following the Little Bighorn disaster that some companies were filled to overflowing with inexperienced recruits termed "Custer Avengers." For the coming movement, Mackenzie would command the cavalry battalion, which comprised eleven mounted companies—B, D, E, F, I, and M from his own Fourth Cavalry; K of the Second; H and K of the Third; and H and L of the Fifth. The battalion was divided into squadrons, with Captain Mauck commanding five companies of the Fourth Cavalry and Major Gordon commanding the remaining unit of the Fourth plus those of the Second, Third, and Fifth. Mackenzie's battalion numbered twenty-eight officers and 790 enlisted men. The infantry battalion fell to the command of forty-nine-year-old Lieutenant Colonel Richard Irving Dodge, Twenty-third Infantry. A grandnephew of famed author Washington Irving, Dodge had headed the army escort during the previous year's expedition to the Black Hills, was then at department headquarters in Omaha, and would join the expedition November 10 at Fort Fetterman. Dodge's battalion consisted of four batteries (C, F, H, and K) of the Fourth Artillery acting as infantry under the command of Captain Joseph B. Campbell, and six companies of the Ninth Infantry (A, B, D, F, I, and K), two of the Fourteenth (D and G), and three of Dodge's own Twenty-third (C, G, and I), all under Captain William H. Jordan. Dodge's command totaled thirty-three officers and 646 men. (Companies K, Second Cavalry; E, Ninth Infantry; and C, G, and I, Twenty-third Infantry, actually joined the expedition later at Fort Laramie.) Crook's expedition thus included sixty-one officers and 1,436 men. On October 31, per regulations, the available troops were formally mustered and inspected at Camp Robinson.[28]

A large complement of Indians scouts augmented this force. In addition to the one hundred Pawnees recruited on Sheridan's direction and commanded by the North brothers and Lieutenant Cushing, Crook ordered the enlistment of agency Indians at Red Cloud and Spotted Tail. Many of the officers disapproved of the enlistment of the Sioux, who they distrusted. "If they fail to cut the throats of half the command," wrote newsman Jerry Roche, "they would at least quarrel with their old enemies, the Pawnees."[29] Yet hiring Indian warriors to help his troops find and fight their relatives was a central component of Crook's philosophy on fighting Indians, and he had applied the principle with positive results for the government earlier in his career in the Northwest and Southwest.[30] The conscription at the agencies was successful, producing seventy-three Arapahos, nine Cheyennes, and seventy-three Oglala and Brulé Lakotas to serve the army. Among the Sioux designees was Charging Bear, who had been captured in the army attack on the village at Slim Buttes in September. The native recruits, outfitted with pistols and rifles at Robinson, were divided into two companies, Company A under First Lieutenant Walter Howe, Fourth Artillery, with Sharp Nose, a prominent Arapaho, as first sergeant; and Company B, under Second Lieutenant James M. Jones,

Fourth Artillery, with Three Bears, a Sioux, as first sergeant. Overall command of the Indian scouts on the campaign—Sioux, Cheyennes, and Arapahos, as well as the Pawnees—would presently devolve upon capable First Lieutenant William P. Clark, Second Cavalry, assisted by Second Lieutenant Hayden DeLany, Ninth Infantry. Whether the well-known traditional mutual enmity of the Lakotas, Cheyennes, and Arapahos on the one hand and the Pawnees on the other was considered during the enlistment process is not known, but the matter would intermittently pose concerns in the weeks ahead.[31]

As with his previous incursions against the tribes, Crook had a number of seasoned staff officers to accompany his command on the Powder River Expedition. His adjutant was Captain John G. Bourke, a scholar and ethnographer who left important chronicles of Crook's movement; First Lieutenant Walter S. Schuyler and First Lieutenant Clark, aides-de-camp; First Lieutenant Charles Rockwell, Fifth Cavalry, commissary officer; and Major Joseph R. Gibson, chief medical officer. The number of guides, scouts, packers, and interpreters included veteran frontiersmen like Baptiste ("Big Bat") Pourier, Tom Moore, William Garnett, and David Mears, already well known for their service in 1876. As on the previous expedition, Crook's chief of scouts was Frank Grouard.[32]

At Camp Robinson, preparations consisted of assembling supplies on hand at the post and forwarding them by wagon under escort overland to Fort Laramie, where Crook and his staff worked out the campaign's details. Many items on hand at Robinson were judged unserviceable, and officers spent considerable time inspecting quantities of clothing, equipment, and ordnance stores to determine their worthiness for the expedition. Other provisions, notably surplus ordnance stores and ammunition deemed unnecessary for the campaign, were transferred to Camp Sheridan, with proper invoices and receipts duly exchanged.[33] Instructions prohibited all cavalry officers from carrying carbines and likewise insisted that all men carry sabers, an unusual decree since other field commands had long since dismissed the weapon as virtually useless for fighting Indians. Nevertheless, orders tasked company commanders to "have the Sabres of their men sharpened on a Grind Stone and carried strapped to the saddle."[34]

Sufficient warm clothing and equipment for a winter campaign was of particular concern for Crook and his officers. He directed department officials to ship two thousand sets of sealskin caps, gauntlets, and pairs of overshoes to Fort Fetterman without delay preparatory to his soldiers' arrival at that post. Other quartermaster items scheduled for delivery at Medicine Bow Station on the Union Pacific included large quantities of blankets, woolen mittens, rubber blankets, ponchos, cavalry jackets, uniform coats, and buffalo as well as rubber overshoes.[35] According to orders of October 26, wall tents and the smaller "common" tents were to be transported for the use of officers, their servants, medical staff, and senior noncommissioned officers. Common soldiers would carry shelter tents "at the rate of one (1) piece [or one-half of the tent] to each enlisted man." Besides blankets, each man took an overcoat "and a change of underclothing." All Sibley tent stoves at Camp Robinson were to be taken along, and orders were placed for more to be received at Fetterman. Each man "will be supplied with two hundred and fifty . . . rounds of Carbine or Musket Ammunition, and One hundred . . . rounds of Pistol Ammunition for the Cavalry." Officers could carry only a valise for their clothing and "no large mess chests." Individual companies were responsible for securing their own food provisions and forage for their animals. Upon leaving Camp Robinson, each unit was to carry four days' rations and, for cavalry, one day's forage.[36]

Each cavalry company was assigned two six-mule teams to transport its property, much of it related to horse equipment, while infantry companies and battalion headquarters each received one six-mule team. On Crook's direction Mackenzie sent off a request for horseshoes "fitted for setting and roughed with toe and heel caulks" so as to improve the animals' traction on ice and snow. Beyond this, the other cavalry equipment requisitioned consisted of standard articles such as curry combs, horse brushes, saddle blankets, nose bags, girths, lariats, spurs and straps, curb bridles, carbine slings and swivels, carbines, and revolvers besides assorted rivets, needles, harness leather, and thread for facilitating field repairs.[37] In addition to clothing and equipment, Crook desperately needed wagons and mules to move his supplies forward. A request to Brigadier General John Pope, commanding the Department of the Missouri, initially brought only the response that Pope had already sent eighty wagons and more than five hundred mules to the Sioux war country and that his department could spare no more. But a prod from Sheridan freed up eighteen more wagons and one hundred more mules. Beef for the expedition was to be delivered on contract to the new cantonment being raised near Old Fort Reno along the Powder River.[38]

After forwarding whatever supplies were available at Camp Robinson, the officers and men assembled for the campaign started themselves over the road for Fort Laramie on November 1, the infantry (including the artillerymen) leading the way at 8:00 A.M., followed four hours later by the cavalry battalion. The route led southwestwardly, tracing for ninety miles part of the old fur-trade trail between Fort Laramie and Fort Pierre along the Missouri River. From Camp Robinson the road (sometimes called the "Red Cloud Trail") passed through rugged terrain en route to the Niobrara River, then continued past Rawhide Creek to finally reach the North Platte River eight miles below Fort Laramie.[39] Corporal James Byron Kincaid, Company B, Fourth Cavalry, recorded details of the march in his diary, writing that on the first day out, the men went eighteen miles and camped at White Earth, near the head of White River. "It was cold with some snow on the ground. We had no tents and had to spread our blankets on the snow." The next day they covered twenty-five miles amid sleeting conditions, bivouacking in the snow at Rawhide Creek without wood for fires. "Imagine the 1,200 wet and hungry, and half frozen men scattered over the prairie . . . with snow ten inches deep, hunting [for] Buffalo Chips." On November 4 the soldiers camped about two miles below Fort Laramie on the North Platte.[40]

Fort Laramie stood near the confluence of the North Platte and Laramie Rivers. Purchased by the army in 1849 from the American Fur Company, its position on the overland trail and as a jumping off point for Indian expeditions to the north in earlier years had ensured its development into the principal government station of its time on the northern plains frontier. The post had lately been home to units of the Ninth Infantry, soon to be replaced by troops of the Third Cavalry fresh from the recent expedition. Fort Laramie was eighty miles from Cheyenne, Wyoming, where supplies for the post, formerly hauled by wagons up the Oregon Trail, were now unloaded from Union Pacific freight cars. In 1876 the post contained barracks and mess facilities sufficient for eight companies, assorted frame and adobe officer quarters, workshops, and administrative buildings in addition to the commensurate quartermaster and commissary supply stores, stables, and collateral corrals and holding pens for livestock. The arrival of the component parts of Crook's expedition put so great a strain on existing grain stores at the fort that it alarmed the post's commanding officer, Major Andrew W. Evans.[41]

At the fort General Crook and his staff had been overseeing preparations for the imminent march. On November 2 word had come of a clash two days earlier between Sioux and Shoshones in the Big Horn Mountains. The Shoshone chief, Washakie, requested that Crook go after the Lakotas using Shoshone scouts recently recruited for service and arrived at the newly raised Cantonment Reno. Crook demurred, perhaps anticipating trouble between those scouts and the Sioux recruited from Red Cloud and Spotted Tail Agencies.[42] In a related matter, an attempt by Lieutenant Clark to organize all the Pawnees with the other Indian scout tribal components under regular army officers failed after Captain North refused to accept any authority but Crook's over his scouts.[43]

Company K of the Second Cavalry was detailed to Crook's headquarters. Some of the other cavalry companies were filled beyond capacity, Company L of the Fourth, for example, reportedly containing 118 men. Many were recent enlistees with little training or camp experience. In arranging for the march, Crook's quartermaster had appropriated all available grain stores at Fort Laramie for the use of the animals accompanying the expedition. In anticipation of harsh winter weather, uniforms for both officers and men scarcely subscribed to regulations. Second Lieutenant Homer W. Wheeler remembered, "I wore a suit of heavy underwear; over that a suit of perforated buckskin, a blouse and cardigan jacket; leggings and moccasins (made by the Indians with the hair inside), a soldier's overcoat which was very heavily lined with overcoat material, with fur collar and wristlets, [and] a sealskin cap and gloves."[44]

As preparations went forward for the movement to Fort Fetterman, Fort Laramie bustled with activity. Besides being the assembly point for some two thousand soldiers, "there was a constant stream of wagons, ox and mule teams, mostly on their way to or returning from the Black Hills," recalled Luther

North. "Scouts, trappers, hunters and Indians were coming and going in all directions." Among the notables who gathered at Jules Ecoffee's roadhouse a few miles upriver from the post were Captain Jack Crawford, the "Poet Scout," then en route to Cheyenne; Baptiste Pourier and Baptiste Garnier, known respectively as "Big Bat" and "Little Bat," both having served during Crook's late summer campaign; and Willis "Bill" Rowland, soon to join the small contingent of Cheyenne scouts.[45]

Occasions for such camaraderie were rare and brief, however, for Crook notified his commanders to be ready to move just one day after their arrival from Camp Robinson. On November 5 the troops pulled out on the road north, some two thousand men followed by four hundred pack mules and two hundred wagons. The move was so sudden that the Pawnees and their leaders were unprepared when Lieutenant Clark called to them that Crook had already left and Mackenzie was starting away. "All we could do was to break camp and follow," wrote Luther North, "and from that time until the return of the expedition . . . , we never knew when we were to move camp."[46] The command struck out along the "river" road, tracing the south bank of the North Platte and passing into a snow squall as the day wore on. Crook and his staff crossed an iron bridge and followed the north bank, or "hill" route.[47] The general had learned that morning of Colonel Miles's fight with the Sioux north of the Yellowstone River and the subsequent surrender "of all hostile Indians belonging to the Missouri River Agencies," and although the notice of the Indians' yielding was premature, the news likely inspired Crook to press forward.[48] It took three full days' marching for the troops to cover the eighty-plus miles to Fort Fetterman. Crook and the scouts arrived on the night of Tuesday, November 7, although the troops and wagons did not completely get in until the ninth. The trek was tiring and cold, and the men hitched their "A" tents together at night, using sagebrush and buffalo chips to fuel the fires in their portable stoves.[49]

Fort Fetterman overlooked a plateau on the north side of the North Platte River at the stream's junction with La Prele Creek. Established in 1867 for the purpose of protecting emigrants on the nearby overland trail as well as for facilitating communications and support between Fort Laramie and the Bozeman Trail posts to the north, the fort lay 160 miles from the Union Pacific Railroad at Cheyenne and had served as Crook's departure point into the Indian country during his two previous movements. A typical frontier military station, Fort Fetterman was laid out on a more or less square grid and contained barracks for three hundred men besides the requisite officer quarters, administrative buildings, magazines, supply warehouses, stables and corrals, and collateral outlying structures, all mostly built of adobe. The post received quartermaster and subsistence stores during the winter via a wagon road from Fort D. A. Russell, near the railroad at Cheyenne, through Fort Laramie, a route that covered 160 miles. During the summer warfare period, most supplies reached Fort Fetterman by way of the then snow-free shortcut from Medicine Bow Station west of Cheyenne along the Union Pacific, a route half as long. The adjoining military reservation occupied an area of sixty square miles, and timber for the post was drawn from pine stock on the western fringes of the Black Hills some distance east. Occupying a dry, high-plains environment, the sage-dotted surrounding countryside was sparse and open in all directions. In 1875 an army captain described the post to his mother as "an isolated place . . . not much for scenery being on the dead *level* plains."[50]

As before in 1876, Fort Fetterman would provide logistical support for Crook's command as it probed the Sioux country to the north. The post remained the only permanent government installation in the region after the abandonment of the Bozeman Trail forts following Red Cloud's War of 1866–68, and on General Sheridan's direction troops from Fort Fetterman had played an essential role in raising the support cantonment along the Powder River. Supplies bound for the cantonment, and ultimately for Crook's troops, came into the fort, where they were inspected, stored, and forwarded as needed. At the end of October, Captain Edwin M. Coates, Fourth Infantry, who commanded there, reported more than 680,000 rounds of ammunition on hand; subsistence stores for the expedition were so plentiful that they had to be placed in vacant barracks buildings. Its situation as the post closest to the war zone had made the roads in and out of Fort Fetterman, along with the small ranches in its vicinity, ready targets for marauding bands of Sioux and Cheyennes throughout the summer of 1876, especially in the wake of their various encounters with the army. The small garrison of one hundred men at Fort Fetterman had been unable to respond effectively, and as these activities increased, Captain Coates had expressed fears that he would be unable to defend the fort itself if attacked. Throughout most of October, the Indian threat had remained high, with the raiders attacking several ranches and hay trains in the area, wounding several citizens, and driving off stock.[51]

Following their arrival at Fort Fetterman, Crook and his men occupied the ensuing days making last-minute preparations for their expedition. The troops bivouacked on the flat along the river north of the post, with the infantry farthest from the post. Their hours were filled with routine activities, including drill; reveille was at 6:00 A.M., sick call at 4:00 P.M., and guard mount at 4:30 P.M. Ammunition was distributed, weapons checked, and, for the cavalry, forage piled into wagons. Lieutenant Colonel Dodge, who was to command the battalion of infantry, reached Fort Fetterman with Companies C, G, and I,

Twenty-third Infantry, on November 10 and issued orders placing Major Edwin F. Townsend, Ninth Infantry, in charge of the
infantry component (replacing Captain William H. Jordan, who
resumed command of his company). Dodge directed that strength
charts for the battalion henceforth be prepared three times per
month. The next day he issued allowances for the infantrymen,
including three blankets per man, an overcoat, fur cap, gloves, and
overshoes, leaving it "optional with the men whether they take the
fur articles or not." All excess personal baggage was to be properly packed, identified, and turned over to the care of the Fort
Fetterman quartermaster, to be retrieved at the conclusion of
the expedition. Meantime, assignments of enlisted personnel
were made in the expedition's commissary department to assist
in packing and transporting the food on which the men would
subsist. Each company also carried in its wagons the "proper
allowance" of shelter tents for both officers and men. Similar
assignments of clothing and materiel went to Mackenzie's cavalry
troopers. As for marching formation, Major Townsend directed
the companies of each infantry regiment to march in a rotating
order reflecting their commander's rank, with the leading company each day to be in the rear the following day. On the eleventh
Dodge detailed twenty-two men to escort supplies to Cantonment Reno, which was under construction seventy-five miles to
the northwest. But the next day Crook's planned movement
from Fort Fetterman was delayed by a snow storm.[52]

One incident that occurred during the layover at Fort Fetterman forecasted trouble between the Pawnee and Lakota
scouts. The Lakotas accompanying the column had not yet
received arms, and during the trip from Fort Laramie, two of
them had approached on horseback and counted coup on two
Pawnee warriors in the Indians' traditional fashion. Captain
North managed to keep his scouts from retaliating, but once at
Fort Fetterman, the Sioux challenge to the Pawnees flared

once again, this time over the assignment of the ponies that had
been taken from Red Cloud's and Red Leaf's people. One of the
Lakotas, Three Bears, went to the herd with Lieutenant Clark to
select a mount, but the animal chosen had been previously
picked by Frank North. The Pawnee herder directed Clark and
Three Bears to North, who claimed the horse and would not
turn it over to the Sioux. The matter, which heightened tensions
between the Indian camps, was resolved in a meeting with Crook,
who sided with North. Captain North then suggested that the
Sioux receive all of the remaining ponies after his scouts had
been mounted, an arrangement to which Clark and Three Bears
assented. The incident, however, intensified the feelings between
the respective tribesmen, more so after the Lakotas learned that
the Pawnees had previously selected the best mounts from the
herd. Luther North remembered that the Sioux scouts "said
they would kill the horses that Frank and I had chosen, but they
never tried it."[53]

It was possibly this event that brought about Crook's meeting with the Sioux and Arapaho scouts on the evening of
November 8, during which the matter of the ponies arose. During the session, Three Bears asked that the Sioux receive half the
animals being driven by the Pawnees, to which Crook agreed.
Three Bears spoke of his concern that the agency families, effectually hostages of the government for the good behavior of the
"local" scouts, be properly rationed in their absence. He also
expressed hope that the monies derived by the sale of the Black
Hills be used for purchasing livestock and equipment for distribution among the people. Another Sioux, Fast Thunder, spoke
for self-determination of the Oglalas in selecting an agency, and
the Arapaho Sharp Nose gave a conciliatory speech, assuring
Crook of his fellows' intention of fighting the Northern Sioux
"until you have got through with them." For his part Crook delivered the government line, lecturing the Lakotas about their need

for discipline to instill among themselves the rudiments of husbandry and telling them that its practice would make them "wealthy, powerful, and happy."[54]

A hot topic of conversation during the stay at Fort Fetterman was the news coming in about the disputed presidential election, in which both Republicans and Democrats claimed victory and for which no resolution would come forth until March 1877, when Rutherford B. Hayes would be determined the victor.[55] By November 13, Crook's command, provisioned and equipped, was ready to take the field. In his journal for that date, Colonel Dodge noted: "Heavy fog & mist this A.M. but the sun finally came out bright & clear. The cold last night was intense—13° below zero at 8 AM."[56] Dodge issued orders directing his command to break camp at 7:30 A.M. the next day, with the two battalions to lead the march on alternate days. The following excerpts give specifics of the manner of the infantry movement during Crook's campaign:

On the march a distance of no less than sixty paces will be maintained between the rear of the leading and the front of the rear battalion. . . . The troops will precede the wagons. . . . Battalion Commanders will see that the march is conducted in good order—that the files do not crowd each other and that the leading file takes a short and regular step. The leading battalion will regulate the halt which must be at least ten (10) minutes in every hour. The following are the hours for calls: Reveille 6 A.M. Guard Mounting 4:30 P.M. . . . The Guard will consist of one Captain Officer of the Day and the lieutenants and enlisted men of one entire company. The Guard will be the rear guard of the column and will bring up every thing.[57]

A turn toward colder weather had begun during the time the soldiers had been bivouacked along the North Platte; however uncomfortable, the freezing temperatures portended success in the field during the campaign ahead, an objective sought by many of Crook's officers, who understood that the Indians were more apt to remain secure in their villages during severe weather. "We begin to fear that Crazy Horse may surrender without a blow," penned Adjutant Bourke. "A fight is desirable to atone and compensate for our trials, hardships and dangers for more than eight months."[58] On November 13, the eve of departure, those prospects were closer at hand than anyone yet realized.

Chapter 3
Cheyenne Interlude

AT DAYBREAK ON FRIDAY, NOVEMBER 14, amid temperatures hovering at fourteen degrees below zero, Crook's command began its trek from Fort Fetterman, fording the icy North Platte and setting a course along the road leading northwest. Delays in crossing kept the last of the infantry column from actually getting across the river until after 10:30 A.M. Besides the 168 wagons, seven ambulances, hundreds of horses and mules, and a beef herd accompanying the expedition, Crook's army departing the Platte totaled more than 1,750 officers, men, civilians, and Indian scouts—the largest of any field command to have operated against the tribes in 1876. The troops, wagons, and Indians stretched along the old Bozeman Trail, the road traced by civilian entrepreneurs in 1864 to run between east-central Wyoming Territory and the gold fields in western Montana Territory. Largely abandoned in the wake of the Indian war of 1866–68, following which the army had withdrawn from the area, the trail in 1876 nonetheless provided ready military access through the "unceded Indian Territory," specified in the 1868 Fort Laramie Treaty, to the Sioux War country of northern Wyoming and southeast Montana. In Wyoming the Bozeman Trail linked reliable water sources, and from the North Platte the road ran to Brown's Springs, a branch of the Dry Fork of Cheyenne River, then successively passed Sand Creek, Antelope Spring, and other tributaries before reaching the Dry Fork of Powder River. From there it proceeded northwest to cross the Crazy Woman

Fork of the Powder, Piney Creek (near the site of the abandoned Fort Phil Kearny), and Tongue River before diverging north toward the Bighorn River in Montana.[1]

The army column snaked over the plains during the day's march, headed by Mackenzie's cavalry battalion. Colonel Dodge reveled at the "beautiful and exhilerating sight [of] Cavalry, Artillery, Infantry, Indians [scouts], pack mules & wagons. The ground was covered with snow, but the day was perfectly lovely. . . . I have never seen so large and well fitted a Comd in Indian warfare." In the afternoon, twelve miles out, the infantry troops pitched their tents along Sage Creek, while the cavalry-men pressed on several miles, searching for pools in the brack-ish stream to water their horses. With scant grass available, the animals feasted on baled hay brought out from Fort Fetterman. Wood for the cooking fires and for heating the tents also had to be drawn from the post.[2]

Crook's movement was directed immediately toward the recently raised Cantonment Reno, the supply base from which he planned to lead his troops north to strike at the villages of Crazy Horse and other Tetons known to be wintering in the tra-ditional hunting territory below the Yellowstone near the head-waters of the Tongue and Powder Rivers. Following the Little Bighorn encounter and the postbattle scattering of the occu-pants of the massive village whose warriors had destroyed Custer, the Oglalas, Hunkpapas, Minneconjous, Sans Arcs, and collateral groups of Tetons, together with some Cheyennes, had journeyed east beyond the Little Missouri River to hunt and prepare for winter. Some of the people were en route to the agencies, expecting to live off government annuities until spring. Most of the tribesmen were within the confines of the Great Sioux Reservation when General Crook's troops had found the village of American Horse at Slim Buttes in September. Many of the people who fled from that village joined Crazy Horse after

the engagement as the Tetons turned back toward the Yellowstone and Powder River country. While Sitting Bull and the
Hunkpapas and Sans Arcs gravitated northwest into the buffalo
lands north of the Yellowstone, the followers of Crazy Horse
and other leaders headed toward the familiar haunts adjoining
the Powder, Tongue, and Rosebud south of the river. There,
beginning in September, the soldiers of Colonel Nelson Miles
monitored their presence from positions on the Yellowstone,
notably from the cantonment erected at the mouth of Tongue
River. Miles's evolving strategy was to place his force between
the two large bodies of tribesmen on either side of the Yellowstone and prevent them from ever joining together again. He
used able scouts to amass intelligence of the Indian positions,
which was conveyed to the military hierarchy; such information
had prompted Crook's movement toward the Tongue River in
November.[3]

The country passed through was familiar to many of Crook's
staff, much of it previously traversed by them during the general's earlier campaigns that year. The objective point, Montana's
upper Tongue River watershed, lay more than two hundred
miles distant from Fort Fetterman, and the intervening tract
would afford the troops few areas of interest, presenting topog-
raphy of which, according to Lieutenant Bourke, "the less said
the better." His description, drafted the previous February,
mirrored a sentiment likely expressed this time out:

*[The country] is suited for grazing and may appeal to the eyes of a
cow-boy, but for the ordinary observer, especially during the winter
season, it presents nothing to charm any sense; the landscape is
monotonous and uninviting, and the vision is bounded by swell after
swell of rolling prairie, yellow with a thick growth of winter-killed buffalo grass, with a liberal sprinkling of that most uninteresting of all
vegetation—the sage-brush. The water is uniformly and consistently*

bad—being both brackish and alkaline, and when it freezes into ice the ice is nearly always rotten and dangerous, for a passage at least by mounted troops or wagons. . . . Across this charming expanse the wind howled and did its best to freeze us all to death, but we were too well prepared.[4]

The land comprised vaguely defined hunting grounds awarded the Indians in the Fort Laramie Treaty of 1868. Unknown to Crook and his officers as they wended their way toward Crazy Horse's camps, the country penetrated adjoined that presently occupied by a large body of Northern Cheyenne Indians, staunch allies of the Sioux throughout the conflict with the army in 1876, who had been mandated by their own 1868 treaty to reside in and hunt the same region.[5] The Cheyennes, or *Tsitsistsas* ("The Human Beings," or "The People"), as they called themselves, were Algonquian-speaking tribesmen whose agriculturalist forbears had migrated from the area of the western Great Lakes to occupy the buffalo prairies east of the Missouri River by the late seventeenth century. With the acquisition of horses their movement continued, and through the ensuing decades the Cheyennes ventured into lands beyond the Black Hills as far north as the Yellowstone River and south to below the Platte. By the middle of the nineteenth century, the people had separated into northern and southern bodies that nonetheless maintained strong family and band relationships. In the intertribal conflicts that occurred in competition for lands and game resources, the relatively small Northern Cheyenne tribe (approximately twelve hundred people in 1876) became noted fighters who forged strong alliances with the Northern Arapahos and Lakotas. Together, the three tribes variously fought warriors of the Kiowas and Crows, and in the central plains they forced the Kiowas and Comanches south of the Arkansas River.[6]

The basic living unit among the Cheyennes was the band, which represented an adaptation to the reality of a plains existence that could not sustain large, horse-centered tribes except during the summer, when bands often converged and traveled together. The life of the people was grounded in *Esevone*, the Sacred Buffalo Hat, and the *Maahotse*, the four Sacred Arrows, which represented the two Great Covenants of the Cheyennes that united them with the Creator. Through these entities and the sanctified worship and renewal ceremonies related to them, the people received spiritual sustenance and guidance in all aspects of their being, and all creation was continually blessed and renewed. The Sacred Buffalo Hat and the Sacred Arrows, forever in the charge of hereditary keepers, helped manifest the divine quality and purpose of Cheyenne existence. Politically, the complexities of life and society were guided by two bodies. One, the Council of Chiefs (or Council of Forty-Four), comprised older, respected leaders—peace chiefs—whose deliberations governed the day-to-day routine of the tribe such as moving the village and deciding the beginning of the annual buffalo hunt. The council included four Old Man Chiefs, or Priest-Chiefs, one of whom was the Sweet Medicine Chief, who represented the root and core of the people's spiritual existence. The other body comprised the various warrior societies whose own chiefs— fighting men—maintained tribal discipline, oversaw the hunt and ceremonies, and provided offensive and defensive leadership against external enemies. Each Cheyenne band usually had four chiefs represented on the chiefs' council, and with band dispersement appearing commonly after the mid–nineteenth century, these men made decisions for the band that the full chiefs' council had formerly made for the entire tribe. While Northern Cheyenne tribal bands often moved independently of each other, the cohesive nature of the society demanded that they maintain relative proximity and contact with one another.

Familial communication often mandated interactive visits with individuals' or families' home villages or bands, and trips to see Southern Cheyenne kinsmen were common.[7]

Like the Sioux and other tribes, the Northern Cheyennes touched pen to the 1851 Treaty of Fort Laramie, an instrument designed to restrict the tribesmen from areas of major emigrant traffic and settlement by prescribing them their own reserved lands. Many government promises went unfulfilled, however, and not every band of every tribe subscribed to the protocols, factors that created longstanding confusion. Moreover, the Sioux, Cheyennes, and Arapahos began forcibly resisting white intrusions into what they considered their land. In the course of events, troops were sent to protect American citizens. Continued emigration thus inaugurated a period of contention and conflict between these tribes on the one hand and the U.S. Army—the instrument of the federal government—on the other.[8] Trouble between the army and the Cheyennes arose in the 1850s following the killing by Sioux of Second Lieutenant John L. Grattan and his small command near Fort Laramie. The government mounted a campaign to punish the tribesmen for the Grattan affair and for the continued disruption of citizen travel on the overland trails. On September 3, 1855, Brevet Brigadier General William S. Harney with an army of six hundred infantry, artillery, and mounted troops found camps of Brulé and Oglala Lakotas along Blue Water Creek in Nebraska and delivered the Indians a demoralizing blow. The Battle of the Blue Water, in which eighty-five Sioux died compared to but four soldiers killed, set a tone of mutual distrust and enmity that characterized relations between the federal government and the Lakotas and their allies for the balance of the nineteenth century.[9]

For the Cheyennes, the episode of momentous consequence in terms of their relations with the United States was the horrific destruction of a village of mostly Southern Cheyennes at Sand Creek, Colorado Territory, by Colorado volunteer troops in November 1864. Responding to widespread raiding by these Indians and their Arapaho allies in Kansas and Colorado, the territorial governor directed that they be punished for killing citizens and stealing livestock. One body of Cheyennes under Black Kettle, desiring peace, settled in November on a tract near Fort Lyon in southeastern Colorado, where authorities said they would be safe from attack. On the twenty-ninth, however, Colonel John Chivington and nearly 700 soldiers with howitzers attacked Black Kettle's village of approximately 500 people along Sand Creek, killing as many as 150, many of whom were women, children, and the elderly. Even though federal authorities quickly denounced Chivington's actions as "a foul and dastardly massacre," news of the butchery swept the plains. To the north, members of the Lakota bands, together with Northern Cheyennes and Arapahos, many of whom had friends and relatives at Sand Creek, prepared to respond when opportunity presented. The significance of Sand Creek cannot be overstated, for it affected Indian-white relations immediately and over succeeding decades.[10]

Following Sand Creek, the tribes mobilized for a period of major confrontation that now appeared inevitable. Vengeful parties of Cheyennes, Lakotas, and Arapahos struck back early in 1865, notably attacking Julesburg along the South Platte River in Colorado. Raiding activities proceeded in Wyoming against emigrants traveling the Bozeman Trail to the Montana gold diggings as well as along the mail and telegraph lines, and repeated skirmishes took place between war parties and troops from Fort Laramie. This fighting peaked during late July 1865 in the Platte Bridge and Red Buttes fights, in which a detachment of cavalry came under attack while attempting to reinforce the escort of an incoming supply train near present-day Casper.

In an encounter in which the Northern Cheyennes played a significant role, the wagon party was wiped out, and the troops who had sought to relieve them made it back to Platte Bridge Station. Punitive campaigns against the tribesmen led by Brigadier General Patrick E. Connor in 1865 brought several engagements to the Powder River country in which the Cheyennes and their Lakota and Arapaho allies eventually forced the troops' withdrawal back to Fort Laramie, having succeeded only in deepening existing animosities.[11]

The Northern Cheyennes played a major role in Red Cloud's War following government attempts to establish a military presence along the Bozeman Trail. Troops erected two new posts, Fort Phil Kearny and Fort C. F. Smith, in Wyoming and Montana, respectively, and regarrisoned a station along the Powder River, Fort Reno, previously raised and abandoned by Connor. Their presence in the country these Indians regarded as their own (even though technically they stood on land occupied by the Crows) gave them much indignation, and with growing frequency warriors ran off livestock and attacked fatigue parties from the posts as well as army and civilian trains negotiating the Bozeman Trail. The intermittent warfare climaxed on December 21, 1866, when the Indians fell on a column of eighty men under Captain William J. Fetterman from Fort Kearny and killed them all. In the summer of 1867, two engagements, one known as the Hayfield Fight near Fort Smith and the other the Wagon Box Fight near Fort Kearny, in which small bands of soldiers came under attack by large numbers of Sioux and Cheyennes, helped restore morale to the troops in the wake of the Fetterman encounter. But despite these successes, the Indians gave no indication of slackening their resolve to rid the country of troops and civilians. Plans to send a major campaign against the tribesmen collapsed due to seasonal considerations as much as to politics. Mounting costs, along with the development of alternative routes for reaching the gold country via the new transcontinental railroad, determined Washington to concede, at least temporarily, the objective of militarily occupying the disputed lands. Federal authorities extended peace overtures, and in the Fort Laramie Treaty of 1868 the Northern Cheyennes, Sioux, and Arapahos seemingly won the day. Most notably, the government conceded maintenance of the Bozeman Trail, agreeing to close Forts Reno, Kearny, and Smith. Only Fort Fetterman—Crook's jumping off place in 1876—would remain at the periphery of the disputed region.[12]

The Northern Cheyennes experienced repercussions from events transpiring among their southern kin; friends and relatives died or were injured in the conflicts with soldiers during the years following Sand Creek, most notably as a result of the troops' winter attack on Black Kettle's village along the Washita River in Indian Territory in 1868, in which the peace chief was killed. In the conflict that arose during the 1870s respecting the army's dealings with the so-called "Northern Sioux"—those Lakotas who spurned the 1868 accord, remaining in the Powder River country and refusing to settle on the reservation—the Northern Cheyennes had continued their cultural alignment with the Tetons, and particularly with the Oglalas, with whom many of them had intermarried.[13]

Among the Northern Cheyenne leaders, two men—Morning Star and Little Wolf—had emerged by midcentury to guide their people as steadfast defenders of the traditional lifeways. Morning Star belonged to the *Omissis* band of Cheyennes—the largest band and the one traditionally occupying the country between the Black Hills and the Big Horn Mountains; Little Wolf belonged to the *Sutaio* band. Morning Star, born around 1808, was known among the Lakotas as Dull Knife; Little Wolf was born around 1830. Both had proven themselves able warriors. As a young man, Morning Star had participated in a raid against enemy Pawnees and had captured a young Pawnee girl, who was raised by his family; years later, she became one of his wives. Beyond that, little appears to be known of the early lives of either chief, but by the mid-1850s Morning Star and Little Wolf had drawn the attention of army officials at Fort Laramie because of their bands' occupation of the area north and south of the post. Both men at the time had reached stature as warrior leaders and had negotiated with military authorities there over disputes arising from the Indians' confiscation of livestock in 1856, following which Little Wolf had narrowly avoided being killed by the troops or captured and imprisoned at Fort Laramie. Military records indicate that at the time, Morning Star's village stood along the South Platte River. In 1866 the chief signed an agreement authorizing the government to erect posts in the Powder River country, an incident that purportedly angered many of his people and affected his standing among them. Both episodes ultimately weakened tribal unity and contributed to the tenuousness of Cheyenne government in the future.

During Red Cloud's War, both Morning Star and Little Wolf took part in the ambush killing of the soldiers under Captain Fetterman near Fort Phil Kearny. Less than two years later, each was signatory to the Treaty of Fort Laramie by which the government surrendered the region, and Little Wolf personally started the blaze that consumed the abandoned Fort Kearny. Under terms of the Fort Laramie treaty signed on May 10, 1868, the Indians would accept as their home either the tract established for the Southern Cheyennes and Southern Arapahos below the Arkansas River in Indian Territory "or some portion of the country and reservation set apart and designated as a permanent home for the . . . Sioux Indians"—the Great Sioux Reservation in Dakota Territory as specified in the previously concluded Sioux treaty. The Indians further surrendered to the federal government "all right, claim, and interest in and to all territory outside the two reservations . . . except the right to roam and hunt while game shall be found in sufficient quantities to justify the chase." The tribes were given one year to permanently attach themselves, as they variously might prefer, to agencies in the specified reserves or to one to be established along the Yellowstone River to serve the Crows. Yet in the funding appropriated to implement the treaties with the Sioux, the Northern Cheyennes and Arapahos were somehow overlooked. With the establishment of Red Cloud Agency in 1871 to serve the reservation Lakotas, the Cheyennes and Arapahos, who continued to roam the "unceded Indian territory" between the North Platte and Yellowstone Rivers, drew annuities at that place, an arrangement eventually sanctioned by the Sioux Agreement of 1876 at those tribesmen's behest despite longstanding congressional designs to move them south.[14]

Thus, by the accords of 1868, the Northern Cheyennes continued to occupy the country adjoining the Big Horn Mountains in eastern Wyoming, with some taking rations with the Sioux at Red Cloud Agency. But many of the tribesmen, the people of Little Wolf and Morning Star among them, managed an arrangement with the government whereby they received their supplies at Fort Fetterman closer to their zone of domicile, the commanding officer serving as ex-officio agent for the Cheyennes. At one time late in 1870, nearly all of the Cheyennes and Arapahos must have camped in the vicinity of the post, with approximately 300 lodges of the former and 150 of the latter, besides 350 lodges of Sioux, reported as present. The tribesmen, described as "friendly," came to Fort Fetterman almost weekly, usually holding lengthy talks with the commander before receiving their rations. Lieutenant Colonel George A. Woodward recalled Morning Star and Little Wolf visiting the garrison peaceably. Morning Star was "tall and lithe in form, he had the face of a statesman or church dignitary of the grave and ascetic type. His manner of speech was earnest and dignified, and his whole bearing was that of a leader weighted with the cares of state. Little Wolf had a less imposing presence, but looked more the soldier than the statesman." Woodward cited no major difficulties with the Indians during his tenure at the post. When, in May 1872, a war party attacked an army supply train along the road from Fort Laramie and killed a sergeant, Morning Star and Little Wolf determined that the culprits belonged to Old Bear's band and delivered up the mule the dead man had ridden. "Having properly acknowledged this evidence of good faith on their part," wrote Woodward, "I made Little Wolf and his companions a present of some rations, and they set out to rejoin their people." In his meetings with the Cheyenne leaders, Woodward strove to promote their acceptance of the plan to remove them to Indian Territory. He also labored to keep them away from Red Cloud Agency, "because I knew that the influences to which they would be subjected there would be opposed to the realization of the government scheme."[15]

With the relocation of Red Cloud Agency in 1873 and the establishment of Camp Robinson to oversee the station the following year, the quasi-agency relationship involving Fort Fetterman ended, and the Cheyennes and Arapahos henceforth were directed to go to Red Cloud for their provisions. By the mid-1870s, Little Wolf and Morning Star were recognized as two of the four Old Man Chiefs in the Council of Forty-Four, honored positions that reflected not only their bravery but also their generosity, even-tempered natures, and abilities to use good judgment on behalf of the tribe. Moreover, Little Wolf received the supreme recognition of his tribe by becoming bearer of the chiefs' bundle, which contained the sweet root granted the people by Sweet Medicine in their early history. By this signal distinction, Little Wolf, now effectually the incarnation of Sweet Medicine, presided over the Council of Forty-Four whenever

that body convened. In November 1873, as members of a Cheyenne and Arapaho delegation to Washington, D.C., Little Wolf,
Morning Star, and other chiefs met with President Ulysses S.
Grant and Interior Department officials to vocally protest the
government design to move the people south to Indian Territory. Declaring that they had never agreed to such a proposal in
the 1868 document, the Indians departed the Executive Man-
sion determined to resist the removal. The government did not
revive the matter until the Black Hills negotiations of late 1876
following the principal fighting of the Great Sioux War.[16]

Early in 1876, when the army opened its offensive against
the Lakotas, some of the Northern Cheyennes were hunting in
the Powder River country of southeastern Montana. Old Bear's
camp, in which Little Wolf was present, stood along that stream
when Colonel Joseph Reynolds's cavalry struck them on the
morning of March 17. Because the troops had moved into the
area from Fort Fetterman, passing along the broad corridor
between the Black Hills and the Big Horn Mountains—the
unceded treaty lands that coincidently composed the Cheyennes' traditional lands—to strike this village, a societal paranoia
had likely appeared among them by mid-1876 that suggested
that they, and not the Teton Sioux, were the primary objectives
of the army operations. And the Sioux might have shared this
belief. Following the assault on Old Bear's people, the Cheyennes sought and received help from the Lakota camps of
Crazy Horse and Sitting Bull. Thereafter, as the tribes traversed
the region, the Cheyenne camp took the lead, for they had been
the ones attacked by the soldiers. Moreover, Crook's second
offensive that year took an almost identical course into the heart
of Cheyenne country around the Tongue and Rosebud before
the coalition of tribes stopped the soldiers and turned them
south on June 17. A week later when Custer struck the immense
Little Bighorn village, it was situated in a traditional setting in

Cheyenne country. The Northern Cheyennes had led the way to the Little Bighorn, and their camp circle stood farthest north in the village alignment. After Major Marcus A. Reno's charge on the southern end of the village had been deflected by the Indians in the opening stage of the engagement, Custer led his battalion directly toward the Cheyenne camp only to be soundly repulsed and then completely destroyed by warriors from all camps. Little Wolf was not present during the battle; he and his few lodges arrived after most of the fighting was over.[17]

If indeed the Cheyennes considered themselves the particular targets of the army during the first half of 1876, that perspective was doubtless reinforced in their consciousness within weeks of the Little Bighorn clash. Many of the followers of Morning Star had remained at Red Cloud Agency throughout the period of early fighting with the troops. Pressures by government agents on them to join their southern kin, coupled with knowledge of the fighting with their relatives in the north, influenced as many as six hundred agency Cheyennes to start north for the Yellowstone country to support them. On July 17 a small advance body of the Red Cloud Agency Cheyennes encountered a command of the Fifth Cavalry under Colonel Wesley Merritt at Hat, or Warbonnet, Creek in northwestern Nebraska. In the ensuing skirmish one Indian was killed (reportedly at the hand of William F. "Buffalo Bill" Cody, who was scouting for Merritt) as the Cheyennes turned back. The main body of tribesmen also turned about and headed east, the Fifth Cavalry in pursuit. Before gaining the agency, Morning Star's band pulled away, likely under darkness, circumventing the troops and moving west in the direction of the unceded tract and the Big Horn Mountains. In late July these Cheyennes camped in the mountains, where the people of Little Wolf and the other leaders joined them after separating from the Lakotas following Little Bighorn. There they hunted and prepared for winter much in the manner of previous years. Those Cheyennes who returned to Red Cloud Agency after the skirmish with Merritt joined with the agency Sioux in conceding the Black Hills to the U.S. government in the agreement signed in September.[18]

Although aware of the Cheyennes' participation as collaborators with the Lakotas in the warfare in 1876, Crook's troops moving out from Fort Fetterman had their sights set on the Sioux camps known to be wintering south of the Yellowstone in the area of Rosebud Creek and Tongue and Powder Rivers. Despite the reasonably good relations that had evolved between the army and the Cheyennes during the years since Red Cloud's War, likely because of the nearby proximity of Fort Fetterman to their domicile, concerns among military authorities over the Indians' role in the recent fighting increased after Morning Star left the agency. In September concerns mounted with word that warriors were en route north from Indian Territory to aid their brethren in the conflict, a fear seemingly without much basis. And late in October Colonel Mackenzie had learned from a tribesman that the "hostile Cheyennes" were at the Rosebud, ostensibly with the Oglalas. Mackenzie sent a Cheyenne runner to the camps with word that the troops would be coming "through the Big Horn country." "I told this Indian to tell the Cheyennes that those who come in would lose their arms and horses but would get plenty to eat." The colonel also called on General Sheridan to send Captain Richard H. Pratt "and the best selection of [Southern] Cheyennes that Pratt can make" to Fort Fetterman to help train the Cheyenne, Arapaho, and Sioux scouts enlisted from Robinson. The suggestion was apparently ignored.[19]

But it was the large bodies of Sioux and not the Northern Cheyennes who were uppermost in Crook's thoughts as his column, stretching out more than five miles along the road, wended north toward Powder River. On November 15 the troops passed under leaden skies, and cool breezes brought "a slight but chilly rain" by midafternoon, when the column approached the South Fork of Cheyenne River. Traveling some eighteen miles, in camp they found enough wood and water, but grass was scarce. Colonel Dodge noted the "magnificent view" attained of the distant Laramie Mountains as the command passed over the divide between the Platte and the Cheyenne drainages.[20] On Thursday Crook's force moved twenty-one miles to the North Fork of Wind Creek, a branch of the Cheyenne. Bourke reported watching the Lakota scouts chase and bring down an antelope, shooting it from their ponies, and then chasing it until it collapsed from exhaustion. "Before it had time to die the Indians had surrounded it and divided the carcass into a dozen pieces."[21] On the march that day, the column encountered hilly terrain, and the soldiers labored with ropes to pull the wagons up the slopes. "Great numbers of the men have the diarrahea," wrote Sergeant James S. McClellan.[22]

At the end of each day's march, the routine had the command jostling about for a place to camp, a condition of affairs that Dodge believed intolerable and due largely to Crook's inattention to such matters. "All the choice spots . . . [were] appropriated by him, his Indians [scouts] & pack mules," he complained. "These two last are his hobbies & he rides them all the time."[23] Furthermore, Dodge confided to his journal about Crook's deficiencies as a commander: "There is no doubt about his courage, energy [or] will—but I am loath to say I begin to believe he is a humbug. . . . All the Hd Qr animals, the pack mules & the mules of the supply train are above us—while his Indians wash the entrals of the beeves in the stream from which his troops have to drink below. The Cavy & Infy are nobodies. The Indians & pack mules have all the good places. He scarcely treats McKenzie & I decently, but he will spend hours chatting pleasantly with an Indian, or a dirty scout."[24] Dodge visited with

Mackenzie, found him compatible, and worked out arrangements with him for alternating their respective infantry and cavalry commands' first use of the road on successive days. That night mail reached the command from Fort Fetterman, including news about the presidential contest making Hayes the apparent winner.[25]

On the seventeenth the troops rolled out of their blankets to face frigid temperatures and a driving snowstorm "blowing right into our teeth," penned Bourke. Many of the infantrymen, not expecting such weather, were without their overcoats. "They plodded along," reported Colonel Dodge, "wind dead ahead . . . without anything but their own stout hearts to protect them." When one man suddenly broke into a chorus of "Marching through Georgia," "at least a hundred voices joined in at once."[26] By midday the storm had passed and skies were clear, and after moving about twenty miles, the column camped at Buffalo Springs along Dry Fork by midafternoon. Toward dusk, fifteen Arapaho scouts rode off to determine the identity of several presumed Indians seen off to the east of the column. The scouts trailed and eventually surrounded the party, only to discover that they were white men ("Horse thieves, perhaps," noted Bourke). That night three Shoshones made their appearance in company with two white men. They had come from Cantonment Reno, now within twenty miles away, where one hundred of their warriors had arrived to serve the expedition as scouts. The Shoshones brought Crook news of Sioux trails running toward the west side of the Big Horns in the direction of the sources of the Crazy Woman and Clear Forks of Powder and Tongue Rivers.[27]

The next day, Saturday, Crook's command arrived at the newly built cantonment after passing down Dry Fork to its junction with Powder River. An officer described the Powder as "a murky, discolored pea soup kind of a stream, almost as filthy as the Missouri itself." Some of Colonel Mackenzie's teams became stuck in the mire of the bed during crossing and had to be extricated by soldiers pulling with ropes. The troops bivouacked in the bottom on the east bank below the post.[28] Over the next three days, Crook and his officers would complete their final preparations before moving against the Sioux.

Lieutenant General Philip H. Sheridan commanded the Military Division of the Missouri in 1876. He and George Crook were classmates at West Point, but their friendship soured after the Civil War. Although Sheridan broadly conceived operations for the Great Sioux War, he disliked Crook's advocacy of the use of Indian scouts and apparent inattention to detail, and he grew increasingly critical of his department commander. The relationship finally ruptured altogether in a disagreement over Crook's conduct of the pursuit of the Chiricahua leader Geronimo in 1886, and the two remained at odds until Sheridan's death in 1888. Courtesy Jerome A. Greene.

Brigadier General George Crook as he appeared in a photograph taken in January 1877 in Cheyenne, Wyoming, by photographer Daniel S. Mitchell. Crook's performance throughout 1876 became a topic of criticism within the army hierarchy, despite the fact that his commands were always in the thick of the action and secured two of the earliest army victories in the Great Sioux War. His oversight of the Powder River Expedition, including Ranald Mackenzie's successful attack on the Northern Cheyennes, helped seal Crook's reputation among the public as one of the army's preeminent field commanders by the end of 1876. Courtesy Paul L. Hedren.

Camp Robinson, Nebraska, in an 1876 view looking west, as photographed by Daniel S. Mitchell. Officers' quarters appear right of center in the distance. In the foreground is Camp Custer, one of three temporary facilities raised to accommodate troops arriving for Crook's expedition. Courtesy U.S. Military Academy Library.

Red Cloud Agency in 1876, looking north. A stockade ran along the agency perimeter and connected the buildings. The tall structure in center was the issue bastion, and the segregated buildings at either side of the agency were the posts of independent traders. Courtesy Nebraska State Historical Society.

Deposed by Crook as federally recognized chief of the Lakotas following a flurry of dissent late in October 1876, Red Cloud, the Lakota leader who purged the army from the Bozeman Trail in the 1860s, had since remained a peaceful though intimidating presence on the Great Sioux Reservation. This image was taken outside the post guardhouse by photographer Stanley J. Morrow following the forced return of Red Cloud and Red Leaf as preparations proceeded for Crook's campaign against Crazy Horse. Courtesy South Dakota State Historical Society.

General Crook at Red Cloud Agency proclaiming Chief Spotted Tail as chief of all the Sioux on October 24, 1876, replacing Red Cloud following the army's surrounding of the Oglala leader's camp a day earlier. Crook and Spotted Tail appear in the center of this image by photographer Stanley J. Morrow. Courtesy U.S. Military Academy Library.

In 1876, at the behest of General Sheridan, Captain Frank North reprised his role as organizer and commander of the Pawnee scouts and led them on the Powder River Expedition. Courtesy Nebraska State Historical Society.

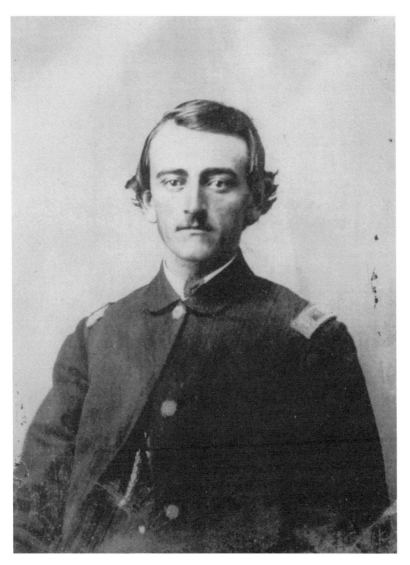

Luther North assisted as brother Frank North's first lieutenant. Courtesy Nebraska State Historical Society.

Lieutenant Colonel Richard I. Dodge commanded the infantry battalion of the Powder River Expedition. His journal accurately reflects the trials of campaigning in winter conditions while delivering a sound indictment of General Crook's organizational practices and leadership abilities. Courtesy The Newberry Library, Chicago.

Sharp Nose, an Arapaho, served Crook superbly as a first sergeant of Indian scouts on the Powder River Expedition. Lieutenant John Bourke called him "the inspiration of the battle-field. . . . He handled men with rare judgment and coolness, and was as modest as he was brave." Photograph by Daniel S. Mitchell. Courtesy Smithsonian Institution, National Anthropological Archives, NAA-55,703.

Crook's cavalry battalion on parade at Camp Robinson in October 1876, shortly before departing on the Powder River Expedition. This picture by Cheyenne, Wyoming, photographer Daniel S. Mitchell shows elements of the Fourth and Fifth Cavalry, and possibly parts of the Third and Second Cavalry. From *Motor Travel* (January 1930). Courtesy Wisconsin Historical Society.

Fort Laramie, Wyoming Territory, in 1876, a view to the northwest. Crook's command likely entered the venerable post from Camp Robinson along the roads in the foreground. A mainstay military presence throughout the northern plains since the 1850s, Fort Laramie played an instrumental role in operations of the Great Sioux War, including the Powder River Expedition of late 1876. Courtesy National Archives.

Chapter 4
Cantonment Reno

CANTONMENT RENO STOOD ON THE LEFT (west) bank of Powder River some three miles upstream from the site of the former Bozeman Trail post of Fort Reno, abandoned since 1868. The erection of the new post had been urged by General Sheridan and directed by Crook following their mid-September strategy meeting at Fort Laramie. As with the Tongue River and Glendive Cantonments along the Yellowstone, Cantonment Reno was to symbolize to the Sioux and Cheyennes the government's determination to occupy the country immediately and permanently and thus prevent any assembling of the tribesmen such as had occurred during the previous spring and summer. The posts, moreover, were designed as staging areas in the heart of the disputed territory from which military campaigns might operate with mobility against the tribes, thereby making the Indians' traditional existence untenable and promoting their movement to the reservation agencies.

The site of Cantonment Reno, as well as its name, was selected on October 14, 1876, by Captain Edwin Pollock of the Ninth Infantry. Pollock's command consisted of Company E, Ninth Infantry; Companies B and E, Fourth Infantry; and Company K, Twenty-third Infantry, the latter two units arriving within a few days, escorting building and campaign supplies from Fort Fetterman. Complaining that he had "the poorest government [wagon] teams I have ever seen," Pollock established the post on level ground with close proximity to water, and his

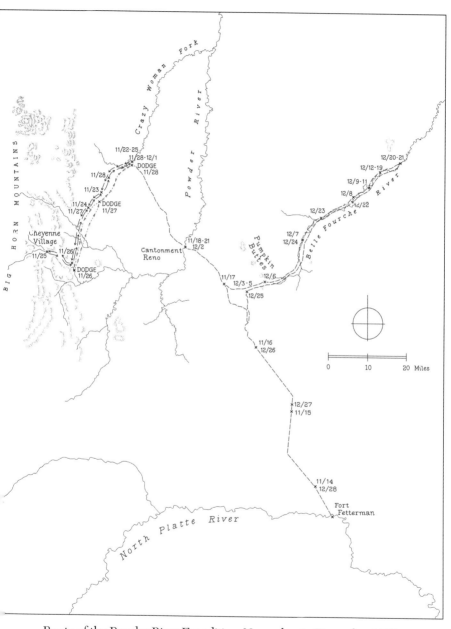

Route of the Powder River Expedition, November to December 1876

men raised many of its buildings of squared logs hewn from the
abundant cottonwoods along the Powder, although some wood
came from the sawmill at Fort Fetterman. The men laid out a
perimeter embracing a parade ground 475 feet by 520 feet. A
storehouse ready to receive provisions for the upcoming expedition was critical, and beyond the necessity of sheltering the
soldiers and officers sent to build the post, immediate efforts
were geared toward erecting that building. The men hurriedly
threw up a skeletal framework 210 feet by 21 feet covered with
tarpaulins. It had double doors at either end; its dirt floor required
that goods subject to dampness placed within be set on poles
covered with sagebrush. "To have built this house of logs . . .
would have consumed weeks of precious time," reported Pollock. "By making the frame and covering it with Paulins, the store
house was built in nine days." Simultaneously, the troops dug two
frost-free cellars, each 12 by 40 feet and roofed, in which to store
perishable goods. Following that, they began construction of
enlisted men's quarters. There were fourteen of them, each 15
by 20 feet, built of logs, and having windows. Four more, measuring 15 feet square, doubled as first sergeants' quarters and
orderly rooms. Dugout structures to serve as kitchens and mess
houses were seemingly partially completed by the time of the
expedition's arrival. All of these facilities were provided with various heating and cooking stoves hauled out from Fetterman.
Future work for the cantonment included the erection of officer
quarters, commissary and quartermaster offices, corrals, stables,
and a hospital.[1]

Despite initial difficulties obtaining wagons, trains loaded
with provisions bound ultimately for Crook's command lum-
bered out of Fort Fetterman with regularity, and the need for
sheltering these goods after delivery to Reno was immediate.
As an example of the necessities required, early in October

Captain Edwin M. Coates reported two supply trains bound from Cheyenne "loaded with potatoes, grain and clothing, [and weighing] one hundred sixty thousand pounds." Coates wired department headquarters and received approval for replacing the clothing with onions at Fetterman and sending the trains on to Cantonment Reno. General Crook predicted that his horses would need up to 26,000 pounds of forage daily, and in anticipation of this, 200,000 pounds of grain were sent to Reno while 300,000 more remained in storage at Fort Fetterman. By the time of the expedition's appearance on November 18, tons of rations, clothing, equipage, and supplies—reportedly enough to sustain the men for five months afield and most of it freighted from Medicine Bow Station on the Union Pacific—had reached Cantonment Reno.[2]

Upon gaining the cantonment on the morning of November 18, Crook and his staff began preparations for finding and meeting the Sioux. To that end, in the evening the general sent out six Arapahos and eight Sioux rationed for four days. Acting on suspicions that the Lakotas had filtered down into the Big Horn Mountains and had gone west of that range, the scouts were instructed to search along the base of and into the mountains, now rising prominently scarcely twenty-five miles west of the new post. The scouts were specially chosen because it was believed that other Indians in the area would know of the traditional Sioux-Arapaho friendship and would be induced to approach them without fear.[3] In addition, by the time Crook reached the cantonment, he had been joined by Frank Grouard, his chief of scouts from his earlier campaigns in 1876 and a skilled frontiersman valued by Crook. Recovering from an illness, Grouard had reached Fort Fetterman two days after the command departed and overtook it at its first camp, along Sage Creek.[4]

During the three days that the command remained at Cantonment Reno, various administrative matters occupied Crook and his officers. On the nineteenth, Colonel Dodge requested from his company commanders "the names of all men . . . who by reason of sickness, age, or any other reason whatever may not in their opinion be able to stand the hardships of a pack mule campaign on which there will be no facility for carrying those who give out." Such individuals were to report for medical examination. "We want on the campaign all the men possible, but no man who is likely to become a burden," said Dodge. Furthermore, all soldiers whose term of service expired before December 15 would remain behind for discharge, and the necessary inventories of government property, including arms, in the possession of such men were made prior to their return to Fort Fetterman.[5] Dodge also issued an order directing his command be divided into four battalions (one each of the Fourth Artillery, the Ninth Infantry, the Fourteenth Infantry, and the Twenty-third Infantry) for the purposes of "drill in battle"; on the afternoon of November 21 the designated units fell out in the prescribed formation "for skirmish drill."[6] Preparing for exigencies, Captain Pollock requisitioned mattresses for the forty-four iron bunks and slats that had arrived for use in a post hospital at Reno.[7]

On Sunday, November 19, two incidents occurred at the cantonment. One involved payment of the troops, for which the departmental paymaster, Major Thaddeus Stanton, had arrived with Crook. Stanton had played a courageous role in Crook's summer campaign, where he earned the sobriquet "The Fighting Paymaster" for his deeds. Now his dispersal of money to the troops brought on an evening of pervasive intoxication throughout the post and surrounding bivouacs. "You never saw such a drunken crowd in your life," one enlisted man of the Fourth Cavalry wrote his brother. After a number of shots rang out in the infantry camp that night, Dodge complained to General Crook about the uncontrolled revelry; the general refused to order the trader's store closed, but Captain Pollock finally shut it down. In addition, the Indian scouts received pay too. "It was very amusing to see them paid," wrote an observer. "Some had one day's pay due them, others more, and they could not understand why they were not all paid alike." Adjutant John Bourke reported that "a degraded wretch" was caught purveying the whiskey to both troops and Indians. "His cart was confiscated and the heads of his barrels knocked in." Nonetheless, one soldier wandered off drunk into the night and a raging snowstorm only to be found frozen to death the next day.[8]

The other matter concerned Crook's Indian scouts and consisted of his efforts to make them get along and hopefully contribute to the operation at hand. Awaiting the command when it reached Cantonment Reno were ninety-one Indian men, mostly Shoshones and already enlisted as scouts, with nine women and four children. They had been at the cantonment for three weeks, having arrived from their agency near Camp Brown, Wyoming—west of the Big Horns—on October 27 in response to Crook's earlier call for their recruitment. The Shoshones, with their venerated chief Washakie, had served Crook during the past summer and had performed bravely at the Battle of the Rosebud in June. Now they were back, this time without Washakie, who cited a bout with rheumatism and other health concerns for a man of his age (he was in his seventies) during a winter campaign. Instead, Washakie's eldest son, Ko-na-ya, headed the assembly. Thomas Cosgrove, an old-time frontiersman, accompanied the Shoshones from their agency and served as their spokesman. The Shoshones at Cantonment Reno were ready to campaign, doubtless motivated by revenge after having learned of an attack by Northern Cheyennes on a village of their people in the Wind River range in late October that had left five of their kinsmen dead.[9]

The presence of the Shoshones boosted Crook's Indian scout contingent to more than 350 people. Besides the Shoshones, Pawnees, Lakotas, and Northern Cheyennes present, apparently fifteen Bannocks (related to the Shoshones), one Ute, and one Nez Perce were present, and plans called for recruiting even more scouts among the Crows in Montana to help find and cripple the Sioux. Four interpreters facilitated communication between these Indians and the command.[10] The fact that several of the tribes had not only recently been fighting the army but moreover held age-old traditions of enmity against each other created unsettled feelings among all and perhaps motivated Crook in his decision to meet once more with the tribesmen and lay out his expectations for them. Certainly the cool demeanor that the Pawnee scouts had manifested toward the other Indians, particularly the Sioux and Cheyennes, registered concern as something that should be speedily confronted and quelled in the interest of campaign harmony.

On the morning of the nineteenth, before Crook's headquarters, all the Indians assembled, standing in a circle with Crook, Dodge, other officers, and the interpreters in the center. As enlisted soldiers, all except a handful of Sioux and Cheyennes wore the U.S. uniform. In his remarks, which had to be interpreted sentence by sentence for each tribe represented, Crook stressed unity and friendship among all for the common good of all and called on *all* the tribesmen to don uniforms. The buffalo were becoming extinct, he said, and the Indians were decreasing in numbers too, while the whites were "getting stronger every day." "We don't want to kill the Indians," he told the scouts, "we only want to make them behave themselves. We want to find the [Crazy Horse] village and make the Indians give up their ponies & guns, so that in [the] future they will have to behave themselves." In engagements he urged them not to kill women and children in the enemy camps and instead to capture

them as insurance that the men would surrender their arms and
ponies. "I want you now to be all friends together, just like soldiers are. You must remain friends and stick to this thing right
through until it is ended." The reward for the scouts lay in the
livestock and plunder they apprehended, which would be distributed equally, but Crook enjoined them not to "let the enemy
get away just in order to capture horses." He further cautioned
the Indians about wasting ammunition, then reiterated the need
for them to forget past rancor, shake hands, and be friends.

Several of the Indians responded to Crook's manifesto elo-
quently and subserviently, the latter attitude particularly reflecting knowledge by the Sioux and Cheyenne scouts that their
families, still at the agencies, were effectually prisoners guaran-
teeing their own good behavior. Among those who spoke was
the Arapaho Sharp Nose, who echoed Crook's sentiments regarding the tribesmen making peace with each other and pledged
loyalty to the general. The Pawnee Leading Chief, replete in
military uniform and with his head and face covered in vermil-
ion, brown, and yellow paint, also addressed the body, empha-
sizing the racial commonality of all the scouts and the civilized
traits that the Pawnees had exhibited in embracing farming,
and he called upon "all to be good friends." Ragpicker, a Shoshone, then spoke in support of friendship, differentiating
between the "bad Sioux" and the Sioux scouts and scolding the
former for being "always the first to break peace." Three Bears,
the Lakota, responded that he was happy to be at peace with
the others. He stepped forward, shook hands with Leading
Chief, and presented him with a horse. Another Sioux, Keeps
the Battle, then gave up two ponies to a Bannock and proposed
that his tribe treat with the Shoshones the following spring. On
that note of peacemaking, the council soon ended. Lieutenant
Bourke, who transcribed notes of the meeting into his diary, in
describing the uniformed majority, noted that "a few sported

magnificent war bonnets of feather work and other warlike regalia." For the Indians, recorded Bourke, "the rest of the day was filled with drilling, parading and charging on horse-back, exchanging visits, smoking the pipe of peace and friendly singing or grunting . . . [and performing] the Pony Dance, which is a rhythmic movement on horse-back to the accompaniment of a melancholy chorus."[11] From the time of the meeting forward, relations between the various tribesmen exhibited marked improvement. The Shoshones, who did not know the Pawnees well, were drawn especially closer to them on learning news from them about their relative Comanches in Indian Territory.[12] In a long-term sense, the relationship between the Shoshones and Arapahos fostered at Cantonment Reno in November 1876 improved to the extent that it contributed to the eventual decision to locate the Arapahos in the Wind River country of Wyoming rather than to remove them south.[13]

Rain fell, turning to snow during the night of November 19–20. Crook planned to move from the cantonment in the morning, but the departure was again delayed to await information from the scouts who had been sent out earlier. Early word had it that the Sioux were gathering west of the Big Horns, and the general prepared dispatches reporting the information to Sheridan. The sun appeared as the day passed slowly, with no further whiskey sales to inspire the men, many of whom were still drunk or down with hangovers from the previous night's bacchanal. Paymaster Stanton prepared to head south on the morrow, while the Indian scouts held a powwow and dance "in which there was mutual serenading, plenty in quantity, wretched in quality," as Bourke recorded. Twenty men started on the back trail to Fetterman, including those soldiers too sick to proceed on the campaign and those scheduled for discharge. Breaking the monotony of the day, two parties of famished Black Hills miners appeared at the cantonment, having barely escaped the night's snowstorm to find succor with the troops. The thirty-four men provided Crook with information about recent Indian trails they had encountered in their trek west. These trails, apparently running between the Nebraska agencies and the Tongue River country, further confirmed in the general's mind the location of Crazy Horse's people.[14]

In preparation for the march north, on Tuesday the twenty-first the cavalry units moved a couple of miles down Powder River and reestablished their bivouac. Crook issued orders directing the entire command to start north the next morning. For the balance of the day, the troops variously drilled and prepared themselves and their animals for the coming expedition, when they would leave behind whatever niceties the cantonment afforded. Confidence was grounded in the sheer size of the expedition compared with previous outings. "The column is too long to suffer a repulse from any force that the Indians can possibly bring to bear at this season," opined an observer. "The exciting rumors of defeat and massacre, so ripe during the last campaign, will be wanting in this. . . . Nothing but the flight of all hostiles north of the Yellowstone, or their ignoble surrender, can or will prevent the Powder River expedition from being a success of magnitude, if not the crowning mercy of this infernal war."[15]

But that afternoon events transpired that would ultimately redirect Crook's efforts away from Crazy Horse and toward a quarry much more within the present reach of his command. The fourteen scouts dispatched to search for traces of the Sioux returned to the cantonment bearing a prisoner. He was a young Cheyenne captured some forty miles north at the Crazy Woman Fork of the Powder River. The young man (Bourke referred to him as a "boy"), whose name was Many Beaver Dams, had let his guard down after the Sioux and Arapaho scouts, devoid of distinguishing army clothing, told him they were a war party going to fight the Shoshones. Relaxing in their company, the Cheyenne offered the news of the moment, including detailed descriptions of the recent locations of the various Indian encampments, including that of Morning Star's Cheyennes in the Big Horn Mountains. With the knowledge gained, the scouts pulled their revolvers, seized and bound him, and then started for the cantonment.[16] There Crook interrogated him, but the Cheyenne's answers had by then become purposefully vague and contradictory, although he evidently allowed that he lived in a camp of five lodges near the head of Crazy Woman Fork and that his absence had likely already alarmed his village into striking north to join Crazy Horse. Crook wrote a message to be telegraphed to Sheridan: "Scouts returned to-day and reported that Cheyennes have crossed over to the other side of the Bighorn Mountains and that Crazy Horse and his band are encamped on the Rosebud near where we had the fight with them last summer. We start out after his band to-morrow morning." Rumors of the nature of the information the Cheyenne gave to Crook quickly swept through the command, with one pervasive scenario depicting the imminent mass surrender of the tribesmen.[17]

At dawn on November 22, the command pulled out of Cantonment Reno and began its movement toward a snow-covered northern horizon. Although the sun shone for a while, the temperature was so cold that the men's canteens froze solid. On Crook's direction the column deviated from the Bozeman Trail and proceeded four and one-half miles east to take up its march along an old supply road branch that had run between Fort Laramie and Fort Phil Kearny to the north. The troops passed some twenty-five miles to gain the south fork of Crazy Woman Fork, where Crook called a halt along its banks at a point where wood, water, and grass were plentiful. Dodge believed the distance to be underestimated, grumbling that "it is 28 [miles] if an inch." The place of bivouac was open and, while not particularly comfortable, was admirably suited for defense. Late in the day the scouts killed three buffalo not far from camp and returned with the meat. Still contemplating a strike against Crazy Horse, whose village was estimated to be one hundred miles farther north, the general ordered Captain John V. Furey to park the supply train at Crazy Woman, while the pack train, provided with rations for ten days, would move out next morning with the troops, each man to carry one hundred rounds of ammunition and but two blankets, "rather cool covering for such nights as we have had of late," wrote the *New York Herald*'s correspondent. "To-morrow," remarked Bourke, "our line of direction will turn N.W. and Crazy Horse's village will be the objective point." In making their preparations the cavalry and foot soldiers were busy far into the night. Under this date Colonel Dodge entered in his journal: "The Cheyenne prisoner . . . is now saying that he lied as to the whereabouts of Crazy Horse's camp. If he did Crook will hang him." Anticipating the next day's march, Dodge issued a circular calling on the infantry company commanders to reduce each company to thirty men to be comprised of those "most likely to stand the hardships of the campaign."[18]

But Crook's immediate objective changed soon after dawn on Thursday, November 23. Sitting Bear, a Cheyenne spy sent out by Mackenzie from Camp Robinson in October to gain intelligence on the Indians with Crazy Horse as well as to deliver to them Crook's ultimatum of surrender of their arms and ponies, suddenly appeared waving a white flag from a distant hill. Pickets admitted him, and the enlisted Indians scouts soon conducted him to the general. Sitting Bear said that he had been in the Oglala village but had left to seek out that of the Cheyennes. En route he had encountered Many Beaver Dams, who had become lost from his small party. They had traveled together, but when Sitting Bear sent him to follow a trail toward the mountains, the young man had been intercepted by the scouts. Sitting Bear also brought news that the small camp of five lodges to which Many

Beaver Dams had belonged had been spooked by the advancing soldiers and had started away to join Crazy Horse. Furthermore—and most important—Sitting Bear had learned the location of the Cheyenne village, which had moved from the place Many Beaver Dams had reported it to be. Believing that the Crazy Horse village—still more than one hundred miles away—would now be fully alerted to Crook's advance, the general made a decision to seek out and attack the Northern Cheyenne village reported in the Big Horns. As soon as the decision was announced, fourteen Pawnees and Shoshones galloped out of camp and up the Crazy Woman in the direction of the foothills, hoping to gain signs of the now-targeted camp. These Indians were to enter the Big Horns at the first pass they encountered. If they found evidence of the village, they were to come out of the mountains and report to the advancing command. Unaware of these developments, the infantry had geared up, ready to pull out according to the previous night's orders, but at 9:00 A.M. Dodge received a note from Adjutant Bourke stating that the foot soldiers would not move. "I returned at once & ordered the tents to be pitched again," wrote the colonel. "The men were quite delighted & yelled lustily." Instead, the infantry and artillery soldiers would promptly follow the cavalrymen's trail.[19]

According to William Garnett, who interpreted for the Lakota scouts at the Crazy Woman camp, Crook's decision was inspired by the Sioux during an audience they held with the general in which they urged him to immediately seek out the Cheyenne village. "They told the General that their plan was to go against the Cheyennes while they were so far from the [Crazy Horse] Sioux and use them up [defeat them], and then turn on the latter and finish them, thus destroying the hostiles in detail. They told him to send out some companies of soldiers two or three miles in different directions, for there were scouts of the enemy watching the movements from his camp at distances, [and] to push these back so far that they could not see what Crook was doing—could not see movements of troops from his camp."[20] It is not known if the scouts' suggestions determined Crook's course or whether they simply coincided with his own evolving plan. It is possible that he indeed contemplated such a movement, that is, following up an attack on the Cheyenne village with a swift advance north to find and strike Crazy Horse while the snows remained deep and the Indians' movements were inhibited by the season. Regardless, it was likely this plan would later motivate Crook to dispatch Louis Richard and Louis Shangrau, in company with five Lakotas, from Crazy Woman to Camp Robinson with instructions to return with as many additional Sioux scouts as they could recruit.[21]

Mackenzie received orders to ride southwest to the head of the stream, strike into the mountains and find the Cheyenne camp, and then surprise and destroy it. In compliance, at noon of the twenty-third, all of the Indian scouts and the cavalry battalion were put in motion up the south fork of the Crazy Woman in the direction of the Big Horn Mountains. Divided into squadrons under Captain Mauck and Major Gordon, the command consisted of the ten companies of the Third, Fourth, and Fifth Regiments—Company K of the Second stayed behind with Crook—plus the Indian scouts, in all about eleven hundred officers and men. The Indians were under overall command of Lieutenants Clark and DeLany, though with the Pawnees governed de facto by the North brothers and Cushing and the Shoshones guided by Tom Cosgrove. The Indians composed approximately one-third of the command. Adjutant Bourke offered to go with Mackenzie and was assigned to the colonel's staff. Other volunteers included Lieutenant Walter S. Schuyler, who was placed in charge of the Shoshones; Second Lieutenant James N. Allison, Company K, Second Cavalry; and Lieutenant Jones, Fourth Artillery, the latter two filling positions with the companies. Closely following the departing column, the 250-mule pack train bore the requisite ammunition, blankets, and provisions to sustain the troops. Bourke noted the appearance of the command as it moved forth: "There are few sights more inspiriting to a military observer than a compact, well-disciplined column of cavalry, 'fined down' to a minimum of impedimenta, moving rapidly, silently and with malice aforethought along the trail of an enemy. Especially is such the case when the march is made in the depth of winter, in a flurry of snow, by day or by night, when the fur-clad veterans, gleaming from head to foot in an additional coating of crystal rime, and with heavy beards matted with the ice of frozen breaths, bring back to recollection all the childhood legends of Santa Claus and Jack Frost."[22]

The command traveled ten or twelve miles southwest before halting for the night a dozen or so miles from the central mountains of the Big Horn Range. The soldiers made bivouac near the foothills along a small stream that joined the fork of the Crazy Woman they had been following. The camp was "well hidden, and with sufficient fuel, plenty of cold clear water and abundant grazing."[23] After bivouac, a detachment of four Sioux and four Arapaho scouts rode out under orders to find the Cheyenne village. A larger group of Pawnees and Shoshones soon mounted up and followed behind them. That night, amid increasing cold, the men devoured their meager rations and tried to sleep, many with expectations of the major fighting to come.[24]

Next morning, before leaving camp, some of the soldiers went to work with picks and shovels erecting a causeway so the cavalry horses, scouts' ponies, and pack animals could pass over the stream. The troops kept on their diagonal route, experiencing considerable difficulty crossing numerous narrow, yet cavernous, cut-banked streams and nearly losing a Fourth Cavalry trooper who almost drowned after his horse fell from a bank. At each stream much digging had to be accomplished to build

slopes that the animals could navigate. While the column negotiated the terrain that morning, a shot suddenly rang out. It was
discovered that one of the packers had discharged his weapon
accidentally or at some game; regardless, the offender was
immediately turned out and sent back on his own. At noon and
after passing some ten miles, the column approached a rocky
spur jutting from the Big Horns. By then the surrounding flat
country had transformed into a land of pink buttes, red clays,
and deep red sandstone rocks. As Mackenzie's column halted,
and as the pack train pulled up to the left of the troops, off in
the distance some of the Arapaho scouts who had been out all
night rushed forward, circling their ponies about and giving off
shrill whoops, cries heartily answered by the scouts with the
command, who promptly mounted their war ponies and raced
them forward. The event was misinterpreted by the cavalry
officers, who believed that the Cheyennes were attacking and
threw out lines of skirmishers in anticipation of a clash. But the
deployment was soon called off as the scouts came closer, their
excitement induced by word they brought that the Cheyenne
village had been found. "It was not very distant from where we
had halted," wrote Bourke. The scouts could not discern the
size of the camp nor the number of ponies in the herd, only
remarking that there were "heap ponies!" present. Two of the
scouts, Red Shirt and Jackass, had remained in the mountains
to observe the camp. Mackenzie considered the information,
then—probably on the advice of Frank Grouard, who suggested a night march timed to reach the village at dawn—put
his troops under cover of a projecting rock ledge to await darkness, with orders that no fires be lit to attract the attention of
the Cheyennes. There the men passed the afternoon in the cold
with little to eat, checking their weapons and assuring that their
horse equipments were secure. Quipped a packer, "Our spread
for dinner was frozen beans, frozen bread, with snow balls and

pepper on the side." A soldier recalled eating "hardtack and raw bacon, but it tasted good to a hungry bunch."[25]

Mackenzie's evolving plan against the Cheyennes was in keeping with his years of campaigning against Indians on the frontier. Just thirty-six, the young New York native had amassed much combat experience since graduating from the U.S. Military Academy in 1862. Mackenzie, as an officer of engineers, took part in numerous engagements during the Civil War, including Second Manassas, Fredericksburg, Chancellorsville, Petersburg, Winchester, and Cedar Creek, all in Virginia, as well as Gettysburg, and between 1862 and 1864 he received no less than eight battle wounds. Appointed colonel of a Connecticut artillery regiment little more than two years after leaving West Point, Mackenzie was promoted brigadier general of volunteers in October 1864 and by war's end had earned brevets of brigadier general and major general "for gallantry and meritorious service." In the postwar West, the young officer made his mark as commander of the Fourth Cavalry and between 1870 and 1874 led campaigns against several tribes on the southern plains. In 1871 he received a severe arrow wound in a fight near the Brazos River in Texas. He fought Comanches in 1872 at McClellan Creek in Indian Territory, and in the following year he pursued Kickapoos and Lipan Apaches into Mexico, where he attacked and defeated them. During the Red River War, Mackenzie assailed Southern Cheyennes at Tule Canyon and Comanches, Kiowas, Cheyennes, and Arapahos at Palo Duro Canyon in Texas.

Known as a brave leader and often in the thick of the fighting with his men, Mackenzie was often seen as erratic, reticent, and antisocial. Ill health and injury plagued him through much of his career; a bout of sunstroke when a child reportedly affected him later in life when he acquired sustained mental problems, ultimately forcing his retirement. Intelligent yet irascible, Mackenzie could be an unyielding opponent in war and a staunch disciplinarian who often drove his men to their limit when in the field. During the Civil War, then-General Ulysses S. Grant regarded him as "the most promising young officer in the army," an opinion more than amply validated by his subsequent career. In 1876 he was viewed by the army hierarchy with favor, much like Custer had been; General Sheridan saw Mackenzie as a veteran leader, responsible and dependable in all matters. On the frontier the Indians saw his disfigured right hand—two fingers had been blown away by a gunshot wound at Petersburg in 1864—and named him "Bad Hand," a sobriquet by the tribesmen that followed him throughout his tenure in the West.[26] Following the Little Bighorn, Mackenzie's transfer with his regiment to the northern plains to oversee the Sioux agencies was in keeping with the high regard of officialdom for his capabilities. His performance during the Powder River Expedition was to fulfill military expectations in a most resounding way.

Chapter 5
Imminence of Attack

DESPITE THE HOPES OF GENERAL CROOK and Colonel Mackenzie that their advance had not been detected by the Cheyennes, the tribesmen had, in fact, been tracking the army's movements since the troops left Camp Robinson. They as well as Crazy Horse's people knew that Crook had recruited Indian auxiliaries from among their own peoples, and they knew that scouts from the other tribes also had enlisted. The Cheyennes in Morning Star's village were kept informed by their own scouts of the location and pace of the troops as they left Fort Laramie and later as they departed Fort Fetterman for Cantonment Reno. But they did not know that Crook's scouts had captured Many Beaver Dams, who described where Morning Star's camp had recently been located. Thus, when Crook pulled out of the cantonment and headed north, Morning Star's people believed that he was going off to find Crazy Horse. They did not know that Sitting Bear, the Cheyenne spy who infiltrated the Sioux village before being discovered and fleeing to Crook's army, had delivered to the troops updated news of the location of the Cheyenne village.[1]

As an example of the Cheyennes' intelligence-gathering activity, several warriors arriving in Morning Star's village following a hunt reported seeing many horse tracks along Powder River. Camp headmen directed four young men—Hail, Crow Necklace, Young Two Moon, and High Wolf—to find the horse trail, follow it, and report back. The four traveled all day, and

90

the next morning from a ridge they sighted the troops and Indian scouts bivouacked at Cantonment Reno. They watched all day as the soldiers turned their horses out to pasture, as the scouts drove their own animals across to the other side of the stream, and as the troops later returned to drive their mounts back toward camp. After sundown, two of the Cheyennes, Crow Necklace and Young Two Moon, approached the cantonment, expecting to meld with the other tribesmen and escape notice. They found the Cheyenne scouts and recognized two of them. Then they visited the Pawnee camp and cut loose three ponies to take with them. Young Two Moon recalled that the Indian scouts "did not have tents but [employed] shelter of bent willows covered with canvas or [canvas placed] over lodges built of poles." The two then approached the Arapaho camp seeking food. They turned loose of the Pawnee ponies, replacing them with three others taken from the Arapahos. When they rejoined their comrades, they found them asleep and their own mounts gone, having wandered off in the night. The four started back to the Cheyenne village riding the Arapaho ponies, eventually overtaking and recovering their missing stock. This infiltration apparently occurred on the night of November 19—the evening when so many of the soldiers got drunk after they were paid. In any event, the four men returned to the location of Morning Star's village the next day only to find that the Cheyennes had moved over a divide to camp along the Red Fork of Powder River. When they reached the village, they reported what they had seen. Young Two Moon later related that he warned the headmen that "it will be a big fight" if the soldiers reached the camp. Some of the people urged that the group start north to seek out and join the Lakotas.[2]

Crook's movement north rather than west gave the Cheyennes some relief, quieted their apprehensions, and fostered a sense of security that in the end was unwarranted. In short, they dropped their guard. The Cheyennes' numbers had increased with the arrival in early November—the Month of the Freezing Moon—of more people from Red Cloud Agency. These included Standing Elk, Black Bear, Turkey Leg, and their followers. The two former leaders had been among those who in September signed the agreement giving away the Black Hills. But they had become alarmed following the capture of Red Cloud's and Red Leaf's bands and the seizure of their horses, an incident that impelled them to leave and join Morning Star and Little Wolf in the sanctioned hunting grounds. Also present in the village was Old Bear, meaning that three of the designated Old Man Chiefs were together. Other members of the Council of Forty-Four were also there. Present too were the two most important holy men in the tribe, the keepers of the Two Great Covenants: Black Hairy Dog, a Southern Cheyenne, Keeper of the Sacred Arrows; and Coal Bear, Keeper of the Sacred Buffalo Hat. All told, Morning Star's camp now numbered as many as twelve hundred people, possibly including as many as three hundred warriors—practically the entire Northern Cheyenne tribe—all occupying 173 lodges nestled in the southwestern part of a walled canyon that stretched along the Red Fork of Powder River.[3]

The canyon ran almost four miles east to west, its north side formed of a precipitously sloped rocky surface rising fifteen hundred feet above the canyon floor. Scrub mahogany dotted the upper reaches of the mountainside, while close to the floor stunted cedar trees abounded. South of the spring-fed Red Fork, which measured but a few feet across and swiftly coursed along the south side of the bottom, a series of sandstone bluffs shot up, extending the length of the canyon and forming a barrier several hundred feet high on that side of the stream. Inordinate iron content gave the rocky terrain and gravelly soil a deep red hue that translated to name the watercourse.

The site afforded an ideal refuge for the Cheyennes against the cold blasts of northern winds while at the same time exposing them to warmer Chinook breezes from the west. A camping ground traditionally used by the people, in 1876 it possessed the additional advantage of providing visual protection from army columns in the area.

So secure was the canyon that it contained but few points for entrance and egress. One was at the extreme lower end of the canyon floor at a gorge where the stream took its exit between the converging north and south walls. Another lay three miles west along the south wall, where a break opened in the perimeter of high-rising bluffs. Yet other openings lay to the west and northwest, where the canyon terminated among a series of flat irregular hills through which branches of the Red Fork had eroded deeply in entering the canyon From the narrow easternmost entrance, the canyon floor gently descended as it opened rapidly to the west. The expansive floor was occasionally disrupted by sharply rising buttes and intersected by wide and deeply gorged washouts evolved from traces of intermittent tributary springs running from the northern mountainside to the Red Fork, along whose banks grew occasional willow thickets, box elders, and cottonwoods. From approximately midway along the canyon's course and continuing to the higher ground at the west entrance, the sage-dotted plain averaged about one mile in width; measuring from crest to crest across the gorge, the distance was much greater.

Here along the canyon's bottom, the people of Morning Star had raised their white lodges on either side of the stream, hoping to pass the winter days in their accustomed manner, hunting pronghorns and buffalo on the nearby plains and grazing most of their ponies east of, or downstream from, the village on the available grass adorning the south margin of the canyon floor. Most of the tipis stood on the south side of the Red Fork.

They were arranged more or less in scattered formation, though clustered according to band and chief, and faced generally to the east. Some were made of tanned and dehaired buffalo hides sewn together with sinew thread, others of heavy canvas obtained at the agencies. Each conical family lodge ran approximately twelve to fifteen feet in diameter and measured some fifteen feet in height. Somewhere in an open space among the dwellings stood a large council lodge, together with the tipis housing the holy articles of the Buffalo Hat and the Sacred Arrows. As of November 24, there was no snow on the ground.[4]

On that day the Cheyennes learned of the closing proximity of the soldiers. A man named Sits in the Night went down toward Powder River to look for some of his horses and saw people whipping them and driving them away. He reported his observation when he returned to the village, and some of the people began to believe that the troops would soon attack them. Also that morning a blind man named Box Elder, who was the most revered holy man among the Cheyennes after Coal Bear and Black Hairy Dog, saw a vision of soldiers and Indian scouts approaching and charging into the camp from the east. When the vision ended, Box Elder beseeched his son to spread the word of the coming danger. At that, Crow Split Nose, chief of the Elk Scraper Society, which was responsible for the order and safety of the village, told the people to take precautions. He suggested that the women and children tear down the tipis and carry them to the west end of the canyon and build breastworks with them. Some of the people followed the advice and packed their ponies, ready to move the lodges.

But Last Bull, chief of the Kit Fox Soldiers, a rival society to the Elks, arrogantly defied Crow Split Nose and called in his police and directed them to permit no one to leave the village. Last Bull threatened to strike with his quirt anyone who tried to evade his order. The Fox Soldiers then turned back those who had already started for the place Crow Split Nose had indicated, even cutting the packsaddle cinches of their loaded mounts. Apparently believing in the security of their location and that the troops would not attempt to penetrate the mountain fastness in darkness despite the abilities of their Indian allies to lead them, Last Bull told the people, "No one shall leave the camp tonight." He further directed that the people stay up and dance through the night in celebration of the recent victory over the Shoshone hunting party, and a pile of wood was gathered by the Elk and Crazy Dog Society members to start a bonfire for that purpose. The two Cheyennes met soon after to restate their positions, Crow Split Nose reiterating his concern over protecting the women and children while the men defended the camp. But Last Bull held firm, recalling for Crow Split Nose how the Elks had spurned Last Bull's own warning the previous winter before Crook's soldiers had surprised Old Bear's village on Powder River in Montana and telling him, "You will not be the only man killed if we are attacked by the white soldiers." Last Bull directed his Fox Soldiers to be on guard through the night. They then went through the village, forcing the families to attend the dance, even though many did not want to go. Thus was the decision made for the tribesmen to stay in the village in spite of the signs of imminent attack.[5]

Meantime, Mackenzie's command had remained in place on the edge of the mountains through the afternoon of November 24, awaiting darkness. The troops mobilized as dusk fell, about 4:00 P.M. Orders directed against smoking, lighting matches, or talking above a whisper. Items carried on the men's saddles and the pack mules were to be firmly secured to make no noise. Then they set out, moving their horses at a rapid walk in columns of twos until dark. Since leaving the wagons with Crook, the men advanced in light marching order. They wore a mix of military and winter civilian clothing to ward off the freezing temperatures that might be expected in Wyoming Territory in November and December, donning heavy overcoats of canvas, kersey, or buffalo over their issue blue blouses and trousers. Outer garb included the issued sealskin caps and gauntlets as well as buffalo and rubber overshoes; thick scarves were common. Heavy underwear was a priority, and many of the men wore several sets at once or had special ordered underclothing made from blankets. Scant extra clothing was transported in the men's saddlebags, while blankets and overcoats (when not being worn) were mounted on the saddle. Each soldier carried a strapped, quart-size tin canteen full of water. For weaponry, each trooper carried a Springfield carbine, pattern 1873, fixed in a leather socket attached to his saddle stirrup and secured to his person by a snap hook and leather sling. In a holster belted about his waist he toted a Colt's patent .45 revolver and carried requisite .45/55 cartridge ammunition for the carbine in a box or rudely made cartridge belt, with more rounds stuffed in his pants pockets. He also carried a pattern 1858 light saber secured in scabbard and worn on a saber belt around his waist. Another necessity mounted on the belt was a sheathed hunting knife. On this campaign Colonel Mackenzie's own dress reportedly consisted of regulation officer blouse and trousers with a heavy blue overcoat, fur cap, and overshoes.[6]

With his force thus equipped, Mackenzie planned to execute the army's familiar tactic that had been used with success in Indian operations since before the Civil War—a rapid, bold assault on a village whose occupants were normally asleep that would surprise, terrorize, and psychologically dishevel them before they could recover and mount a productive defense of their homes and property. While not a formally prescribed stratagem, it had evolved in use over time, generally with greater success during winter against otherwise highly mobile peoples constricted in their movements by the season's frigid weather and lean ponies. The act of sweeping down suddenly and striking warriors and their families together, threatening, capturing, or killing noncombatants in the process, while simultaneously driving off and destroying the pony herd and then burning the village and its contents, though seemingly immoral by modern standards, nonetheless offered means of success to a frontier army charged with protecting white citizens. The army considered it a way to fulfill the government's mission and consequently practiced it to advantage when opportunity dictated. Most recently during the Great Sioux War, part of General Crook's command had employed the maneuver at Slim Buttes in routing the mixed village of Sioux and Cheyennes. Mackenzie himself had successfully utilized the "dawn attack" scenario previously against tribesmen in Texas. Now he forged ahead, determined to implement it against the Northern Cheyennes.[7]

The march turned laborious as the column began its winding ascent into the mountains. *New York Herald* correspondent Jerry Roche described a movement around the base of a conical hill before passing into and through a "deep red sandstone cut" for an eighth of a mile. This, according to Lieutenant John Bourke, was sufficient "to prevent our being seen for any distance." Then the force undertook a tedious climb up another hillside, formed of what Bourke called "dwarfed knolls of . . . red ferruginous clays," looking back from which the troops gained a spectacular view of the remainder of the column stretched out behind. Newsman Roche reported:

For about a mile the land now spread out level to our view, and as we advanced "Sharp Nose," one of our Arapahoes, called attention to two black specks away to the left. Before any white man present could do more than barely discover their existence he told us they were the two Sioux scouts who had remained behind to learn something more about the village. About the same time that we noticed their approach they

discovered our advance and guided their course so as to head us off.
In about twenty minutes they joined us and just as they reached us
the pony ridden by Jackass, one of the Sioux scouts who was a little in
advance of the other, stumbled and fell over completely exhausted.
Jackass himself, who, by the way, is a brave, bright eyed, handsome
young Indian, was about as tired and hungry as the pony, and could
not tell us what he had seen until after he had eaten a few mouthfuls
of hard bread and bacon. . . . Then, with flashing eyes and in eager
haste, he said he had seen some of the ponies and counted eleven of the
lodges from a hill overlooking the village. He said we could reach the
village at midnight by marching onward steadily. He could not give us
any idea, however, of the size of the village either from the number of
tepees he had counted or the number of horses he had seen.[8]

By this time darkness fully enveloped the command. The men
pressed ahead, aided by a rising moon and the North Star,
trekking through narrow defiles, surmounting craggy hills, and
often wading cold, deep, and brisk mountain streams. On reaching one major watercourse, probably the North Fork of Powder River, they halted to water their horses and tighten their
girths, then forded the stream and continued moving generally
south of southwestwardly. Here the Indian scouts mounted
their war ponies, which they had been leading, and turned their
other animals loose to graze. The scouts with Lieutenant Clark
took the lead in the formation, and the Arapaho Sharp Nose
was in front because he knew the country best of all. Colonel
Mackenzie and the cavalry followed behind, and the pack train
came last. While the advance proceeded slowly across the rough
terrain and crusted snow, there was much activity as riders
passed back and forth to the head of the column to consult with
Mackenzie and his staff.

   At one point the command reached a broad, high-walled
valley estimated to be three miles long and one-half mile wide,

so level that the men likened it to a racecourse. "The ground was like a carpet," wrote Private William Smith, and it allowed the cavalry horses to close up in columns of fours and move along silently at a gallop. Near the end of this valley, the Indian scouts began making active preparations for war, stripping down, changing into special clothing, and painting their faces. The column then moved into more difficult terrain, and the cavalrymen had to dismount and lead their animals single file perhaps as many as twenty different times in their progress. In this fashion the march proceeded, at some places the column stringing out for several miles along its course. Commented one soldier, "If the hostiles had of known we were coming they could of killed every man of us in some of these places." At other points the route was tortuously twisted. "If we could have gone in a direct line from the point where we halted in the afternoon to the [Cheyenne] camp," reported Roche, "the distance would not have been over ten miles, but along the route we were obliged to move we must have marched over twenty miles." First Lieutenant Henry W. Lawton wrote, "At our pace we were three hours going one mile." And Sergeant McClellan recorded of the march: "sometimes the head of the column would be checked [while the rest closed up]. . . . This would cause us to sit in the saddle for half an hour at a time. I was so sleepy and tired I could not keep awake." One time when the troops halted to wait for the column to catch up, the men dismounted and lay down under the trees in spots bereft of snow. "As we rested," remembered one of the packers years later, "the moon shone on the scene, making a wonderful picture."[9]

The night was cold but not unbearably freezing, and Trooper William Judkins kept his overcoat strapped to his saddle during the ride; other soldiers probably did likewise. Soon after midnight—with no village yet near—the moon set, but for the illumination of starlight, plunging the men into total darkness and causing them to grope along for several hours through some of the roughest country yet encountered in their advance. Somewhere along the back trail, a firearm discharged, and Mackenzie became momentarily irate and cursed loudly when he heard it.[10] At one point Frank North directed his brother to move aside and count the Pawnee scouts as they filed by to ensure they were all present. Luther North recalled: "While they were passing me I saw a good many cavalrymen that had fallen out of ranks also pass, and many of them were smoking [against orders]. I noticed another thing and that was that a great many men were sick at the stomach; even some of the Pawnees were so. I don't know why this was so; perhaps the high altitude and the cold had something to do with it."[11]

Presently, the route, as defined by the scouts moving in advance, abruptly turned to the right, and the soldiers found themselves at the Red Fork of Powder River moving in a northwestwardly direction. Wrote Bourke: "Our progress became slow, painfully slow, the pathway was naturally difficult, and hereabouts so cut into by little ravines and 'cut-banks' with frozen sides as to be practically impassable. At one point, the whole column was delayed one hour and two at another. General Mackenzie's natural impatience was aggravated by the solicitude of our Indian guides, who kept coming back every few moments to urge the column forward, saying in a low tone to the interpreters that the hostile village was at hand."[12] All the time, the Indian scouts kept going out and returning to the column with the latest information about the village, and as the troops drew nearer some of the scouts heard the throbbing of drums above the ripple of the stream off in the western distance and Mackenzie was notified of the dance revelry going on in the camp.[13] Just before daybreak, the head of the army column gained the portal leading into the east end of the canyon harboring Morning Star's village. One of the Indian scouts approached

Mackenzie and took him away to investigate the situation. Lieutenant Bourke remembered dismounting with one of the scouts. "We threw ourselves on the ground and then heard with startling distinctness the thumping of the drums, the sleepy intonation of the tired out 'medicine men' and warriors and the patter of languid feet. The dance was almost over, but the dawn had almost come." After ten or fifteen minutes the colonel returned.[14]

The situation was one that Mackenzie neither expected nor relished, but on balance the circumstances probably worked to his advantage. Despite the hour, the camp occupants were mostly awake, a factor that flew in the face of the tactical norm of army surprise attacks on Indian villages. Success was usually assured when the soldiers could approach a sleeping camp with sufficient time to execute a surround, then attack while one or more units simultaneously drove off the pony herds. In this instance the village still lay nearly a mile distant, and there had been no thorough reconnaissance that would permit an estimation of its size, warrior strength, and its defenders' capabilities when under attack. Furthermore, the command had no knowledge of the darkened terrain before them. But given these circumstances, there was also advantage in the situation confronting Mackenzie, both in the drumming and singing emanating from the lodges as well as the unrelenting cascade of the rippling waters of the Red Fork, which would combine to cover much of the noise of the advancing command. The colonel was no doubt relieved to learn that the sounds from the village in no way indicated that the Indians had learned of his approach. Furthermore, the nighttime revel had tired the participants and, unknown to Mackenzie at the time, there were no sentries posted despite the Cheyennes' knowledge that troops were operating in the vicinity.

Trying to gain further intelligence of the status of the village and its immediate physical environs prompted Lieutenant Clark to dispatch several more scouts ahead to reconnoiter before the assault got underway. Presently, one Indian returned with information that the tipis were located on either side of the stream and that there were two or three herds of ponies nearby. Meantime, the soldiers in the fore of the column had dismounted, waiting for those troops still behind and negotiating chasms to close up. Those standing with their mounts tightened their cinches and otherwise adjusted their equipments. Fearful that some sort of ambush might greet his cavalry, Mackenzie directed that the Indian scouts take the lead into the canyon ostensibly to drive off and capture the Cheyenne mounts, an order with which the overanxious allies readily complied. The scouts, already riding their war ponies, now stripped away all encumbrances preparatory to the engagement, crowding ahead "like race horses coming to the score" to await the signal to begin moving forward.

When the last company was reported up, Mackenzie assembled his officers and issued his orders for the assault. His initial plan had been to arrive early enough to surround the village, but that was now too late. He told them to prepare for a dash, following the scouts as they charged forward, and if there occurred an ambush, the Indian scouts would receive the brunt while the troops opened fire from behind. Luther North recalled Mackenzie's instructions thus: "The General gave us [scouts] orders to keep up the lefthand side of the creek; when he gave the order to charge the Shoshone scouts were to follow us up that side of the creek, and the cavalry was to keep up the right-hand side. Our scouts with the Shoshones were to pass around to the left of the village, and the soldiers to the right, and we would have the village surrounded."[15]

Mackenzie arranged his army units for the attack. Major George A. Gordon's battalion was in front. Accompanying Gordon was his battalion adjutant, Second Lieutenant Augustus C. Tyler, and six companies with their officers, each positioned in order of rank seniority: Company H, Fifth Cavalry, Captain John M. Hamilton and Second Lieutenant Edwin P. Andrus; Company K, Third Cavalry, Captain Gerald Russell, First Lieutenant Oscar Elting, and Second Lieutenant George A. Dodd; Company F, Fourth Cavalry, Captain Wirt Davis and Second Lieutenant J. Wesley Rosenquest; Company L, Fifth Cavalry, Captain Alfred B. Taylor, First Lieutenant Edward H. Ward, and Second Lieutenant Homer W. Wheeler; Company H, Third Cavalry, Captain Henry W. Wessels and Second Lieutenant Charles L. Hammond; and Company M, Fourth Cavalry, First Lieutenant John A. McKinney and Second Lieutenant Harrison G. Otis. The second battalion was headed by the senior captain, Clarence Mauck, with First Lieutenant Wenz C. Miller as adjutant, and consisted of the following four companies and their officers: Company D, Fourth Cavalry, Captain John Lee and Second Lieutenant Stanton A. Mason; Company I, Fourth Cavalry, Captain William C. Hemphill, Second Lieutenant James M. Jones (Fourth Artillery, attached), and Second Lieutenant James N. Allison (Second Cavalry, attached); Company B, Fourth Cavalry, First Lieutenant Charles M. Callahan; and Company E, Fourth Cavalry, First Lieutenant Frank L. Shoemaker and Second Lieutenant Henry H. Bellas.

Final preparations seem to have taken an inordinate amount of time, but the moments were necessary to close up the column; to gain new information with which to coordinate the attack among unit commanders, their other officers, and the leaders of the Indian scouts; and to ensure that it was light enough to shoot. At the staging area Mackenzie addressed the scouts and their commanders, telling them to capture the pony herds but not to shoot unless they were fired upon by the Cheyennes. The Indian scouts were placed in order, the Pawnees in the lead followed by the Shoshones and then the Arapahos, Lakotas, and Cheyennes.[16] From behind a hill on the right of the column, the morning star glowed brighter; finally, the first streaks of dawn shot across the valley to the west. The scouts leading the way, troops filed forward in column of fours through the pass to cross the brisk-running creek, its rocky protuberances on either side hemming the command. Then they began their gentle descent to the valley floor. During the passage, First Sergeant Thomas H. Forsyth removed his greatcoat and sealskin gauntlets, strapping them to his saddle. Observing this of his ranking non-commissioned officer, First Lieutenant John A. McKinney did the same and called over to Forsyth to "stick with him, no matter what happened."[17]

As the light slowly improved, the valley could be seen by the troops and scouts for the first time. Once through the gap, Mackenzie made a hurried final placement of his men. The Arapaho, Shoshone, and Sioux allies quickly divined the presence of the Cheyenne pony herds, and they could scarcely control themselves at the prospect before them. As William Garnett remembered: "[They] were chafing to spring on the village as daylight was breaking and they could hear the strains of music and other sounds of merriment. . . . [They] knew that the village was all unconscious of the presence of any foe, and the scouts could scarce restrain themselves, so great was their desire to make the attack a perfect surprise and success. It was with the greatest difficulty that they could be held in check from breaking forward and bursting upon the village, and Three Bears, the chief sergeant of the Sioux, was kept busy in pressing the overanxious ones back into their places in the lines."[18]

The situation with the scouts momentarily grew critical. One of them, a Lakota named Scraper, had somehow managed to advance down the grade ahead of the others. Mackenzie saw him and cried out, "What is that man down there?" Told that he was a Sioux, the colonel instantly pressed white scout Baptiste Pourier and interpreter Garnett to go after him. When they reached Scraper, Garnett told him that Mackenzie wanted him back with the other scouts. The Indian, who was busy tying the cords of his war bonnet beneath his chin, was apparently upset at having been passed over for an appointment as a noncommissioned officer among the scouts. He responded: "I never allow anybody to think before me in a case of this kind. . . . I'm a-going." Then a Lakota sergeant named Fast Thunder rode up. But Scraper again moved out in the lead, and the others followed him down the slope.[19] Back at the pass, the Arapaho sergeant Sharp Nose approached Mackenzie and asked if his men were ready to go. The scouts swarming in the lead, Mackenzie and his staff led Gordon's battalion out of the gorge and down the threshold into the valley below.[20] Less than a mile away in the smoke and mist, most of the Cheyenne lodges remained hidden in the ghostly twilight. The drums had stopped throbbing. It was Saturday, November 25, 1876—five months to the day from the army's catastrophe at the Little Bighorn.

Chapter 6
Triumph and Despair

COLONEL MACKENZIE'S CAVALRY ADVANCED into the canyon at a trot, passing out of a grove of cottonwoods and hesitatingly feeling its way along the unfamiliar turf on the widening north side of the stream. The Indian scouts, given the go-ahead through Adjutant Joseph H. Dorst, meantime burst forward, moving rapidly along the east side of the Red Fork toward the village, 1.25 miles away to the west and mostly hidden from view in the clinging darkness and by willow thickets and cottonwood trees. The opening action occurred in their front and involved the two scouts, Scraper and Fast Thunder, and the interpreters Baptiste Pourier and William Garnett. These men had kept advancing on the left, ahead of the other scouts. Presently, they reached a trail leading to the village and found themselves amid the Cheyenne pony herd. Soon they encountered a solitary Cheyenne man apparently watching the animals. The man appeared perplexed, then caught with the realization of what was happening, he raised his revolver and fired at the scouts—the first shot of the fight—turned, and ran toward the village. Garnett called to his colleagues, "He fired first, now fire!" and the men all discharged their weapons. "This was the beginning of the battle," he remembered. Soon other Cheyenne herders appeared to engage the four men, who were together bent on trying to keep these Cheyennes checked while the remaining scouts came up behind to drive off the ponies.[1]

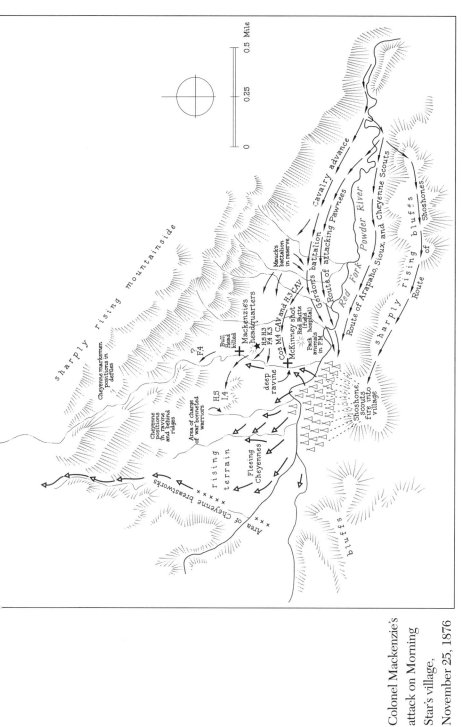

sharply rising mountainside

Cheyenne marksmen
positions in
defiles

Cheyenne
positions
in ravine
and behind
ridges

Area of charge
of war bonneted
warriors

rising terrain

Area of Cheyenne breastworks

bluffs

Fleeing
Cheyennes

? F4

H5
I4

Bull
Head
killed

H5 H3
F4 K3

Mackenzie's
headquarters

deep
ravine

Cos. M4 CAV and H,3 CAV

McKinney shot

Red Butte
(field
hospital)

Pack
animals
in P.M.

Shoshone
scouts
fire into
village

Mauck's
battalion
in reserve

Gordon's battalion

Route of attacking Pawnees

Red Fork Powder River

Route of Arapaho, Sioux, and Cheyenne Scouts

sharply rising bluffs

Route of
Shoshones

Cavalry advance

0   0.25   0.5 Mile

Colonel Mackenzie's
attack on Morning
Star's village,
November 25, 1876

The main body of Indian scouts, meanwhile, had begun their advance along the south side of the Red Fork as Mackenzie had directed, but it must have frustrated them badly. So constricted was the area between the stream and the sharply rising terrain on the south that the scouts had to advance in single file, and thus more slowly than anticipated. Frank North and his brother were in the lead, the Pawnee scouts "strung out behind" and followed by the Shoshones and others. North kept abreast of the advancing cavalry column across the Red Fork to the right. At one point, Mackenzie, through one of several Pawnees he had kept with him, directed North to cross back over to the cavalry side of the stream. The captain complied, leading his men down to the Red Fork and through a boggy bottom, a move that consumed valuable time in the growing daylight. Luther North said years later that this delay permitted the Cheyennes to get their women and children out of the village and into the rocky hills to the west and northwest before the troops struck. Although unstated, the cavalry presumably continued its advance, with the Pawnees, now stripped to trousers and shirtsleeves and armed with carbines and revolvers like the soldiers, gradually catching up. The Shoshones, however, did not cross, instead following Lieutenant Walter Schuyler to the left and up the slope of a five-hundred-foot-tall hill—later called Mackenzie Hill—that extended for approximately three-fourths of a mile along the south side of the Red Fork, its abrupt, north side directly overlooking the Cheyenne village and its west and northwest edge facing the areas of the Indians' eventual withdrawal from the camp. When the Pawnees and the Shoshones diverged from the route, only the Arapaho, Sioux, and Cheyenne scouts under Lieutenants William Clark and Haden DeLany proceeded ahead toward the village as originally intended.[2]

What happened next is not altogether clear. Several of the statements point up the confusion that seems to have reigned, at least momentarily—and intermittently—in the ensuing action, and some incidents seem to have occurred more or less simultaneously in the course of events. The initial advance of the troops up the valley was tentative because of darkness and of irregularities in the terrain, and they were forced to dismount on several occasions to cross ravines transecting their front. Reporter Jerry Roche wrote, "Our progress was comparatively slow in consequence of the roughness of the country through which we were moving."[3] At a point perhaps one-half mile from the Indian encampment, Mackenzie sent Lieutenant John Bourke to direct Major George Gordon's battalion forward, keeping Captain Clarence Mauck's men in reserve. The colonel, mounted on an iron gray horse, personally rode forward with his staff at the head of Gordon's command.[4]

As the four scouts on the far left, across the stream, opened fire on the Cheyenne herders and attempted to stampede the ponies, some of them climbed atop a high red sandstone butte on the north side of the creek overlooking the village. From here they fired on the increasing number of Cheyennes running toward them from the camp to save the ponies. According to participants, the Pawnees advanced on the village howling and blowing "hideous-voiced wind instruments" that sounded to Roche like "the prolonged shriek of a steam whistle" and, in fact, were probably war whistles fashioned from eagle wing bones. Adding to the tumult, the assaulted tribesmen began beating a loud drum to warn their fellows. Dogs began to bark and bay. The cracking sound of gunfire now sporadically echoed through the valley, accenting the pounding hoofs and screams of frightened animals. Some of the advancing scouts, probably mostly Arapahos and Sioux under Lieutenants Clark and DeLany, had approached along the base of the mountain occupied by the Shoshones and penetrated the southeast side of the village. This action forced many of the people to run west and northwest, but a number of the warriors fled northeast toward the ponies and drove some of the animals into an especially cavernous dry ravine that cut across the bottom from the north and debouched into the Red Fork just west of the prominent Red Butte occupied by Pourier, Garnett, and the two Sioux. Clark, DeLany, and the scouts were thus first into and through the camp and were subject to much of the initial retaliatory firing of the fleeing Cheyennes. In this opening action the scouts rapidly went about their own devices, leaving the two officers briefly and suddenly alone in the village to face the fire of the warriors.[5]

Into this growing melee appeared the van of Mackenzie's troopers and the Pawnee scouts. Four companies of Gordon's command, H of the Fifth, K of the Third, F of the Fourth, and L of the Fifth, racing forward in column of fours at a full gallop, thundered around the south side of the Red Butte, then forded the creek and approached the village on the heels of the scouts.[6] As the Pawnees arrived, a Cheyenne marksmen took aim on Luther North, but North fired first, killing the man and later discovering that he had been one of Morning Star's sons.[7] The presence of the Shoshone auxiliaries on the high hill to the south caused the column to halt, however, because those Indians had begun leveling heavy gunfire into the camp. Apparently, Mackenzie and his orderly entered the partly deserted village and now were separated from the balance of the command. The excited colonel, bullets flying about him, consulted briefly with Clark, then dispatched his orderly with instructions for the horsemen to charge in. The appearance of these troops, with Company L in the lead and headed by the Pawnees, who killed several Indians in the village, pushed more of the tribesmen beyond the lodges and likely accelerated the passage of additional warriors around their right front, through the stream, and into the steep-banked washout.[8] Company L's Lieutenant Homer Wheeler noticed a number of Indians attempting to drive off ponies, and he and three enlisted men managed to thwart them and recover the animals. In so doing, the soldiers cut off the warriors from the village, causing them to funnel into the mouth of the washout. This action helped set the stage for the most dramatic part of the assault.

As it became apparent that some of the warriors, trying to save the ponies from capture, had been pressed into the gulch near the base of the Red Butte and were trying to move up that rugged zigzag defile to escape,[9] Mackenzie sent Lieutenant Henry W. Lawton to direct two companies (H of the Third Cavalry and M of the Fourth, operating as the rear units of Gordon's battalion but far in advance of Mauck's second battalion reserves) to thwart the movement and intercept the Indians.[10] Immediately the units raced ahead, rounded the Red Butte on its north side, and approached the largely unseen ravine in column of fours. Company M led the way with Memphis-born First Lieutenant John A. McKinney, an 1871 West Point graduate, out in front, and Company H of the Third under Captain Henry W. Wessels following close behind. As the troops, pistols raised, closed on the gulch, they suddenly drew point-blank gunfire from fifteen or twenty warriors hidden therein, a volley that ripped into the thirty-year-old McKinney, knocking him from his saddle with four gunshot wounds, three of them mortal. McKinney's horse was shot under him, and as the lieutenant fell he screamed to his men, "Fall back! Fall back!" Two men, First Sergeant Thomas H. Forsyth and Private Thomas Ryan, dismounted and rushed to the officer's side, their weapons blazing at the Indians. Two others, Sergeant Frank Murray and Corporal William J. Linn, also hurried forward. Within moments a bullet grazed Forsyth's head and another struck Linn in the right hip joint, yet both were able to continue to discharge their weapons into the ravine while protecting the fallen lieutenant.

The abruptness of the assault, together with the succeeding volley, caused Company M to reel to the right, back from the ravine, and many of the panicked cavalrymen started to retreat up a rise twenty or so yards to the rear. Adding to the confusion, the wounded horse of McKinney's trumpeter, George Hicks, slumped atop its rider, pinning the man's leg and trapping him, but using the animal as a breastwork he was able to twist around and open fire on the warriors in the gorge. At the roar of gunfire and the sudden halting and repulse of McKinney's first ranks, the men of Wessels's Company H, riding directly behind, skewed their mounts sharply to the right to avoid a collision with McKinney's horses and pulled up along the ravine on their flank, tumbling from their saddles at Wessels's barked command to "Dismount and Fight on Foot!" and mixing in with the remaining horsemen of Company M. Although McKinney's second in command, Second Lieutenant Harrison G. Otis, soon moved up and managed to help restore order, it had been Wessels's prompt action near the ravine that had saved the teetering command from a possible rout.[11] Meanwhile, Forsyth and Linn, both wounded, remained at the scene close to the ravine, and with Sergeant Murray and Private Ryan they surrounded and protected the stricken McKinney until he could be moved to the rear. Their action in staying at the ravine also most certainly saved Trumpeter Hicks from being killed. Forsyth's head injury shortly rendered him unconscious.[12]

Things now happened rapidly, confusedly. The led horses were rushed to a point east of the Red Butte out of the line of fire, and the remaining soldiers of the two companies—seemingly moving in undisciplined bunches—advanced on the ravine and opened a fusillade that killed some of the tribesmen. "Just as we swung out of the saddle," remembered Sergeant McClellan, "those in the gully poured in another volley, which passed over our head."[13] By the time of McKinney's fall, Mackenzie had

returned from the village. Instantly grasping the situation, he
directed Gordon to send Captain John Hamilton's Company H
of the Fifth and Captain Wirt Davis's Company F of the Fourth
to support the units under Wessels and Otis. Major Gordon personally escorted these companies ahead, the units arriving to
assist the others in driving the Indians to the north and capturing
some of the ponies. In bolting forward with his troops during this
second rush, Lieutenant Otis's cap was struck by an Indian bullet, which turned it completely backward on his head without
injuring his person. When some of the warriors attempted to
capture the army casualties near the gorge, Captain Hamilton
reportedly fought them back with his saber, wounding one or
two. Eventually, the soldiers, deployed as skirmishers, were able
to spread to their right, many running along the gulch and keeping up their fire, wounding and killing other Indians trying to
flee through it. "The company stood fire like a brick and we had
some hard fighting," one enlisted man recorded.[14] So close was
the combat along this line that Bourke reported Hamilton's and
Davis's men involved in vigorous hand-to-hand fighting and subjected to firing from warriors to the west, which was relieved
only after the Shoshones with Lieutenant Schuyler managed a
long-range response from their hilltop position.

    As the troops of Otis, Wessels, Hamilton, and Davis pressed
the warriors to the north for perhaps a quarter mile, many of
the men took cover behind a butte to protect themselves from
Cheyennes firing from ridges and hillocks to the west and north.
Into the void to their left Mackenzie sent one of Mauck's reserve
units, Captain William Hemphill's Company I, Fourth Cavalry,
but the gunfire of warriors from ravines in their front soon forced
the troopers to pull back beyond range. Soon after, Hemphill and
Hamilton were ordered to take two high knolls situated on the
right, on the high ground adjoining the mountainside and a
short distance ahead of the washout ravine, so as to protect the

right flank. Possibly twenty warriors died in the encounter along
the gully, including eight whose bodies fell into the hands of the
troops, although many Indians managed to get away through
tributary draws. These survivors took up positions opposite the
ravine or behind boulders on the mountainside and returned
fire on the troops. At one point during the fighting, the soldiers
trained their carbines on a warrior who daringly stepped from
his cover to dance and parade some three hundred yards in
front, but they kept missing him with their shots until a bullet at
last found its mark, and the dancer did not reappear. After a time,
Companies K and H, Third Cavalry, under Russell and Wessels
took up dismounted positions between the village and Hamilton's flankers, while three companies of the Fourth—one of
them McKinney's shaken unit—stood in reserve behind the Red
Butte on the left. Thereafter, fighting settled into a long-range
duel between the soldiers stationed behind knolls and ridges
east of the ravine and the warriors ensconced behind hillocks
and rocks to the west at the base of the north mountain wall.[15] At
least one other Indian was killed during this protracted exchange,
as described by Sergeant McClellan:

*An Indian jumped out of a hole on my right front, and at once pulled
down and shot at me. I was so surprised that for an instant I thought
all I had to do was to fall and pass out; but in an instant I realized that
he had missed; so, shooting from the hip, I finished the Indian. Taking
no chances, I rushed forward and put one or two more shots into him
with my revolver. As I was about to bend over to take the Indian's gun,
one of our Pawnees rushed up and took the coup. . . . I took the gun
and belt from the dead Indian, thinking that the extra gun and ammunition would come in handy if the fight lasted long. The Pawnee
reported the incident to Maj. Frank North, and as the gun and belt
had the name of Little Wolf on it, we thought at the time that I had
killed Little Wolf; but when the Indians surrendered at Camp Robin-*

son the next spring, it was shown that in the rush Bull Head, a half brother of Little Wolf, had taken and fought with the latter's equipment. Little Wolf escaped the catastrophe.[16]

The episode with McKinney's faltering company was evidently more serious than reported at the time, and it might have stirred controversy among the command because many of the unit's men were fresh recruits—"Custer Avengers"—who had enlisted out of patriotism after the Little Bighorn disaster and who lacked either experience or military discipline. In later years Lieutenant Dorst of Mackenzie's staff remembered what he had witnessed from another vantage:

I noticed a whole troop suddenly breaking to the rear. I was on elevated ground about 300 yards behind the line. . . . The men were riding rapidly back in a confused mass, and a line of dismounted men that had been formed to their left and rear then broke for about 300 yards and was coming too. I noticed men still further to the left who had stopped firing and were looking to their right and rear. The Indians set up a general yelling and more than redoubled the rapidity of their fire. The incident made a strong impression on me, as I was alone and could overlook the whole scene. I could not surmise what had happened, and one sight of these retreating men brought my heart into my mouth. In another moment, however, the mounted mass wavered, then turned and went forward again followed by the others. [What happened was that] the troop had been advancing at a gallop . . . , when it encountered a number of Indians in a deep and impassable ravine. Its commanding officer [McKinney] had then ordered it to fall back, doubtless for the purpose of dismounting it, but at the same instant he was shot down, as were also a number of men. With the exception of four or five big soldiers at the head of the troop, all turned about and started to the rear on a run. The 2nd Lieutenant went with them without being able to exercise any control. One or two other officers who happened to be in their way tried to stop them, but

*produced no effect. Lieut. Lawton, who was close by, then rushed at
them and succeeded alone in stopping them and turning them. No one
but a man of extraordinary force, perfect coolness and great determination could have done it. It was the most critical moment of the
whole engagement.*[17]

While Lieutenant Lawton may indeed have played an important
role in turning the fleeing troopers back toward the line, Captain
Wessels seems to have confronted and rectified the problem
near the edge of the gorge.[18] After anxious moments, McKinney
and the other wounded were borne away to a spot behind the
Red Butte where contract surgeon Dr. Louis A. LaGarde
attended them. On examination, LaGarde found the officer shot
through the head, spinal column, arm and stomach, and body,
yet the lieutenant recognized the doctor, calling him by name,
and muttered a few words about his mother before he died.[19]

Only about fifteen minutes had elapsed between the time
the cavalry column had forged into the valley and McKinney's
wounding. There was much occurring all along the line, from
the village at the left front to the ravine and along it to the north
mountainside. Far above the action the Shoshones continued
to deliver volleys—"showers of molten lead," said Bourke—
against the Cheyennes, some of whom had taken refuge on a
high ridge directly west of the scouts' position and were largely
beyond their range.[20] So much was going on simultaneously
that an enlisted man recalled that "it would have required a man
with 100 eyes to see just how the whole thing worked out."[21] As
the movement along the washout was taking place, and almost
simultaneously with Hamilton's and Hemphill's seizure of the
two knolls on the right, Captain Alfred Taylor's Company L swept
through the length of the village, driving out any remaining
tribesmen in the west end and securing the bluffs to the southwest, from which the sheltered warriors still annoyed the com-

mand with desultory fire. One man was killed and four of Taylor's horses were lost in this action, and the captain himself barely missed being shot, a bullet grazing his coat. The movement was followed by the rapid arrival of Mauck's reserves, who, dismounted, raced through to the west side of the village and clambered up the bluffs, driving out the remaining Indian marksmen and securing prominent ground commanding many of the ravines north and west of the village. This was a critical position, its occupation mandatory for the troops' ultimate control of the engagement. Correspondent Roche recounted that the "ravines were full of hostiles who had the advantage of the advancing troops to the extent of being in a position to fire at the approaching masses while comparatively secure themselves."[22] Shortly after this position was secured, a veteran soldier of Company L was fatally shot while manning a line just beyond the village.[23]

While news of McKinney's death spread through the command, Mackenzie took steps to consolidate his position and gain information about the location of his adversaries.[24] As the gray twilight of dawn yielded to day, the troops remained scattered from the bluff overlooking the village, to the Red Butte—now occupied by Luther North and some of the Pawnees with the scout Frank Grouard—and across the plain to the two red knolls adjoining the north mountainside, east of which the majority of troops guarding the large washout were now congregated.[25] From their position overlooking the village, the Shoshone scouts continued an intermittent fire against targets now mostly beyond their range.[26] In all reality, from this point forward, reported Bourke, "the enemy . . . gave up all hope of recovering their village or of even doing anything more than annoy us with the fire of their heavy rifles."[27] Luther North maintained that Indian fatalities were few for the duration of the fighting. "After the first charge into the village I doubt if there were many Indians killed, although we were exchanging shots with them all day."[28]

Distressed at the loss of their ponies, the warriors opened a heavy barrage from behind rocks and ridges in the soldiers' front that gradually lessened during the course of the day. Mackenzie properly discounted the notion of charging the Indians across unfavorable terrain, for his losses would have multiplied rapidly. Initially, his response was to lay down a steady fire on the positions, generally from five hundred to fifteen hundred feet distant, and try to inflict more casualties. With that objective, the gunfire along the ravine soon increased in volume, turning to deafening volleys as the soldiers leveled round after round at Cheyennes hidden in their front. The sound reverberated across the valley, and after a time, during which it became apparent that the Indians were not leaving their positions, some officers became anxious over the apparent waste of ammunition by the troops, many of whom it was discovered were discharging their pieces in the direction of the warriors without taking careful aim. Mackenzie dispatched Lieutenants Clark, Bourke, Lawton, and Dorst to caution the company commanders against wasting cartridges and to fire only at close-range targets.

With the soldiers bunched more or less behind the gorge on the northern and southern sides of the valley, it became necessary for staff officers, company officers, and orderlies to pass across the plain with orders and information through a kind of no man's land, racing a distance of perhaps five hundred yards, usually through a deadly hail of lead sent by warriors secluded in coulees or behind hillocks to the west. "If not able to hug the cover of a favorable ravine," penned Bourke, "[they] were compelled to ride full tilt."[29] Mackenzie personally made the trip several times, constantly and recklessly exposing himself, commented Bourke, each time drawing much fire in his passage. "Those officers who served on his staff that morning will long remember the whistling of the bullets flying about their heads as they carried the General's orders from point to point."[30] The

North brothers were among those running the gauntlet, and at least one enlisted man died while making the attempt. The warriors, observed Bourke, "understood perfectly that the immobile and silent ranks under cover were the companies of soldiers, and that those who had to essay the passage of the 'dangerous space,' as we soon learned to term it, were either officers high in rank or orderlies carrying important dispatches."[31]

Meantime, the Indians moved about, seeking advantages in the rough terrain from which they might draw carbine fire from the troops. Shrewdly cognizant of the range capabilities of the soldiers' weapons, they accordingly positioned themselves to return fire appropriately with their longer-range rifles. Roche recounted an example of their savvy: "A party of braves would creep behind some projecting ledge of rock or hospitable ridge far enough to get just beyond range of our guns, and then would make a wild charge forward howling savagely to draw out our men, from whose bullets they considered themselves safe, but whose exposure would give them the very chance they sought."[32]

At one point soon after the troops took position along the north end of the gully, Captain Davis advanced Company F, Fourth Cavalry, to a bluff fronting some rocks behind which some warriors were hidden. These Indians had killed and scalped Private John Sullivan, Company B, Fourth Cavalry, at a forward position, and his body could not be immediately claimed.[33] After a time Davis's unit fell back, whereupon eight or nine warriors raced out from their cover in pursuit. Davis's men then suddenly dropped into a dry ravine, turned, and opened fire on the pursuing Indians, killing several and driving away the others. A few of the warriors took refuge in a nearby cave or defile on the right where Davis's troopers found and killed them.[34] By now all of the troops were dismounted, the horses having been taken to protected areas in ravines and behind bluffs. Dead animals, killed in the tumult of the early hours, lay scattered about the field.

Within an hour of Mackenzie's attack, most of the Cheyenne noncombatants had made their way through ravines and behind ridges to the western recesses of the canyon.[35] Some watched the engagement playing out behind them, although most, still shaken by the assault, began moving away from the scene, momentarily at a loss over what to do. On the field Mackenzie established his headquarters behind a butte east of the large washout and near the north mountainside, although at one point in the proceedings the colonel advanced as far as the twin knolls to consult with his officers. It was mainly behind Mackenzie's headquarters promontory that the staff officers and battalion commanders congregated. Gunfire was directed into the post from warriors hidden in recesses above the troops on the mountainside, in positions directly to the front right of the troops, and in ravines to the southwest. One Cheyenne, apparently armed with a long-range Sharps rifle, played havoc with the men, and every discharge echoed "like the roar of a cannon from hill to hill." Finally, one of Captain Davis's soldiers took bead on the Indian and dispatched him.

By late morning a directive ordered firing to cease along the front since the warriors had moved beyond effective carbine range. Soon after word reached Mackenzie that the pack train had followed the soldiers through the night and at last arrived, the animals having borne their packs for nearly twenty-four hours, and was pulling up in a protected area among some willows behind the Red Butte on the left. The news was significant because included in the beasts' loads were some thirty thousand cartridges, which all but assured Mackenzie's victory. About this time, some of the cavalry horses were moved across the plain to be watered in the Red Fork. Roche noticed a soldier riding a horse and leading another. "This man had not gone fifty yards from the bluff before his led horse fell, hit by a bullet from the hills, and he was wounded himself." Having passed over the space himself, the correspondent could relate. "Before I had crossed the field, though going at full speed, at least a score of balls whistled past my ears."[36]

One of the objectives of the troops and scouts during the engagement was to capture and corral the Indian ponies, accomplished following the initial attack when several hundred head were taken. As the fighting wore on, however, a herd of about one hundred animals grazed unconcernedly some one hundred yards from a ridge to the southwest where Cheyenne marksmen were posted. Several times parties of the different groups of Indian scouts had tried to advance and take the ponies, but all had failed and were met by the successive jeers of the other scouts, who watched this entertainment. Finally, Luther North asked his brother to let the Pawnees try, and Frank North assented on condition that his scouts would indeed bring in the animals. Luther took only one man, a scout named Boy Chief. They circled around via the stream in approaching the herd, then dashed out waving blankets and yelling to drive the animals together and get them moving. After some close calls the two brought the ponies back through the village and across the Red Fork to the position southeast of the Red Butte where the other horses were corralled. The Cheyennes managed to kill several of the ponies, but Boy Chief and North were not hurt.[37]

As the day progressed the temperature rose, and by early afternoon the men lay at their posts in shirtsleeves. Several times during the fighting, some of them noticed a white flag being waved by the Indians, but they ignored it and occasionally had fired at it. During the afternoon, the troops again spotted the flag, this time fluttering from above the hills near the head of the canyon. This time some of the interpreters and Cheyenne scouts, led by Bill Rowland, went forward to the extremity of the twin knolls to communicate with the Indians. Despite the flag, the men dodged bullets in their advance to talk but eventually were allowed to approach closely. Morning Star spoke to them directly, explaining that he had lost two sons thus far in the contest and was ready to yield. But the other chiefs, including Little Wolf, Old Bear, Roman Nose, and Gray Head, were not ready to give up. They told Rowland's group that they had many casualties but were determined to hold out against the soldiers and, if necessary, die. These four told the scouts to go home, that they had no business being there. "We can whip the white soldiers alone," they said, "but can't fight you, too." Other warriors soon approached, trying to trick the interpreters and scouts by saying that they were going to seek help from a large Sioux village nearby.[38] At about two o'clock Mackenzie, possibly motivated by this incident and seemingly convinced that the warriors would not withdraw, sent Frank Grouard and a Sioux scout back to Crook with a message asking that the infantrymen be advanced as quickly as possible so they might deal with the warriors with their long-range Springfields.[39] (Roche took the occasion to send back his first account of the Red Fork encounter, which reached print in New York City only four days later, November 29.) By 4:00 P.M. the Cheyennes' gunfire had diminished sufficiently for some of the soldiers to walk to the pack train and obtain a bite of food.

During the middle of the afternoon, Mackenzie directed Captain North and the Pawnees to destroy the Cheyenne village (although some of the lodges had apparently been torched late that morning), an action purposefully devised to further demoralize the warriors still refusing to leave their hiding places. The Pawnees, animated all day by the events, moved out immediately, and four of the scouts' horses were killed by distant marksmen in approaching the abandoned camp.[40] In the course of the destruction, which carried over into the next day, it was revealed that the Cheyennes had left behind great quantities of ammunition, doubtless accounting for the slackening gunfire from the warriors during the day. The cartridges were subsequently burned in the consuming flames, and at one point a keg of gunpowder ignited, its explosion echoing loudly through the canyon. Many of the tipis still had kettles filled with water, some with smoldering ashes beneath them and looking much as they had when hurriedly abandoned by their occupants earlier. The lodges also contained large quantities of dried meat and undressed hides. Before firing the tipis, the Indian scouts ransacked them and recovered enough buffalo robes to load down fifty pack mules. Garnett recalled that he and some of the scouts went after some Cheyenne ponies south and southwest of the village (about where the ranch road enters the area today). Moving toward the animals, they were fired on by warriors hidden in the timber west of the village as well as by the Shoshones, erroneously, from their bluff-top position to the east. Some of the scouts fired back at the Shoshones, wounding one, and a Sioux scout who was with the latter yelled down: "Hold on; these are Snakes up here; you have shot one of them."[41]

The Pawnees had been in the village for most of the time since the opening attack, and one had killed an elderly woman and scalped her. Some of the soldiers also took the opportunity to plunder for souvenirs. Finally, when the lodges were ignited, everything remaining was consumed by the flames. Said one witness: "The smoke made by the burning rawhide and canvas, mingled with the smoke of the powder, filled the canyon with a dark cloud, the fumes of which, together with the savage yell of the Indians, made an impression on one's mind not easily forgotten."[42]

Over the next several hours, the Cheyennes' gunfire gradually waned, ceasing altogether at sundown. By then all of the soldier dead but one had been retrieved. That man had fallen in an exposed area, and after sunset troops advanced and brought in his body. An enlisted man watched the dead being brought in, "some skelpt [sic] and some striped [sic] of all their clothing."

Soldiers wrapped the remains in canvas for eventual transport across the backs of the pack animals. Nearby, the surgeons tended the wounded despite occasional firing into the hospital area by several Cheyennes hidden in rocks on the north mountainside. Dr. LaGarde recalled his experience at the dressing station where he had attended to Lieutenant McKinney: "The wounded commenced to be brought [in] . . . and I kept putting bandages on these people and dressing them as well as I could under the circumstances; there was a great deal of confusion; there was a troop right by us and the Indians kept shooting in our direction. I could hear the bullets striking into the flesh of the horses, and I must say that I never experienced more difficulty in putting bandages on than at that time. We kept on until the thing got so hot General McK sent Lawton to tell us to move up beyond the hill. . . . [After that] we moved them up to a place of safety and dressed their wounds properly."[43] At Mackenzie's request Captain North sent six Pawnees to rout the marksmen. Stripped to breechcloth and moccasins and wearing bandanas about their heads to distinguish them from the Cheyennes, the scouts went up the near-vertical mountain face and drove out the warriors, killing two of them.

A few of the other Indian scouts continued their firing at dusk, shooting at the Cheyennes moving back out of their defenses to join their families in withdrawing from the canyon. Late in the day, as the firing subsided, Private William E. Smith, one of Mackenzie's orderlies, went to the partly burned village. Earlier, on a previous visit there, Smith had taken a pipe from an old woman, and now he relocated the lodge and discovered the woman "shot all to pieces. I found after words that some of the boys in my company had done it for to get the Bufflow robe [she wore]." Expecting a renewal of the fighting during the night or the next morning, Mackenzie ordered pickets to the high ground around the canyon. Alert to a possible counterattack, he placed his remaining troops in position to protect the partially burned camp and the captured ponies corralled south of the Red Fork in the gap below the Shoshone position. The Sioux, Cheyenne, and Arapaho scouts set up camp to the east, while the Shoshones settled to the west. Near them the Pawnees camped in the midst of the charred tipis and built a fire to cook, but the flames attracted the gunfire of warriors still in the vicinity, particularly that of the man armed with the Sharps buffalo gun, and the scouts eventually raised protective bulwarks of packages of dried buffalo meat taken from the lodges. "We were rite near the hospitle," recorded Private Smith, "and I could hear the wounded groneing all night." Yet Luther North remembered, "we slept the sleep of tired soldiers and knew nothing more until after daylight on the 26th." As the troops and scouts passed the night under arms, snow fell heavily, blanketing the blackened ruins of the village.[44]

During the action of the twenty-fifth, several episodes of a personal nature occurred among the army participants. Reporter Jerry Roche, attempting to observe the fighting and thus render a comprehensive and accurate account for his readership, rode over the field numerous times during the first hour of the contest. In one instance, he wrote:

I galloped across . . . to a ridge where Frank Grouard, Baptiste, Billy Hunter and one or two other scouts and interpreters were shooting at some hostiles on the hills to the left. There I shed my overcoat, attached a picket rope to my bridle and crept to the crest of the bluff next to Frank Grouard, who was evidently too much interested in the work in hand to pay any attention to fresh arrivals at his side. "What are you firing at, Frank?" I inquired. Without turning to see who spoke he opened the breech of his gun, pressed in another cartridge and answered by inquiry in the Sioux language. Again I asked him where the particular Indian was that he was trying to knock over, and again he replied in Sioux and kept on shooting. Then I reminded him that I didn't happen to understand the Indian tongue, and should be obliged if he would answer me in English, and, suddenly recollecting himself, he laughed and pointed to a hill about 800 yards in front, from which bullets were coming in quick succession to the crest of the bluff we occupied. A moment afterward some one on my left knocked over one of the Indians on this ridge and the others crept to safer quarters. Frank did not get his man that time, but he did before the battle closed, and he now rejoices in the possession of a scalp of a hostile Cheyenne.[45]

Roche later joined Grouard in the village, where the hungry scout helped himself to some of the abandoned meat. Soon after, on the right of the line, the correspondent described an incident in which a corporal and a private engaged two warriors, apparently in the area of the twin knolls. The corporal (evidently Corporal Patrick F. Ryan, Company D, Fourth Cavalry) was fatally shot, whereupon the private fired and killed the Indian responsible as the other warrior attempted to flee. Lieutenant Bourke related an unusual incident on the firing line. A soldier, disregarding orders, raised his head and shoulders above cover and was hit by a bullet that passed through his jaw. "Knocked senseless by the blow, he fell forward, but still remaining on his feet, against the bank in front of him. The blood from his wound poured down his throat and choked him to death." Elsewhere, Lieutenant Wheeler saw a trooper have his horse shot from beneath him. "I heard the bullet when it struck the horse, which swayed back and forth several times and then dropped dead." The soldier, fearing he would be charged for losing government property, hurriedly worked to unfastened the animal's bridle and saddle before leaving its side.[46]

Bourke also remarked on the bravery of the opponents. Once he saw a warrior or chief astride a white pony and wearing a tailored war bonnet and carrying a shield appear from a hill fronting the north side of the line. As he rode daringly and tauntingly before the troops, no one was able to bring him down. Finally, Lieutenant James Allison, attached from the Second Cavalry, fired a round that sent the Indian to the ground. But the action was not over; soon another warrior, similarly adorned, appeared, riding quickly forward to swoop down and retrieve the corpse of his colleague, then "turned back to regain the friendly shelter of the rocks and gulches." Before he reached safely, however, he fell, another victim of the soldiers' marksmanship.[47]

By their nature, Indian reminiscent testimony of the fighting at Morning Star's village consists of highly individualized accounts that nonetheless help immeasurably in defining the Northern Cheyenne perspective of the engagement. They describe the attack as starting just as the dance was breaking up and while many of the dancers were returning to their lodges. The cracking sounds of gunfire could be heard in the distance along with the thundering of the charging horses' hoofs and the war songs of the scouts. Then some of the people looked up and saw the Shoshones at their bluff-top position. Almost simultaneously some of those who had been tending the ponies ran back to the camp, yelling out that soldiers were approaching.[48] As the warning cries spread through the village, pandemonium broke out, women and children screaming in terror and running through the camp toward the hills to the west. Some ran into tipis to find their children, grabbing them up or pulling them awake to run, naked, into the cold morning. Warriors likewise hurriedly grabbed whatever arms and ammunition they could before running and driving the noncombatants out of the camp. A Cheyenne named Elk River slashed open the back of his tipi so that his family could escape, then returned to try and save the ponies. Another, Black White Man, managed to get his wife and son aboard a pony and out of the camp before he headed toward the sounds of the gunfire. Some of the girls who had participated in the dance were still loosely tied together in traditional fashion, and when the commotion started, they began to panic, trying to rid themselves of the binding thongs. Finally, somebody cut them apart and they too fled to the west.

As the scouts, then the soldiers, finally struck the village, some of the warriors managed to interpose themselves to slow things down and to gain time for the women and children to escape. When the bullets began striking the lodges, they sounded like hailstones hitting. Black White Man said that he saw several ponies tied in front of his lodge racing back and forth trying to break their tethers. He reached them and cut them loose, then drove them beyond the camp. En route he came upon a small boy who was running toward where the women and children had gone. They continued on together while bullets rained all around them, yet neither was hit. A woman named Iron Teeth was not as lucky as she and her family fled the village. Years later she recalled: "My husband and my two sons helped in fighting off the soldiers and enemy Indians. My husband was walking, leading his horse, and stopping at times to shoot. Suddenly, I saw him fall. I started to go back to him, but my sons made me go on, with my three daughters. The last time I ever saw Red Ripe, he was lying there dead in the snow."[49] Elsewhere during this flight from the camp, the wife of Limpy took a bullet through the chest, making her cough up blood as she ran. Years later, Red Bird recollected his own frenetic flight from the camp:

I make up my mind to save myself, but I don't know which way to go. I start to run across the river. I don't know [if] there was such fighting over there, but my horse is excited and jumps up and down. He wants to go, but I hold him tight. I then struck a deep creek and my horse try [sic] to jump over, but its hind legs fall back, and then I fall. Then the horse jump up and go and now I am on foot. As I started to run, I hear somebody opposite say "lay down." I look, I saw a group of women and children sitting against the rocks, and there were most of the brave young men, all wearing war bonnets and [all] had good guns. And all singing war songs, "All the rocks are the only ones that stay forever." I look up and saw Brave Bear on white horse, charging the enemy and sweeping the main battle ground. He turned to his right toward the mouth of the creek in which we had a refuge, and then his horse was fatally wounded.[50]

The group that Red Bird joined was chased out of their refuge by dismounted soldiers, and they continued their withdrawal to the north. (Red Bird reported that the troops mortally wounded a young girl, daughter of White Face Bull, during this movement; she died days later as the refugees struggled through the snow to reach Crazy Horse's village in Montana.)[51]

Most of the early casualties occurred in the lower, or east, end of the encampment; those people farther up had more time to gather their families and move out, and many of them fled on horseback. If Mackenzie's men had been able to surround the camp as originally planned, such escape would have been impossible, and large numbers of the Indians would certainly have died. Within but a few minutes, most of the people had abandoned the lodges, running northwest along the stream to seek shelter in the ravines and defiles leading north and northwest from the camp. As it was, the loss of the pony herds was imminently devastating because the tribesmen were forced to move on foot, thereby consuming much energy, and they lacked the food provisions that the butchered animals might have furnished them in their flight.[52]

Without the food, clothing, arms and ammunition, and other equipment from their homes, the Cheyennes now found themselves in a desperate situation.[53] Nonetheless, some of the leaders had taken the proper steps to ensure the safety of the

Sacred Buffalo Hat and the Sacred Arrows. Coal Bear, responsible for the sacred hat, was able to secure it in the melee and move out, accompanied by several warriors guarding him and his wife, who was the sacred hat woman and carried the bundle on her back as they made their way to the high ridges to the northwest. With them was Box Elder, the blind holy man, who carried his sacred wheel lance for protection. As they moved, Medicine Bear covered their withdrawal. From side to side he waved a rawhide disk trimmed with buffalo tails, known to the Cheyennes as *Nimhoyoh*, or the Turner, which could turn death away from the people.[54]

Finally, the party reached a dry streambed, probably northwest of the camp, and found there other tribesmen who had fled. With assistance, Box Elder then took a position atop a knoll, where he sat down alone, filled his pipe with tobacco, and began to sing. He offered his unlit pipe to the four directions, and suddenly, witnesses said, it started burning, seemingly without source. Bullets flew about him, but he sat there calmly. Soon a warrior named Long Jaw, bedecked in a red cloth, rushed out on a ridge to the northwest. A dog was running beside him, and he jumped about for a distance of one hundred yards, drawing the soldiers' fire to himself before he ducked down. He shortly reappeared with the dog near Box Elder's knoll, then turned and faced northwest for a time. Up above, near the end of the canyon, women had begun singing strong-heart songs to inspire the warriors. After the fighting was over, the Cheyennes noticed that the red cloth worn by Long Jaw, who was unharmed, contained numerous bullet holes. The warrior later stated that he was thinking about the Creator when he performed this act. "Every jump I made, I asked to be saved. . . . Many soldiers were shooting."[55]

As the party with Coal Bear, which now included a number of women and children, continued on their way, they passed along a small ridge that once more exposed them to the soldiers' bullets. As before, Medicine Bear rode up and waved the Turner, protecting the party from injury. The three men—Medicine Bear, Box Elder, and Long Jaw—were thus instrumental in preserving the lives of many of the women and children as well as in protecting the Sacred Hat, and they continue to be remembered for those deeds within Cheyenne society. Meantime, the keeper of the *Maahotse*—the Sacred Arrows—had also successfully gotten them out of the village. When the shooting erupted, Black Hairy Dog had rushed to the lodge and retrieved the sacred bundle. While carrying them from the village, his wife was grazed in the head by a bullet and dropped the arrows, but she was able to pick them up and move on. Then Black Hairy Dog sought out a high point west or northwest of the camp overlooking the principal fighting area. Gaining it, he opened the bundle, removed the arrows, and ritually laid them out. Black Hairy Dog and his colleagues then performed a ceremony that inspired the warriors fighting the soldiers below, thereby directing the power of the Sacred Arrows against Mackenzie's men. After that, Black Hairy Dog rebundled the arrows and joined a group of families moving away from the area.[56]

When the attack opened, Young Two Moon, outfitted in a double-trailer war bonnet, rode his pony down through the camp. He saw his friend Crow Necklace at a distance, himself war bonneted and riding his spotted horse. The men at one point were on opposite sides of the village, Young Two Moon on the north and Crow Necklace on the south. Young Two Moon started a charge in front of four oncoming companies of cavalry, and sweeping across the village to the south, he arrived to see Crow Necklace fall, fatally shot from his mount. At the point where the Cheyennes in the gorge shot into McKinney and his soldiers, the fighting turned into a major struggle. Yellow Eagle and several other warriors fired the rounds that hit the officer.

When the troops pulled back in the shock of the moment, three of the Cheyennes came forward to count coup on the fallen soldier. Yellow Eagle touched him first and got his gun. After that, the troops restored their composure, advanced, and fired into the ravine, killing at least six of the tribesmen and wounding three (one mortally).[57] Those who got away were able to climb out of the gulch and run across to another farther west. Young Two Moon was also there, and he recalled that the lieutenant, after having been "shot and having coup counted on him, got up and writhed away some distance" before falling again.[58]

Young Two Moon said that after another soldier was shot and fell from his horse, two warriors sprinted forward out of the ravine and took his gun and ammunition belt. Another Cheyenne, Bull Hump, was there too. With his rifle he killed a horse along the washout and, during the confusion that momentarily reigned, managed to cut free one of the saddlebags (the horse was lying on the other), which was full of ammunition. As he started away with his prize, jumping from side to side to avoid the soldiers' fire, he came on two revolvers, which he thrust beneath his belt. Now weighted down with his assorted cargo of rifle, two pistols, and a full saddlebag and determined not to give them up, Bull Hump was forced to walk amid the bullets. Miraculously, he was not hit. The Cheyenne attributed it to all the gun smoke hanging over the canyon, which hindered the soldiers' aim.[59]

After this episode, the final clearing of the village, and the cavalrymen's taking up positions on the north side of the canyon, most of the warriors escaped to ravines and mountainside prominences farther west and north. One of the protectors of the women and children was Little Wolf, who led a number of them up the gulch after the McKinney affair. The chief stood up, drawing many bullets to him as the people in the ravine managed to get down out of sight. Nonetheless, six of his group were

killed. In this vicinity too, the warrior Yellow Eagle led twenty-
five or thirty other men, women, and children through dangerous terrain, at one point each person having to jump up and run
thirty yards to gain cover. At every opportunity the soldiers rid-
dled the position, but only four of the people were wounded. In
yet another location, where a dozen stayed to help protect the
women and children fleeing to the northwest, four men received
wounds: White Frog, Bald Faced Bull, Two Bulls, and Bull
Hump, who had earlier escaped the soldier bullets. Thereafter,
the fighting devolved into intermittent long-range shooting.
Young Two Moon, who was mounted, returned to the northwest end of the canyon, where women and children who had
earlier reached that point were hurriedly erecting breastworks
of stones, intending to defend the position against the soldiers
should they overcome the warriors in front and attempt an
assault there. Already the warrior Brave Wolf and some others
were building fires to keep the families warm. There Young Two
Moon switched horses and started back to the fighting.[60]

Young Two Moon described an encounter on the field with
Many Beaver Dams, the Cheyenne who had been captured by
Crook's scouts and from whom the troops obtained information
about Morning Star's village. Several other Cheyennes saw and
approached him; one, thinking he had arrived with the troops,
wanted to kill him. Many Beaver Dams claimed to have been
traveling on foot with the Arapaho scouts, who had only given
him a pony that morning with which he made his escape. Following a distracting argument on the field, Many Beaver Dams
was taken away to join the women. Then Young Two Moon and
twenty other warriors, all sporting war bonnets, executed a
maneuver to save five men trapped behind a low ridge in front
of the right of the soldiers' position. "They cried charge and
dashed toward the upper (right) end of the gray horse co. . . .
When they made the charge some soldiers that they had not seen

began to shoot at them from one side and turned them. . . . This was the closest they got to the soldiers." In subsequent action the troops moved, and the five trapped warriors—Long Jaw, Little Horse, White Horse, Braided Locks, and one more man who remained unidentified—were able to escape.[61]

At one point during the fighting, one of the Cheyenne scouts named Old Crow made his way to a small hill near the north end of Mackenzie's line not far from where a group of warriors watched the action. Old Crow was one of the Cheyenne council chiefs. The scout called out to his kinsmen somewhat apologetically, telling them that he was leaving ammunition for them at that place. The warriors later found a large number of cartridges. Young Two Moon stated that a man, Crawling, wounded in one leg, was rescued when two warriors, Braided Locks and Hairy Hand, rushed in afoot and carried him to safety. Soon after, Braided Locks was himself wounded, shot through the body. Another man, Yellow Nose, shot through the breast, came to the women at the breastworks for treatment. All they had to bind his wound was a strip of buffalo robe, which they applied hair side in. Yet another warrior, Blacktailed Bull, received three wounds—a bullet in the shoulder, a piece of an ear shot away, and a finger shot off. Finally, Crow Split Nose, the society chief who had earlier counseled defense for the women and children, was shot and killed by soldiers on the north side of the Red Fork as he fought in an area at the foot of the bluff occupied by the Shoshones. A warrior named Dog Speaking led several men in charging forward to claim the body. The firing, however, was too intense, and they merely covered Crow Split Nose with a blanket before seeking cover from the bullets that flew all around. The party succeeded in getting the body in a second attempt.

Young Two Moon also remembered watching the lodges being torched later that day. He wanted to go back to the village and get robes for the women and children, but Indian scouts were everywhere. Those lodges situated on the north side of the stream—ten tipis belonging to Red Robe's camp—were not burned, though, until the next day. After dark on the day of the fighting, Young Two Moon and a half dozen other young men ventured into Red Robe's lodges and retrieved several buffalo robes from one before his fellows' noisy chatter drew gunfire from one of Mackenzie's pickets. Later that evening the tribesmen held a meeting, ultimately deciding against staying behind the breastworks and instead to scatter in bodies of three or five so that the soldiers could not easily pursue them. With what few ponies they were able to retain, the Cheyennes began their trek that night.[62]

The troops, meantime, continued their destruction of the Cheyennes' village throughout the night, most of the work performed by Captain Gerald Russell's Company K, Third Cavalry, and Davis's Company F, Fourth Cavalry. The 173 lodges contained a plethora of goods, ranging from hides to utilitarian tools, guns and ammunition, and virtually irreplaceable handcrafted clothing and artwork. Indeed, the village may have represented the most opulent encampment of its kind ever sacked by troops operating against tribes in the trans-Mississippi West. "Never had so rich and complete a prize fallen into the hands of the Regular Army from the days of its first organization," wrote Lieutenant Bourke. He termed each lodge "a magazine of ammunition, fixed and loose, and a depot of supplies of every mentionable kind."[63]

The soldiers searched the tipis before burning them. Besides the arms (many of which were not destroyed) and the barrels of powder and boxes of ammunition, they contained tons of dried and bundled buffalo meat, along with great quantities of pemmican, meant to subsist the people until spring. Each lodge was burned independently, "most artistically," declared Bourke. In many cases, fat and marrow stored in paunches was laid on the smoldering cooking fires within each tipi, followed by corded wood normally used for fuel. The flames soon erupted in a bellowing, hissing blaze that consumed the canvas or skin lodge, its poles, and everything trapped within. Exploding powder kegs and cans added to the conflagration. Roche reported that "there were 165 fires going in the hostile camp on Sunday morning."[64] Along with everything else, metal shovels, axes, picks, spades, hammers, hatchets, knives, and scissors went into the bonfires to ruin their temper and render them useless. Bullet molds and empty cartridge cases that might be reloaded were destroyed. Containers such as canteens, kettles, pots, tin cups, and frying pans were axed and crushed before burning. China saucers, plates, and cups were shattered; coffee pots, knives, forks, and spoons bent and broken. Lodge poles that had not entirely burned were broken into pieces and thrown back into the fire. Mattresses, pillows, and blankets were likewise destroyed. Saddles were thoroughly broken and bridle reins slashed before being tossed into the flames. Beaver traps and even bottles of strychnine used by the tribesmen to kill wolves were consumed by the fire. The inventory of buffalo meat went the same route, the troops tossing "it in alongside of blazing saddles and steaming fat, to add its quota of crackling noise to the detonation of bursting ammunition"[65] The Cheyennes "did not get away with anything," jotted Lawton, "not a blanket, a saddle or a butcher knife." Newsman Roche agreed, penning that "not a pin's worth was left unburned."[66]

Among the priceless artifacts lost in the demolition, beyond the tipis themselves (including the Sacred Buffalo Hat lodge and the significant lodges of the soldier societies), many of which bore pictographic paintings on the walls, was the vast collection of artwork represented in a village of this size, part of the material cultural composing the Cheyennes' world. Beyond the thousand or so untanned buffalo hides and other skins saved from the destruction, there were stone hammers and mashers; painted war shields; eagle war bonnets; clothing of religious value, including buckskin shirts trimmed with human hair ("savage and civilized," wrote Bourke), and beaded leggings; women's robes and dresses trimmed with carefully crafted beadwork, porcupine quillwork, and elk's teeth; stone pipes with inlaid silver designs; elaborately beaded and quilled pipe bags; "and many other specimens of dress, art and manufactures." The troops also incinerated aged and sacred corn that went back to the Cheyennes' formative times along with sacred objects and bundles that were important to the people as a tribe and as individuals. But saved was a necklace made of beads interspersed among eight human fingers, purported to belong to a religious leader named High Wolf and subsequently donated by Lieutenant Bourke to the Bureau of American Ethnology in Washington, D.C.[67] Beyond a few other pieces that were saved, the treasures of the Cheyenne village went up in smoke, "wiping off the face of the earth," said Bourke, "many products of aboriginal taste and industry which would have been gems in the cabinets of museums."[68] Fortunately for the people, however, the Sacred Buffalo Hat and the Sacred Arrows had survived, rescued by their respective keepers in the opening moments of the onslaught.

The lodges bequeathed a wealth of evidence that these Cheyennes, or a large number of them at least, had participated in the destruction of Custer's command at the Little Bighorn the previous June. Besides some cavalry mounts branded "7C," there were many associative relics found: a pillow case fashioned from a Seventh Cavalry guidon; assorted memorandum books of several first sergeants killed there; a guard roster of Company G; a book with names of crack shots of Company G; army saddles, Shoshone-made saddles (suggesting that some of these warriors had fought Crook's troops and their Shoshone scouts at

Rosebud Creek a week before Little Bighorn), nosebags, horse brushes and currycombs, canteens, shovels, and axes marked with unit designations of the Seventh; company rosters; an officer's dark blue overcoat; two officers' blouses; gauntlets; an India-rubber cape; a buckskin jacket with taffeta lining and a bullet hole in the shoulder, supposed to have belonged to Captain Thomas W. Custer, killed at Little Bighorn; a gold pencil case; field glasses; a silver watch; wallets complete with paper currency and metal coin (the Arapaho scout, Sharp Nose, found a wad of money totaling forty-seven dollars); various letters, some stamped for mailing (and subsequently posted); and many photographs taken from soldiers' bodies or from saddlebags. Also recovered was a hat identified in the sweatband as belonging to Private William W. Allen, Company I, Third Cavalry, who had been killed at the Rosebud on June 17. They found a pass signed at Red Cloud Agency for a Cheyenne man, Roman Nose (not to be confused with the warrior killed at Beecher's Island, Colorado, in 1868), permitting him to leave the reservation to search for lost livestock.[69] One of the ledgers recovered (the discovery was by Sergeant James H. Turpin, Company I, Fifth Cavalry) was in fact the duty roster of Company G, Seventh Cavalry, that had been carried by Sergeant Alexander Brown. This item carried special significance because, in addition to the penciled notations describing the work performed by company members and descriptive inserts about the last march of the unit, various Cheyenne artists had pictographically added visual records of events in their own lives.[70]

A number of gruesome discoveries also occurred. One consisted of the scalps of a young white girl and a young Shoshone girl. Another was the hand and forearm of a Shoshone woman, while another was the scalp of a Shoshone scout killed with Crook's command at the Rosebud and identified by the man's friends, who recognized its hair ornaments. These discoveries brought sadness among the Shoshone scouts. But the item that caused the most consternation was a buckskin bag containing the right hands of twelve Shoshone babies, evidently taken in the recent attack of the Cheyennes on their village. With this knowledge, the scouts opened a long, tormented wailing that continued, mixed with singing, most of the night of the twenty-fifth. "All sympathy was rejected," observed Bourke. "They surrendered themselves to the most abject grief, and letting their hair hang down over face and shoulders, danced and wailed . . . until darkness had passed away." The Shoshones became so saddened by these objects that they refused to take new names, as the Pawnees were doing, in celebration of the victory over their enemies.[71]

That evening Mackenzie tallied his casualties. There had been one officer, McKinney, and five enlisted men killed. One other man would succumb to wounds on November 27, so that total army fatalities at the Red Fork came to seven. Besides them, there were twenty-one enlisted men wounded, most of them flesh wounds, along with one Shoshone scout, a total of twenty-two. A few of the wounded had not been shot but had been injured by their horses having fallen on them or by scratches made from ricocheting slugs.[72] Cheyenne losses were more difficult to calculate. In his all-too-brief report of the affair dated November 26, Mackenzie did not give a figure for them; Crook's report of January 8, 1877, simply stated that the troops had killed "about twenty warriors," a number likely told him by Mackenzie. But Lieutenant Bourke stated that thirty Cheyenne dead "fell into our hands," of which the Pawnees and Shoshones scalped sixteen.[73] Sergeant McClellan reported seeing only eleven dead Cheyennes on the ground but allowed, "I cannot tell just how many Indians was killed."[74] Years later, Lieutenant Dorst made the following statement regarding Cheyenne casualties: "Gen. Mackenzie reported only 25 Indians killed, but that was only the number of dead bodies within our lines. At least half as many more lay all day in front of us, between us and the hostiles, but he would not report them as killed, because no officer had been close enough to them to be able to certify of his own knowledge that they were actually dead. When these Indians surrendered in the following spring we learned from some of their friends that they would not acknowledge the loss of even 20 killed, but did admit that they had altogether about 100 killed and seriously— not slightly—wounded. This makes it certain that the total loss was greater."[75]

The Indians themselves have helped bring some clarity to the matter of their casualties at the Red Fork through various statements made years afterward. Bourke recorded that, when the tribesmen surrendered in the spring of 1877, they had turned in a list of some forty people killed, but they never said how many had been wounded. (The list of fatalities purportedly submitted has apparently not survived.) Another period source reported that the Cheyennes had lost thirty-eight killed and sixty-five wounded.[76] Around 1935 the aged Cheyenne Weasel Bear, who had been in Morning Star's village on November 25, 1876, related that the Indian losses stood at "about 35," although the proportion of dead to wounded in this statement is not known.[77] It is reasonable to conclude that the number of Cheyenne fatalities stood at approximately forty killed, with perhaps double that number wounded in the encounter, bringing total Cheyenne casualties to about 120. But Cheyenne losses did not end once the gunfire ebbed, and those deaths and injuries sustained by the people due to exposure over subsequent days can be directly attributed to the attack of Mackenzie's soldiers on Morning Star's village.

Fort Fetterman, Wyoming Territory, in 1876, a view to the north. Following the government's abandonment of the Bozeman Trail forts in 1868, Fort Fetterman stood alone in monitoring the periphery of Sioux-Cheyenne country in east-central Wyoming. The post became a major debarkation point for General Crook's three campaigns in 1876. Fetterman closed in 1882, after the Indians had been removed to reservations. Courtesy Nebraska State Historical Society.

Little Wolf and Morning Star, a photograph taken in November 1873 during their visit to Washington, D.C. The two leaders had worked for peace with the whites prior to the Great Sioux War, into which they became inextricably drawn by circumstances beyond their control. Courtesy Nebraska State Historical Society.

Part of Crook's command near the headquarters building at Fort Fetterman, Wyoming Territory, prior to setting out for Cantonment Reno. An engraving from *Harper's Weekly*, December 16, 1876.

The Powder River Expedition crossing the Platte River en route north from Fort Fetterman on November 14, 1876, as presented in *Harper's Weekly*, December 16, 1876.

Cantonment Reno, Wyoming Territory, view to the northwest, as it appeared in the summer of 1877, a few months after the Powder River Expedition. In August of that year the post was officially redesignated Fort McKinney, after the officer killed in Mackenzie's attack on Morning Star's village. By mid-1878 the site had been largely abandoned in favor of a new Fort McKinney west of the present town of Buffalo, Wyoming. Courtesy U.S. Military Academy Library.

Colonel Ranald S. Mackenzie, Fourth Cavalry, as he appeared in the 1870s. By the time of the encounter with the Northern Cheyennes in the Big Horn Mountains, Mackenzie had gained considerable experience with Indians in Texas and Mexico, and his previous service during the Civil War won him repeated brevets for gallantry and meritorious service. Considered by many a brilliant military leader, chronic mental impairment eventually forced his retirement from the army in 1884. Courtesy Amon Carter Museum, Fort Worth, Texas.

Four of the Pawnee scouts who served with the North brothers in 1869. Some of these individuals likely joined the Norths in 1876 for duty against the Northern Cheyennes in the Great Sioux War. Courtesy Nebraska State Historical Society.

View looking south-southwest across the ground of the scene of Mackenzie's attack. The pond left of center (not present in 1876) approximates the site where McKinney's troops charged and where the lieutenant fell mortally wounded. Beyond the distant tree line adjoining the Red Fork of Powder River lay Morning Star's village, stretching from left to right. The Shoshone scouts occupied the high bluffs at left and fired into the tipis. Subsequent fighting occurred along the line of the ravine running to the right (north) of the present pond and on into the high ground to the northwest, over which the tribesmen withdrew from the village. Immediately to the left of the pond is the Red Butte, east of which was established a field hospital where doctors tended the wounded and where Lieutenant McKinney died. Photograph by the author.

View to the north from the modern stock pond looking toward Fraker Mountain. McKinney's wounding occurred near the ravine's junction with the pond as hidden Cheyenne warriors opened fire on the advancing cavalry. Troops thereafter spread out along the course of the ravine as it cut north across the valley to engage warriors firing from positions high on the mountainside and in the rugged highlands to the left. Photo by the author.

"The Shooting of Lieutenant McKinney," as romantically depicted in the *New York Daily Graphic*, December 28, 1876. Courtesy Paul L. Hedren.

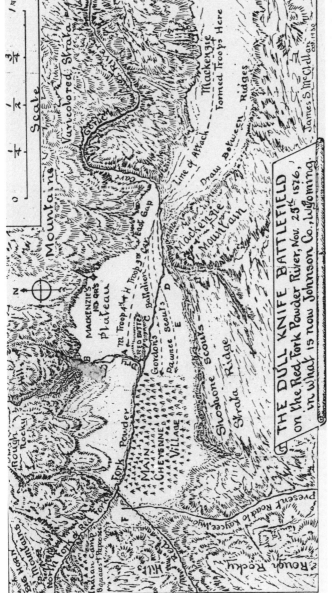

First Sergeant James S. McClellan, Third Cavalry, drafted this map of the so-called "Dull Knife Fight" in 1930. As finalized, it was used to accompany articles by McClellan in *Motor Travel*.

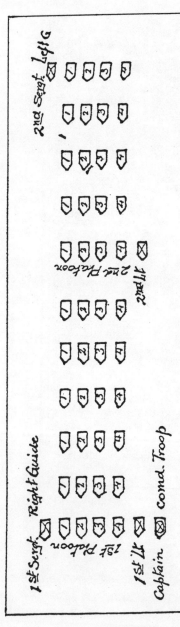

First Sergeant James S. McClellan's diagram and explanation of his company's movement in the opening charge, as prepared in October 1930. "The head or front of H Troop, 3rd Cavalry, formed as it went into the Dull Knife fight, attacking from the . . . east, . . . facing the dry gully or washout. . . . For regularity of the diagram, all officers are assumed to have been present; but in that engagement the 1st and 2nd lieutenants were both absent, so their places were taken by the next in rank, the 3rd sergeant acting as 1st sergeant, etc. This made 1st Serg. McClellan acting 1st Platoon commander, and placed him in the position next to Capt. Wessells that would otherwise have been occupied by the 1st Lt. If the troop were reversed ('about faced'), the relative positions of the officers would be the same; that is, the fours would wheel about on No. 4 as a pivot, but the numbers in the fours would also be reversed. On account of restricted space, the full complement of men is not indicated. Mr. McClellan adds, 'The movement of cavalry at such a time and under those conditions, are rough and ragged; and as this was not a dress parade (you may be assured!), we were not striving for good looks or fine tactical movements.'" *Motor Travel* (November 1930).

Chapter 7
Disconsolation All About

ON SUNDAY MORNING MACKENZIE'S troops continued their destruction of the Indians' possessions and, on the colonel's authority, prepared to move in the direction of General Crook and the foot soldiers. In looking around the scene of the previous day's encounter, the officers found bloody places where Cheyenne wounded had lain. They also discovered another dead tribesman, several dead ponies killed by soldier fire, and some ponies killed by the Cheyennes and stripped of flesh for their flight. Most of the morning was given over to making the wounded comfortable and preparing the dead for the march back to the Crazy Woman camp. The body of Private James Baird, Company D, Fourth Cavalry, was buried on the field near the southeast edge of the Red Butte,[1] while the body of each of the other dead was sewn into a blanket and slung belly down on a packsaddle, "and the diamond hitch thrown over him."[2] Bourke recorded that the bearing animals were at first "restive and frightened, but by the end of an hour or so became reconciled to their ghastly cargo."[3] Under the direction of Lieutenant Wheeler, lodge poles pulled from the burning village along with blankets and gunnysacks were used to fashion thirty travois for carrying the wounded and sick in an inclined position for borderline comfort. Pack mules pulled the poles and blankets bearing the injured, the ends of the poles dragging on the frozen ground and acting as springs to cushion the passengers.[4] Late in the morning the troops corralled the captured ponies and at about noon, amid snow now falling so hard as to obscure the tops of the canyon walls, began moving through the same opening at the east end of the canyon by which they had entered to initiate the attack. As the soldiers departed, several Cheyennes were seen to enter the ruins of their homes, sit down, cry, and sing mournful songs.

The march out was grueling, made more so by the recent snowfall. As Lieutenant Bourke described: "The route became slippery from the impress of hundreds of hoofs; and, where intersected by deep ravines, almost impassable for these 'travois.' In one particularly bad place the frightened mules had to be pushed over the edge of the declivity, and allowed to slide down, sustained by stout ropes held by the enlisted men, and the ends of the 'travois' supported in like manner. . . . [Later] the extremities of the 'travois' poles were secured in the bight of a rope, held by men on horseback riding alongside."[5] Similarly, a packer remembered the travail of the wounded: "The trail was very rough in many places, thru sage brush and over small bushes, causing the wounded much pain. When crossing creeks the drag ends of the travois would be picked up by mounted men and carried across. I saw one dropped by a young cavalryman in the deepest part of a creek. For punishment he was sent back to assist another, and he dropped that in about the same place in the icy water. His hands were so cold he could not hold the travois."[6]

During the march, some of Mackenzie's Pawnees and Shoshones rejoined the column following their reconnaissance of the Cheyenne refugees. These Indians had tried to capture about one hundred ponies they had discovered but, coming in sight of the Cheyennes, became engaged in a brief but spirited exchange with them and were forced to return under cover of the snowfall with only a few of the beasts. The scouts reported that the people they had seen were in a canyon six miles away headed north with their wounded and were in bad shape, "almost naked, without blankets, moccasins or ammunition." After going about eight miles, the soldiers bivouacked along the north side of the Red Fork. Mackenzie composed his brief official report of the encounter, citing the slain Lieutenant McKinney as "one of the most gallant officers and honorable men I ever knew." The Indian allies held a scalp dance before retiring that evening.[7]

On Monday the troops moved out at about ten o'clock, now heading north as they continued to retrace the route of their advance on the night of the twenty fourth.[8] The Indian scouts this day reported another village to the west, and the command, stretched out as they bore the wounded forward, experienced considerable anxiety as they moved along, fearful of a sudden attack. "As we were the last company of the rear guard," wrote Sergeant McClellan, "I felt uneasy for fear they would cut us off."[9] Many of the army mounts, exhausted from the activities of the past several days and nights, played out altogether and were shot on the trail. McClellan recorded in his journal, "Our horses are very week and the snow that has been falling the past two mornings makes the road very slippery."[10] Nonetheless, the soldiers managed fourteen miles before bivouacking along what was probably the south fork of the Crazy Woman. Remembered McClellan: "We would go into camp along some stream, or where water could be secured. The dead would then be taken from the backs of the mules and stood up (on their hands and feet, as they were frozen solid), fires lit and guards posted."[11] In the evening some wandering buffaloes stumbled onto the bivouac of the scouts, who fired on them, creating consternation among the men who momentarily thought they had come under attack by warriors. At each camp the troops arranged their wounded comrades with their heads resting on packsaddles and their feet near a fire.[12]

Meantime, Crook with the balance of his command had waited in camp along the Crazy Woman for word from Mackenzie, passing the hours in skirmish drill and routine camp activities.[13] Some of the officers, the general among them, ventured forth hunting rabbits. On the morning of the twenty-sixth, upon receiving the message sent by Mackenzie the previous day, Crook hurried off dispatches to be telegraphed to Sheridan announcing the colonel's victory in the capture of the Cheyenne village and most of their pony herd and the death of Lieutenant McKinney.[14] Then he ordered Colonel Dodge to ready his soldiers and strike out southwest on Mackenzie's trail of the twenty-third, fully intent on supporting the cavalry as the colonel requested. Dodge got off before noon, his men bearing one hundred rounds of musket ammunition and two days' rations each. These troops moved forward easily until they reached the snow-covered mountains, then things got worse. "We got in camp at a quarter to 11—after eleven hours of the hardest marching I ever saw," penned Dodge. "Bivouacked in snow & in the open air. Many men straggled, indeed it was simply impossible not to straggle. The trail was so narrow that the Com[man]d had to move in single file. . . . In going down one almost precipice one fellow slipped [and] fell on his bottom & gliding swiftly forward was set upon by at least thirty men. A whole Co was down in an indiscriminate heap & the swearing was something terrific."[15]

At the camping place, evidently along the Red Fork yet downstream from the spot where Mackenzie had bivouacked, Dodge and his men encountered Crook and his guard company, who had preceded them. Next morning, following a breakfast of coffee and bacon, the troops plodded forward and soon overtook Mackenzie's trail en route back to the Crazy Woman, whereupon Crook ordered Dodge to countermarch his soldiers. Dodge struck out directly overland for the camp at the Crazy Woman and after traveling six miles reached that stream, moved along it, and set up his bivouac. On November 28 the foot troops continued on the back trail and soon reached their base camp, where Crook awaited them. Dodge entered in his journal: "I doubt if any men ever made a more difficult march in better time than mine did on [the] 26th. The Genl & all are well pleased with our performance."[16]

On the twenty-eighth Mackenzie's troops, still following their earlier trail, marched ten miles along the south fork of the Crazy Woman. "All along the road [today]," wrote one man, "you could hear the report of fire arms as they were shooting played out horses."[17] During the day, one badly wounded trooper, Private Alexander McFarland of Company L, Fifth Cavalry, died from his injuries. His travois was reoccupied by the Shoshone who had been mistakenly shot by the Pawnees and had been riding his pony since leaving the village. His name was Amzi—also given as Anzi and Angzy—and he had been hit in the intestines, injuries believed by the surgeons to be mortal. The attendants gave the man whiskey laced with morphine to keep him comfortable. Amzi not only finished off all the whiskey but also somehow survived and eventually returned to his people.[18] That evening Mackenzie divided the ponies among the scouts, giving a few extra to the Pawnees who had recently gone out. "The Sioux had a regular knockdown over their division," noted Frank North. Later the Sioux and Pawnees danced for each other in a gesture of amity, and the Pawnees turned over to them a large number of the animals. Throughout the march, the tribesmen largely stayed within their own tribal groups. Those who had killed and scalped Cheyennes kept their trophies on their mounts and continued singing of their feats.

At dawn the next day, the soldiers continued downstream until at about 11:00 A.M. the remainder of Crook's command was reached. There they went into bivouac amid rumor that the entire body of troops would soon go into winter quarters. Yet

Crook's announced plans were to move the wounded on to Cantonment Reno, then obtain more rations before pressing north. A pervasive melancholy settled over the camp that evening. Lieutenant Lawton, who was assigned to take command of Company M, Fourth Cavalry, in addition to his other tasks, wrote a friend, "McKinney's death casts a gloom over everybody, and one would suppose we were regretting a defeat, rather than rejoicing over a victory."[19] That evening, at Crook's behest, Captain North sent his brother, Luther, with four Indian scouts to find and monitor the Cheyenne refugees presumably heading north to join Crazy Horse and encourage instead their surrender.[20] Twenty-five men from each company of the Fourth Cavalry made ready to go forward on a moment's notice if the scouts brought word of the Cheyennes' presence nearby. But the scouts found nothing and returned the next day. Lawton pondered subsequent movements and concluded that "we will try Crazy Horse, probably."[21]

At noon on Thanksgiving Day, November 30, Crook, Dodge, Mackenzie, Major Edwin Townsend, Major George Gordon, and their staffs attended Episcopal burial services at the cavalry camp for the blanketed bodies of the five enlisted men killed in the fighting at Morning Star's village. McKinney's remains would be carried to Cantonment Reno, where Captain Pollock had them crated for express shipment by railroad to his home in Memphis, to be accompanied there by Second Lieutenant Orlando L. Wieting, Twenty-third Infantry. McKinney would be memorialized in a regimental general order as a "high minded gentleman, a genial associate and a kindly superior," and a mourning armband would be prescribed to be worn by Fourth Cavalry officers for thirty days in his honor. The funeral procession, headed by infantry buglers playing "The Dead March," included the cavalrymen who had taken part in the encounter, all mounted, as well as the Indian scouts, all of whom "moved with measured tread to the place of sepulture and there halted until the extracts from the Book of Common Prayer had been read." A firing salute followed, rendered by the mounted members of Company D, Fourth Cavalry, which had endured the most fatalities, and then "Taps" was played over the graves.[22] The remains were interred side by side, recalled Wheeler. "Rocks were piled on the graves to prevent the wolves digging up the bodies, and a great quantity of wood was placed on the stones and set on fire, obscuring the grave."[23] Dodge and two other officers then visited Mackenzie's tent, where they found the colonel "very downcast—bitterly reproaching himself for what he called his failure. He talked like a Crazy Man . . . [and] said to an officer that if he had courage enough he would blow his brains out." Mackenzie later confided in Dodge "that he believed he [had] degenerated as a soldier as he got older—that he was a fool, & ought to have captured every Indian—that he regarded the whole thing as an utter failure."[24]

Mackenzie's self-lamentations were, of course, without foundation. From Crook's standpoint, the assault on the Cheyennes had been a major success. And besides the devastation visited upon the Indians during the attack, there had been untold suffering in its wake as the tribesmen confronted what had happened and attempted to save themselves. According to Cheyenne sources, all talk on the evening of the twenty-fifth was of escaping and how best to accomplish that before the troops should gradually advance on their position behind the breastworks at the far western end of the canyon. After dark, the surviving leadership assembled to mull over the circumstances and to choose a course of action. It was decided not to move en masse but to send small parties of three and five people together, ultimately to scatter in every direction away from the soldiers so that the troops would not be able to overtake one large body of people.

A major impediment to be mastered was the mountain on the north (present Fraker Mountain). In the darkness of the night, as snow began falling, the women and children, arranged in small groups, each led by a man, started up the slippery slope in subfreezing temperatures. It is believed that the people ascended following a rivulet line along the westernmost face of the mountain for a distance of approximately 1.75 miles. Passing over the summit, some of the warriors built fires to warm the families as they came along. Some of the people had robes about them, but most lacked any kind of garment appropriate for the frigid conditions. Children and the elderly were given what few robes and blankets were available. Far below, the people could still see the fires set by the soldiers destroying their homes, clothing, and other property in the village. They likely heard the throbbing of drums and the far-off muted tones of flutes retrieved from the village and now being played by enemy Shoshones and Pawnees. Many watching from the heights lacked moccasins; some wore on their feet pieces of animal skin or cloth torn from the clothing they wore. Yet the survival instinct was strong among them, and knowledge that the Sacred Buffalo Hat and Sacred Arrows were safe and accompanying them brought certain relief and meaning to this experience. Some of the wounded people ached mightily from their injuries as well as from the numbing cold, now intensified by whipping winds. One of them, White Frog, who had been shot four times, stumbled along on foot while his wife, Island Woman, held their baby tight to her body to give it warmth. Once in a while during the passage, the men killed one of the ponies they had made away with, opening its abdominal cavity so that the people could warm their hands and feet in the entrails. Despite such efforts, eleven Cheyenne babies reportedly perished that night from the cold (gauged by Lieutenant Bourke to be nearly thirty degrees below zero), and three more succumbed the following night.[25]

On the morning of the twenty-sixth, three mounted warriors rode on ahead at the direction of the chiefs. The three, Young Two Moon, Yellow Eagle, and Turtle's Road, had gone but a short distance when they encountered five Pawnee scouts who were possibly lost, for they were herding some Cheyenne ponies in a direction away from the army command. The three Cheyennes charged down a steep slope on the Pawnees, who fled, leaving behind the ponies. Some other Cheyenne warriors soon joined the three in pursuing the Pawnees over several ridges until the scouts finally got away, losing one of their own horses and its saddle to the warriors. Despite their condition, the Cheyennes had effectually bested the Pawnees and had recaptured about eighty of their own ponies, which thereafter helped them in their journey north. During the day, the village refugees apparently traveled northwest, gaining Arch Creek at or near a point presently known as The Arch, and then continuing northward through the Big Horns along that stream. Two days later a party of warriors traveled back to the village, seeking more ponies that might have gotten away from the soldiers. They found a number of the animals there and rejoined the northbound people with them. The main body plodded on through snow sometimes a foot deep, seeking warmth at bonfires built intermittently along the way by some men moving in advance and eating cooked horseflesh rudely turned on the coals of these fires.[26]

The route of the Cheyennes out of the mountains continued up Arch Creek until they probably reached a tributary of Pass Creek, which they followed down to ford the creek and, soon after, the North Fork of Powder River. While their precise route immediately after is not known with certainty, they eventually debouched from the mountains in the vicinity of Lodge Pole Creek (modern Clear Creek—probably the south fork), traveling northeast and coming down Bald Ridge to where the present town of Buffalo, Wyoming, stands. Then they turned north, eventually arriving on the southern shore of Lake DeSmet, where they camped. From here the Cheyennes continued north, finally gaining Crow Standing Creek (present Prairie Dog Creek), which they followed northwest to reach Tongue River. All during this journey, which evidently consumed about two weeks, the people subsisted entirely on horsemeat. Finally, along the Tongue, they found and succeeded in killing some buffalo for roasting. Wolf Tooth, one of those who had made the journey with no blanket or robe, took the occasion to fashion himself a robe of green hide, which he donned; however, it froze in the cold weather, and Wolf Tooth could not remove it for a long time.[27]

Near the mouth of Hanging Woman Creek on Tongue River, the refugee Cheyennes were surprised by a war party of ten of their own people just back from an unsuccessful attempt to raid the Crows. This party had been camped for the winter with Crazy Horse's Oglala Sioux, and now the people from the burned-out village in the Big Horns went with them, seeking help from these Lakotas. Together, the Cheyennes crossed to the east side of the Tongue, continuing to Otter Creek. At that stream's east fork, they crossed to Box Elder Creek (present Beaver Creek), where they found the Oglala camp along with ten lodges of Cheyennes under White Bull and Black Moccasin—the latter being the only one of the Old Man Chiefs who had not been in Morning Star's village when the soldiers attacked. Now all of them—Little Wolf, Morning Star, Old Bear, and Black Moccasin—were together. Here they found that the Oglalas were themselves in desperate straits and were eating horsemeat from ponies that had died. Nonetheless, Crazy Horse's followers welcomed the newcomers and gave them lodges, robes, tobacco, and packsaddles. Some of the refugee Cheyennes, however, reported that the Oglalas did not treat them well and were miserly in their sharing; in later times this

slight, whether imagined or real, was neither forgotten nor for-
given by the Cheyennes.[28]

Regardless, for the moment, the people from Morning
Star's encampment experienced a modicum of security that
they had not enjoyed for weeks. They never again met the troops
of Crook's late 1876 offensive, although the warriors who had
been in the Red Fork village soon found themselves embroiled
in combat with soldiers on another front. These were men of the
Fifth and Twenty-second Infantry, who in early January 1877
under the command of Colonel Nelson A. Miles started from
the army cantonment at the mouth of Tongue River on the Yellowstone to find and attack the village of Crazy Horse's Sioux.
On January 8, partly in blizzard conditions, warriors from the
village led by Crazy Horse, Two Moon, White Bull, and others
launched a surprise assault on Miles's bivouac along upper
Tongue River. The fighting raged over several hours, with charge
and countercharge made by each force until worsening weather
compelled a ceasefire, and the Indians soon after withdrew to
their village farther up the Tongue. Miles's troops followed
briefly, then turned about and marched back to the cantonment
at the Yellowstone. In the Battle of Wolf Mountains, neither
side sustained more than minimal casualties, but because of the
Indians' already aggravated circumstances, and doubtless the
condition of the refugee Cheyennes, the encounter with Miles
proved of major significance in forcing their ultimate decision
to head for the agencies.[29]

Meantime, the tribesmen at the Red Cloud and Spotted
Tail Agencies had remained compliant since Mackenzie had
dismounted and disarmed the Red Cloud and Red Leaf people
in October 1876. Because so many of the warriors had volun-
teered to go with Crook as scouts on the Powder River campaign, a selective process of dismounting and disarming had
since proceeded, and initially only those men who returned to

the agency from the expedition were subjected to it. As Crook
had earlier advised the scouts in council at Cantonment Reno,
"the families of Indians who are with General Crook are protected and cared for, so that no dissatisfaction may result from
ill treatment of them."³⁰ On Sheridan's insistence, however, Major
Julius W. Mason proceeded to retrieve arms and ponies from the
Red Cloud Agency people, and by early December the tribesmen had yielded 290 ponies and seventy-five guns, a large number of which were "serviceable breech-loaders" (most likely
taken from Custer's dead at the Little Bighorn). When Crook
learned of the procedure, he fumed, telling the Lakota scouts
that it was not of his doing. The animals, as before, were forwarded for sale at Cheyenne and Sidney. Meantime, to assure
supplies of hardtack, bacon, sugar, and coffee for the people at
Red Cloud and Spotted Tail, the War Department complied
with a request from the acting Indian commissioner to provide
such goods if needed, with proviso for either their payment or
return in kind. A real concern lay with the flour ration, already
insufficient in amount for the tribesmen present, a deficiency
that would be compounded if more Indians surrendered.³¹
After Mackenzie's strike against the Cheyennes and Miles's subsequent fight with Crazy Horse, the latter seemed most assured.

By the time of the Wolf Mountains battle in early January
1877, news of Mackenzie's attack on the Northern Cheyennes
at the Red Fork of Powder River had made headlines across the
country. Two days after Mackenzie's fight, the dispatch scrawled
on the battlefield by Jerry Roche was telegraphed from Fort
Fetterman to the *New York Herald*, where it appeared in November 29 editions accompanied by a partial list of casualties. This
was followed on December 1 by a follow-up Roche account
headlined "M'KENZIE'S VICTORY" that offered "Details of the
Fierce Cavalry Fight at Dull Knife's Village." And on December
11 yet another account by Roche appeared, this one consoli-

dated and more reflective, written on November 30 at the Powder River camp and giving further details of the action. Other tabloids got their descriptions of the action in relay from the *Herald*, which was the only paper with a reporter directly on the scene.[32]

Crook's dispatch to Sheridan of November 26, telegraphed from Fort Fetterman, reached the division commander two days later, and he forwarded it to General Sherman, who received it the same day in his Washington offices. On November 28 Crook sent another dispatch enclosing Mackenzie's own report and citing his junior's "brilliant achievements and the gallantry of the troops of his command." "This will," said Crook, "be a terrible loss to the hostiles as these Cheyennes were not only the bravest warriors but have been head and front of most all the raids and deviltry committed in this country."[33] General Sherman duly forwarded copies to the secretary of war, the secretary of the interior, and the commissioner of Indian affairs and on December 2 directed Sheridan to "convey to Generals Crook and McKenzie my congratulations." In addition, the general in chief offered an appreciation for the "brave officers and men, who are now fighting savages in the most inhospitable region of our continent. I hope their efforts this winter will result in perfect success and that our troops will hereafter be spared the necessity of these hard winter campaigns." To Sherman's comments Sheridan appended his own congratulations.[34]

For the men of the Powder River Expedition, such encouraging praise from the army leadership afforded scant consolation, given the reality of their circumstances in the cold, raw immediacy of the Wyoming winter they endured. And despite their significant victory, their campaign was not to end soon. On December 1 a sergeant of Company I, Fourth Cavalry, was killed when his horse slipped on icy terrain and fell on him. Already, Crook was making plans to resume the campaign, his objective now Crazy Horse. From the field the general sent Louis Richard and Louis Shangrau with five Sioux scouts cross-country to the Red Cloud and Spotted Tail Agencies to recruit more of their kin to join Crook's campaign near the headwaters of the Little Missouri. They were also to learn whether any of the Cheyennes from the destroyed village had come in at either place. The scouts further carried dispatches to Major Mason, directing him to send two Lakota spies north to find Crazy Horse's village and, once found, report the information to Crook. While at the Crazy Woman, military routine proceeded too; several men were court-martialed for losing ammunition on the march.[35]

On December 2 the command moved twenty-eight miles from the Crazy Woman to Cantonment Reno, bivouacking after dark southeast of the post. "The wagons did not get in until late and it was about nine before we got supper," complained Sergeant McClellan. At the post Crook arranged to take with him 374,000 pounds (twelve days' supply) of grain, 16,635 rations of hard bread, and 8,279 rations of bacon available, significantly reducing the amounts of these supplies there. He also turned in for storage at Reno a large quantity of flour and more than sixty thousand rounds of rifle ammunition the general deemed excessive for the march. Previously, Crook had sent word to the commanding officer at Fort Fetterman to deliver 200,000 pounds of grain to Reno for his expedition's use besides "the field guns, caissons, harness and ammunition" along with some "experimental canned beef" and sufficient extra carbine and revolver ammunition "to meet the contingencies" of the movement. By late November too, tobacco supplies had grown low, and requisitions went out to rectify the shortage. But worsening weather impeded the arrival of stores from Medicine Bow on the Union Pacific tracks. The supply situation did not improve; in fact, it worsened in December. As Crook's command labored through wintry climes, anticipated grain supplies from Medicine Bow, Cheyenne, and Fort Laramie were slow in getting through to Fetterman for relay forward to Reno and Crook's army. While weather played a role in the delays, so did intimidated civilian contractors who often refused to embark beyond the Platte River to reach Cantonment Reno.[36]

Crook continued readying his command as word passed through the units of the general's destination: the Belle Fourche River in the area south of Mizpah Creek, where scouting reports indicated that Crazy Horse was encamped. In fact, Crook had written Sheridan that he expected Mackenzie's fight, having devastated the Cheyennes, would force movement among the Lakotas too, with Crazy Horse heading east toward Slim Buttes. The general planned to ascertain that objective, then start for his quarry by moving eventually through the northern Black Hills. Mindful of his horses and the insufficient forage, he would immediately start southeast, locate a supply base four-teen miles away at Buffalo Springs along the Dry Fork of the Powder, watch for and harass the tribesmen until the new year opened, and then return to Fetterman. He directed that the seven days' supply of grain expected from Fetterman, on arrival at Reno, be forwarded to Buffalo Springs and decreed that a detail of foot troops—men "least fitted to stand the hardships of the campaign"—be left at the cantonment to manage the exist-ing supplies there. A pioneer unit comprised of "reliable" men with skills in handling tools was appointed to duty with the lead-ing wagon of the supply train. The rear-guard troops received instructions to stay well behind the supply wagons to preempt any attack on them by Indians. The continued dearth of forage, however, was severe and threatened the future of the campaign, for only seventy thousand pounds of grain would yet be avail-able at the cantonment. "That alone," wrote Dodge, "assures us against any further success. Our animals must break down in a week or ten days without forage." An immediate positive note was that the trader at Cantonment Reno had exhausted his whiskey supply, thereby saving the command from revisiting the drinking excesses of the previous month.[37]

Despite the supply problems, Crook got his command underway on Sunday, December 3. The movement angered some officers who had been led to believe that the men would remain in camp through the day. "I was disgusted," wrote Dodge. "[Crook] makes up his mind at the last moment, & then acts at once—expecting everybody else to do the same. He has nothing to do but make up his mind." The Sioux, Arapaho, and Pawnee scouts continued with the troops, but on this day the Shoshones, laboring under a belief that some calamity had befallen their people as evidenced by the findings in the Cheyenne village, left Crook's command at Cantonment Reno and headed for their homes beyond the Big Horns. That evening the soldiers raised their bivouac at Buffalo Springs following a trek of fourteen miles. The supply of water there was "very muddy and not much of it," wrote Private Smith, a sentiment echoed by correspondent Roche, who reported that "a few small, muddy pools of greasy alkali water were all that could be found within miles." The forage train arrived, and a number of Arapaho scouts who had gone out several nights earlier to check the area around the devastated Cheyenne village returned with some ponies found along the refugees' trail.

In the morning Crook decided to remain in camp because of an approaching storm, a decision that provoked another outburst from Colonel Dodge, who questioned the general's ultimate purpose in the movement. "I do not believe he has any definite plan or expectation. He proposes to go a certain distance in a certain direction hoping . . . that something may turn up, but his actions convince me that he either has no plan, or that it is very illy made."[38] Referencing the additional scouts that Crook had sent for, Dodge questioned the practicality of the decision and complained in his journal: "It will take these Indians at least 8 days to get to the agencies—& not less than 10 days more will be required for those recruits to get to the Little Missouri where they are to meet us. We start from here when this storm is over with rations to the 20th Decr. How the recruits are to do us any good, with so small a margin to work on, is a problem for a Brig. Genl. I can't solve."[39] Meantime, Major Gordon and a party accompanied McKinney's casketed remains, along with the wounded from the encounter on the Red Fork, by wagons to Fort Fetterman. Other expedition troops, sick and suffering from frostbite—in all totaling as many as 250 men -as well as played-out horses reached Fetterman on the sixth.[40]

The command laid over December 5 at Buffalo Springs too, and Dodge finally was able to confront Crook and elicit from him specifics of his plan. He learned that the general intended to head northeast, move past Pumpkin Buttes, and follow the Belle Fourche River to its forks before turning north to the Little Powder and following that stream to the Powder. At that point scouts would deploy in all directions, and if they found a village, Crook would start his soldiers for it on pack mules, owing to the poor condition of the horses. If no village was found, the army would march back to Fort Fetterman via Buffalo Springs. When Dodge suggested that the rations would not last that along, Crook allowed that if the chase justified, he would procure rations at the Tongue River Cantonment at the Yellowstone. If no village was found, he would turnabout, retrace his route, and reach Fetterman by December 31 with the rations immediately at hand. Moreover, the purpose for the layover at Buffalo Springs, Crook told Dodge, was to allow time for the scouts to reach Red Cloud Agency, recruit more auxiliaries, and meet Crook's command. Later, Mackenzie talked with Dodge; both concluded that from the forks of the Belle Fourche, the route to Camp Robinson was ten days shorter than by moving back through Forts Fetterman and Laramie, and Mackenzie said he would propose the former route to Crook for those troops and scouts expected to return to Robinson. In the end, as events proved, the matter was academic, but at that moment, penned Dodge, "I feel a great deal better since Crook unburdened himself."[41]

The reality was slowly dawning on all that the successful attack on the Cheyennes would likely remain the high point of the expedition. "The aspect of the campaign at present," opined Bourke, "is that it is more than doubtful if we see another hostile Indian on the trip." Crook began his march northeast on the sixth, leaving a small party at the Buffalo Springs camp and taking a convoluted course along a tributary of the Dry Fork before coming upon a wagon trail used by miners passing between Montana Territory and the Black Hills. "Now," wrote McClellan, "we find how hard it is to travel in this country in winter." In the afternoon the troops, Indian scouts, and lumbering wagons camped in a broad ravine protected from winds and harboring a bountiful spring. They had traveled about eleven miles, and Pumpkin Buttes could be seen to the north. That night some of the cattle stampeded but were recovered to the west the next morning. Snow on the seventh obscured any view of the buttes, and the command struggled through twenty miles of rugged arroyos in gaining the upper Belle Fourche. It was so cold, scrawled newsman Roche, that "one could scarcely pull a trigger without risk of freezing his fingers." The soldiers bivouacked at 3:00 P.M., but many of the wagons did not arrive until after dark. The men used sagebrush for fueling their fires. The Indian scouts made money shooting game and selling it to the command. Roche shot a porcupine and roasted it in the campfire ashes. "The meat," observed Bourke, "is fat and has a greasy, rancid taste, something like pork." By now the mules were worn out, noted Dodge, lacked proper attention, and were "expected to do all the work on half forage of grain." The same was true of the horses. "I think," he ranted, "[Crook] is pushing on now simply from vanity. . . . By the time we reach the Little Powder, it will be a miracle if more than half of us do not have to walk back."[42]

On the eighth "snow in a feeble kind of a way trickled down all the morning," recorded Bourke. The troops passed across eighteen miles of broken lands, "a dreary and treeless waste" that again delayed the wagons, and camped once more along the Belle Fourche. Much of the course paralleled that of the historic route of the Sawyers Expedition of 1865—a private enterprise intent on surveying a wagon road from Nebraska to the then-Montana gold fields; years later Luther North recalled that Crook's command followed "a fairly distinct old trail the greater part of the way" that was likely the Sawyers route.[43] During the march, the infantry soldiers began firing their weapons at game passing by, recklessly endangering the Indian scouts and their ponies and drawing a sharp rebuke from Major Townsend. That evening Dodge once more approached Crook regarding the worsening condition of the animals, more of whom were falling from fatigue. In his journal he condemned not only the administration of Crook but also that of Quartermaster John V. Furey, whom he believed was derelict of his duties. "He leaves the management of his train to understrappers, who neglect it entirely. No mule is ever curried—some of them are cruelly beaten—they get no grazing. . . . Altogether the transportation of this expedition is the very worst managed I have ever seen, & if for no other reason the expn must be a failure."[44]

Saturday brought a repeat of the previous day's marching conditions, but the labor was much shorter, the command traversing but five miles of the wintry terrain. "The difficulty," wrote Dodge, "is that we had to cross the Belle Fourche many times. It is a nasty gulch, with banks from 20 to 30 feet high." As before, the pioneer units labored to cut roads for the train, and again many wagons were stranded far behind and did not catch up until after dark. In addition to the condition of the animals and problems with the wagons, rations began to run low, although the men and scouts felled so much game that the matter was never critical. On December 5 a request for ten days' rations to be delivered posthaste to Buffalo Springs had gone back to the commanding officer of Fort Fetterman, and now on the ninth another missive directed the conveyance of both rations and additional forage to the Belle Fourche camp; fifty wagons immediately started back to Buffalo Springs to bring forward arriving supplies.[45] Near the camp of the ninth were perpetually burning coal veins, and William Garnett remembered how some of the citizens who trailed the troops "preferred to hover round the fires where the banks of earth were warm and the fires were sending up flames four and five feet high."[46] Coal from the outcroppings was subsequently used by company blacksmiths to reshoe some of the cavalry mounts. That evening some of the cattle were butchered and the companies dined on fresh meat. On the tenth the troops laid over, the cavalry only moving downstream a few miles to find new grass. During the forenoon, a group of eleven prospectors with two small wagons drawn by horses and oxen passed the command headed for Montana from the Black Hills. That day too Dodge, on Crook's direction, sent Captain William Jordan, Company A, Ninth Infantry, to escort a train back to Buffalo Springs, load the stores there, and return to the Belle Fourche with the detachment that had remained there. It was General Crook's plan now to strike east to the Black Hills, and word accordingly went over the back trail via scouts for trains en route from Fetterman with supplies for the army to diverge cross-country to Inyan Kara Mountain on the western edge of the hills.[47]

At 2:00 A.M., December 11, two miners appeared in the camp. They were from the party encountered on the tenth. Looking haggard and ill clothed for the weather, they reported how five Indians had jumped their camp, fired on them, and run off their stock, including nine horses. By morning all but one man had come in to Crook's bivouac, and Luther North and a party of Pawnees sent out by the general found the missing miner dead. The scouts trailed the raiders (six of them, according to North) without success. From accounts of the attack as well as the discovery at the site of a moccasin made from uncured buffalo hide, it appeared that the Indians were horseless Cheyennes, doubtless refugees from Mackenzie's attack, although this was never confirmed. Destitute, the miners beseeched Crook for help, and the general allowed them to remain with his command. Later in the day, arriving mail told of another attack on miners at Piney Creek, apparently by other Cheyennes.[48]

Throughout the march, the men of Crook's army were in most respects taxed to their limit because of existing conditions. The weather alternated between good (the eleventh was "balmy and beautiful," wrote Dodge), bad, and worse and was one reason for the frequent layovers in camp. The sites selected for bivouac often lacked the barest of necessities, particularly water, grass, and wood. Where water existed, it usually proved undrinkable because of its alkaline or mud content. At one place along the head of the Little Powder, reported Bourke, "we had to use water from a 'water-hole' swarming with wriggling worms. We boiled the fluid but made as little use of it as possible."[49] Often, sagebrush and greasewood sufficed for fuel in the absence of timber. The troops, however, had plenty to eat; the pack train bore sufficient rations, with even more on the wagons bringing up the rear. Further, game was plentiful in the form of deer, elk, pronghorns, and jackrabbits to augment the army ration. These comforts, noted Bourke, helped compensate for the rough moments, and he relished "the really luxurious living that awaited us within an hour after our wagons had reached bivouac. During my experience on the frontier, never have so much comfort and so much efficiency been combined in the same Expedition. The only drawback is the almost impossibility of getting enough grain for our animals." The horses suffered badly from the constant lack—and consequent but partial rationing—of forage. The command's mounts normally consumed thirty thousand pounds of grain per day—they could not depend on grass for nourishment because the ground was cloaked with snow. The cavalrymen spent considerable time cutting down hundreds of cottonwood trees and peeling the bark for the animals to eat, with General Crook occasionally taking part in this labor. Despite the stockpiles of grain at Cantonment Reno and Fort Fetterman and the assurance of more coming via the railroad, winter storms complicated delivery. At one point the cavalry mounts at Fetterman were used to transport forage to Crook's command. "Yet the supply was inadequate," reported Bourke, "and it seemed as if many of our poor horses were fated to pave with their bones the trail we had followed." Besides his normal responsibilities, the lieutenant took occasion of the march to collect tribal vocabularies of the Indian scouts accompanying the command.[50]

The ensuing days along the Belle Fourche mirrored the preceding ones and, contrasted with the excitement of the attack on Morning Star's village and its immediate aftermath, were decidedly anticlimactic. Bad weather persisted. "Disagreeable nasty night," recorded Colonel Dodge on Tuesday the twelfth, "snow, sleet, & wind." The artillery and cavalry battalions continued down the river, the former traveling in wagons, which were too few to transport the remaining foot troops too. They went only five miles before camping, the wagons returning to bring up the infantry command the next morning. As was typical, idle chatter and rumor constantly passed through the enlisted ranks. "All kinds of reports come in," McClellan jotted in his journal. "Some say that Crazy Horse is only 40 miles from here in a strong position and has rifle pits dug all around his village." On the thirteenth most of the command laid over, Mackenzie's horsemen going down the river several miles to find grass. Nearby the soldiers discovered a tree with nine Indian burials in it. Crook expected the scouts from Red Cloud Agency to arrive at any time, along with the spies he hoped to send into the Lakota camps. "He will not take any risks of roaming about scouting the country with this command," noted Dodge following a conversation with the commander. "If he can not find it, or if it is too far away, he will go in [to Fort Fetterman]."[51]

That scenario became more and more likely over the next week. The command did not go forward. The anticipated scouts and spies did not materialize on Thursday, and Dodge reported that forage and rations were running out. "Not a pound of grain on hand & less than a week's rations." During the night of December 14, something startled the cavalry horses and they stampeded. The troops who had labored each day cutting cottonwood for them to eat relished the respite, and some hoped they would never be found again. But by nightfall the men of Company I, Fourth Cavalry, had rounded them up and brought them back to camp. Also on the fifteenth, a sutler arrived from Fort Fetterman and opened business with five barrels of whiskey. Dodge at first countered the presence of the merchant by issuing an order requiring all whiskey sales to be made to officers for distribution to the men, but he revoked it the next day, partly, it seems, at Crook's request.[52] Some of the officers attended court-martial proceedings for a second lieutenant of the Fourth Cavalry who had committed a minor offense but who Mackenzie wanted prosecuted. News came of the arrival at Cantonment Reno of Captain George M. Randall and seventy-six Crow scouts enrolled at the Crow Agency in Montana Territory. Randall, on Crook's authority, had recruited two hundred Crows, and the group had passed overland to Reno through deadly winter storms that forced many of the enlisted Indians to abandon the march and return to their homes. Those who pressed on reached Cantonment Reno but would remain there to recuperate from their plight before joining the command.[53] Meantime, Crook learned from his scouts that most of the recently discovered trails suggested that the warriors and their families were heading south to the agencies.

The sixteenth saw a continuation of the courts-martial as the troops stayed in camp, and some of them became intoxicated on the sutler's commodity. Private Smith, who had made extra money by renting out his tent to gambling soldiers at night, was one of many to partake of the inebriant at "only one dollar a drink." On Sunday, December 17, the supply wagons arrived with enough forage to keep the animals fed on half-rations for twelve days. Word also came that yet more forage was en route. "Snow and cottonwood is light feed for animals hard worked," penned Lieutenant Lawton. Two days later the command remained bivouacked. The Sioux auxiliaries had still not arrived, angering Crook, while boredom and uncertainty now consumed his men. The Sioux and Pawnee scouts were becoming testy with each other. The enlisted men's gripes increased. "It seems as though Crook did not know his own mind," remarked one. "We are all getting decidedly impatient," groused Dodge. "It is dreadfully irksome to be on such a campaign & doing nothing."[54]

Amid such indecision, on the twentieth the command broke camp at 7:00 A.M. and moved six miles down the Belle Fourche. Crook also ordered the commanding officer at Cantonment Reno to divert trains to the camp of November 16 at Wind Creek, which he intended to reoccupy during his return to Fort Fetterman. If no such train appeared, then one was to be sent from the cantonment loaded with supplies for two days. That night a vigorous wind-driven snowstorm swept in, and one of the cavalrymen who had imbibed too much of the sutler's wares got caught in the tempest and froze to death. The loss portended the end of Crook's expedition. That day he received notification from Sheridan that his transportation costs had exceeded sixty thousand dollars per month, more than double the anticipated cost. His expected Indians not arrived, the location of the Sioux quarry unknown, his animals and transportation failing, and the weather potentially becoming even more unpredictable, Crook dashed off a telegram to Sheridan announcing that "the worn out condition of all the citizen & army transportation in this part of the country makes it impossible to keep this command in the field any longer." He informed the Division of the Missouri commander of his intention to arrive back at Fort Fetterman in eight days and requested that Sheridan have instructions there awaiting his arrival. Then he met with the various Indian scouts, explained the situation, and released the Sioux to start for Red Cloud Agency the next day.[55] The Powder River Expedition was at an end, and rejoiced Colonel Dodge, "I don't believe there is a man in the command who is not happier for the order."[56]

Chapter 8
Outcome

THE HOMEWARD TREK TOOK LITTLE MORE than a week, beginning Friday, December 22. While the days passed much as before, the officers and men, now inspirited with the realization that they were at last inbound, assumed a markedly new enthusiasm in their outlook. "My little wife would be worried at such flying in the face of the Ancient Superstition," wrote Colonel Dodge, "but Friday has always been a very lucky day to me except in minor discomforts." The advance took time because the road needed to be cleared of ice so that the pack mules would not fall down. The soldiers passed thirteen miles before halting in the face of a terrific blowing snowstorm and camping under some high bluffs. Thermometers registered just five degrees. "Altogether it has been anything but a lovely day & if we had to face the storm instead of going before it, we must have lost many men."[1]

Dodge took occasion that afternoon and evening to mull over the deficiencies he recognized in the expedition. He blamed much of the failure of the latter part of the campaign to the presence of insufficient rations and forage brought on by the civilian teamsters' habit of provisioning themselves with a superabundance of bedding, stoves, wall tents, and other creature comforts. Dodge claimed that "the Citizen employees . . . carry more impedimenta than would be required by a force of troops nearly double that we have." Compounding all, however, was General Crook's own lack of ability to organize. "He knows

178

nothing about . . . [organization] & is obliged to trust to others. He asks no questions & believes what is said to him. . . . He thinks his mules break down from hard work when they are neglected & starved. His successes must always be accidents as was this last—& he must fail—because he cannot himself organize, & has not the judgment to select men who can."[2]

Saturday proved to be "a day of terrible hardship & trial for all of us—men & animals"—as the command pushed southwest over frozen ground as "slippery as glass." Every rise had to be worked over with axes and picks so that the mules could gain traction. Plummeting temperatures were forecasted that afternoon by the appearance of a sun dog, an atmospheric phenomenon described by Jerry Roche as shafts of flame on either side of the setting sun so bright that they "presented the singular spectacle of a seeming descent of three suns below the western horizon." Thermometers hovered at between two and minus two degrees all day, and wood was scarce. The troops made eleven miles before camping. "There was a lot of men frozen and during the night 2 mules died from cold," wrote Sergeant McClellan. On the twenty-fourth they made only seven miles, again amid below-zero readings, and bivouacked at the same place they had camped on December 7. "Thermometer went down to –42 below zero and froze," wrote the sergeant. "Had to melt snow to make coffee. This is the coldest we have had yet. . . . I can see lots of men riding in the ambulances with frozen hands and feet." Crook and his senior officers gathered in the general's tent to celebrate Christmas Eve with hot brandy punch. That evening, Captain Randall and his Crow scouts arrived from Cantonment Reno. Bourke observed the Indians to be "handsome," and "the majority very young, but all made of good material." The Crows passed two nights with the command before leaving for home. Despite the holiday, there was no time off for the troops, who, although starting late in the morning because of further civilian incompetence, managed twenty miles across the bleak Wyoming landscape, passing Pumpkin Buttes. Dodge estimated the temperature that morning at fifty degrees below zero—the thermometers were again frozen. "Beards, mustaches, eyelashes and eyebrows were frozen masses of ice," recorded Lieutenant Bourke. "The keen air was filled with minute crystals which often cut the skin, while hands and feet ached as if beaten with clubs." Several more horses and mules were killed or abandoned during the march, which ended at a camp with sufficient wood, water, and grass—and slightly warmer temperatures. "It is a Xmas long to be remembered," recorded Dodge. "I don't care ever to have another like it."³

On Tuesday, December 26, amid sporadic flurries, Crook led his soldiers over a new route directly south for ten miles, after which they reached the old Bozeman Trail between Fort Fetterman and Old Fort Reno. The men reacted like they had found an old friend, and then kept plodding south for another sixteen miles until they gained Wind Creek and camped on their old bivouac site of November 16. There a train loaded with forage met the command. Together with gradually warming temperatures that reached twenty-two degrees by early afternoon, the troops and animals relaxed in a sheltered camp, where spirits were generally high. Next day the march resumed, the men passing seven hours through freezing weather to gain twenty-one miles and raise their tents along the south fork of the Mini Pusa, a dry branch of the Cheyenne River. On the morning of December 28, following an especially brutal night, General Crook departed alone via ambulance for Fort Fetterman, which he reached that afternoon. Three days later he left for Fort Laramie, from there passing down to Cheyenne, where he was to participate in court-martial proceedings against Colonel Joseph J. Reynolds and Captain Alexander Moore, Third Cavalry, on charges preferred by the general against those officers following the Battle of Powder River March 17. The Powder River Expedition, now under Dodge's direction, continued toward Fort Fetterman on the twenty-eighth, marching twenty miles to reach Sage Creek, halting there at midafternoon. The men were little more than ten miles from Fort Fetterman.[4]

They reached the post about midday Friday the twenty-ninth. Fetterman appeared, Bourke wrote, "off to the left, across the North Platte, on a squatty projection of land, [where] a long straggling line of buildings, a dozen or so more columns of smoke and in the centre a flag staff, were discerned and greeted with a cheer. They were not much in themselves, but they constituted Fort Fetterman, the advance post of civilization. Our ponies waited for no spur, but voluntarily struck out at a brisk pace and within twenty minutes we were seated by cheery, hospitable firesides, answering the greetings of warm-hearted friends." There the men and animals rested briefly before starting overland for Fort Laramie, where Dodge would break up the battalions and send the units off to their new assignments. Colonel Mackenzie and the cavalry column departed Fetterman on December 30, the colonel heading for Chicago and meetings with Lieutenant General Sheridan before traveling on to the national capital, where President Grant had requested his presence to command troops if needed in the wake of the disputed 1876 election. Mackenzie would remain in Washington, D.C., until March 1877. On January 1, 1877, Dodge's foot troops, mustered the previous day and recovered somewhat from a night's revelry, overhauled the cavalry, now under Captain Clarence Mauck's command after Mackenzie had pressed ahead to gain the railroad at Cheyenne, and then kept on for two more days until reaching Fort Laramie. After disbanding the command, Dodge left for Cheyenne by ambulance on the fourth, reaching it two days later amid the hubbub of officers lately arrived to serve on the Reynolds/Moore trials and noting, "more rank than

I have seen together since the war." Next day Dodge entrained for Omaha en route to his new station in Kansas, his work in the Indian war at an end.[5]

The cavalry troops, meantime, gained Fort Laramie and remained briefly, after which the Fourth Cavalry units rode on to Camp Robinson, those of the Fifth started for Fort D. A. Russell, the companies of the Third headed to posts along the Union Pacific Railroad, and those of the Second started for Fort Fred Steele, Wyoming Territory. The infantry troops likewise dispersed, with the Ninth Infantry companies bound for North Platte and Omaha, those of the Fourteenth for their home station in Utah, and those of the Twenty-third for Fort Leavenworth, Kansas. The Fourth Artillery men who had served as infantry went to Cheyenne and boarded cars for their home base in San Francisco. The Pawnee scouts under Frank and Luther North reached Fort Laramie on January 6 and then left for Sidney Barracks on the eleventh. The scouts rode into their station nine days later, proudly showing off the scalps they had taken in the encounter with the Cheyennes. Although there was some sentiment for sending the Pawnees to assist Colonel Nelson Miles at the Tongue River Cantonment, this was not done. Instead, sharing encomiums from Crook attesting to their "soldier-like conduct and discipline," the Pawnees were mustered out of service in late April and returned to their homes in Indian Territory.[6]

Crook's exploitive use of the Pawnees and Shoshones—both tribes with longstanding animosities toward the Cheyennes—was viewed as successful. Even his use of Lakota and Cheyenne scouts, where the relationships had to have been more sensitive, even strained, proved effective, although it caused tumult later when the respective antagonists assembled on the reservation. One criticism leveled at the Sioux auxiliaries was that, after the initial charge on Morning Star's village, "many of them relapsed into apparent indifference to everything except plundering the abandoned tepees . . . and trying to run off the horses." A participant complained that "the Pawnees fought like tigers, but the Sioux were engaged in pillaging the village and did not do much fighting. It is the general opinion of the privates and citizens that some of the killed and wounded on our side was the work of our Sioux allies." But Frank Grouard believed that the Lakotas had acquitted themselves well and had participated in "some of the hardest fighting that was done," despite earlier suspicions that "they would not stay with the troops when the emergency of battle arose." Meantime, the returning Shoshones brought word of the destruction of Morning Star's village to people still mourning their own losses in the earlier engagement with the Cheyennes.[7]

Individual honors for the soldiers who attacked Morning Star's people were not presently forthcoming. No soldiers were immediately nominated for the Medal of Honor. The closest such distinction came on November 30, 1876, when Lieutenant Harrison G. Otis, Company M, Fourth Cavalry, presented to Mackenzie a recommendation to recognize three of the individuals who had shielded Lieutenant McKinney as he lay unconscious at the edge of the ravine following his wounding. "I have the honor to call the attention of the Regimental Commander to the gallant conduct of 1st Serg. Thomas H. Forsyth, Serg. Frank Murray, and Corp. William J. Linn, Co. M, 4th Cavalry, as displayed in their successful efforts to defend the person of 1st Lt. John A. McKinney, 4th Cavalry, mortally wounded, from being outraged by the Indians during the fight of November 25, 1876. While thus engaged, 1st Serg. Forsyth and Corp. Linn were wounded; yet all three maintained their positions, protecting the body of Lt. McKinney until its recovery, and I take great pleasure in recommending them to the Regimental Commander for honorable mention."[8] Despite this endorsement, none of the men won recognition for their valor for some time, and

Private Thomas Ryan, Company M, Fourth Cavalry, who had played an important role during the moments following McKinney's fall, did not even receive mention in Otis's citation. But in 1880 Ryan received a Certificate of Merit for "extraordinary gallantry," entitling him to two dollars extra pay each month, for "maintaining his stand with but two of his comrades, one of them disabled, thus rallying the troop in time to rescue the body of his commanding officer." By that time, however, Murray and Linn, mentioned in Otis's initial communication, had left the service and received nothing. In 1891, following a petition by former adjutant Joseph H. Dorst and others, Forsyth was granted a Medal of Honor—the only such recognition accorded any participant in the engagement. Finally, six officers received brevet commissions in 1894 for their performances at the Red Fork. Besides the deceased McKinney, they were Second Lieutenant Hayden DeLany, Ninth Infantry; Second Lieutenant Homer W. Wheeler and Captain Wirt Davis, Fourth Cavalry; and Captains John M. Hamilton and Walter S. Schuyler, Fifth Cavalry.[9]

General Crook's farewell to his troops was published on January 8, 1877. In it he lauded his men for their "courage, endurance, and zeal" in persevering under the undue privations they had abided, "with the mercury exhibiting such extreme degrees of cold as to make life well nigh unbearable. . . . You have endured, with uncomplaining fortitude, the rigors of the weather from which you had less to protect you than an Indian is usually provided with." He continued, "The disintegration of many of the hostile bands of savages against whom you have been operating, attests the success of the brilliant fight made by the Cavalry with the Cheyennes on the North Fork and your toilsome marches along the Powder River and the Belle Fourche." He lamented the losses of Lieutenant McKinney and the others killed "in the lonely gorges of the Big Horn Mountains" and voiced, in convoluted fashion, a rather odd sentiment that "the fostering care, by a grateful country, of those who are personal sufferers in their deaths, prove that Republics are not ungrateful." But overall, returning after a more-or-less subdued campaign and not directly on the heels of the sole successful combat for the troops proved to be somewhat anticlimactic. Concluded correspondent Roche, "We return with peeled noses and cheeks indicative of our incursions into frigid latitudes, badges of our suffering of which we should be proud perhaps, only there is so little poetry in savage warfare that one can put it all in his eye."[10]

In his report of January 8, 1877, Crook gave the reasons for closing his expedition as "exceedingly bad" transportation, inadequate forage, and the frigidity of the weather. Moreover, the Sioux had scattered in the wake of Mackenzie's attack on the Cheyennes and were not to be found. He blamed the transportation problem on a "meagre appropriation allowed me for this purpose," resulting in his "serious embarrassment, it being almost utterly impossible to accumulate with it sufficient forage to enable expeditions to remain out for any great length of time in winter." Crook's explanation amounted to public criticism, and it clearly angered Sheridan, who fired off an endorsement to the report that lambasted his subaltern for Crook's own shortcomings of preparation: "The complaint of want of transportation was unnecessary, and if any one is at fault, it is the Department Commander, who did not make the proper arrangements before he started." This sentiment was echoed by General Sherman, who replied, "General Crook was certainly empowered to provide for his command as liberally as any General that ever took the field at any time." He further chided Crook for his statement regarding the men's lack of protection from the elements during the campaign. "If his men were not properly provided with everything, it was his own fault." Sherman was concerned that Crook's printed address "had gone forth to the world, and will be scrutinized."[11]

And Crook also drew criticism for maneuvering favorable press accounts of his work with reporters like Roche, who broadcast his successes exclusive of the efforts of other commanders (like Terry during the summer campaign). Crook's principal rival for success during the Great Sioux War now became Colonel Nelson A. Miles, who could not be kept from adding his voice (probably privately to his uncle-in-law, General Sherman) to the mounting reproach of the winter campaign. "With all the resources of a Dept. . . . [Crook] started with the great 'Powder River Expedition' of twenty-two hundred men to subjugate or destroy . . . [the Sioux] and that after the engagement of Mackenzie with the Cheyennes, and when within a few days march of Crazy Horse's camp he turned round and marched back to [Cantonment] Reno & then down toward Bell Fourche where there has not been a camp of hostile Indians in two years, camped fourteen days on a sage brush plain & returned to winter quarters, having accomplished nothing, but given the Indians renewed confidence. . . . [Crook] was a failure during the war and has been ever since."[12]

Adding to this judgment, former commissioner of Indian affairs George W. Manypenny asserted that the Cheyennes were where they had a right to be under the accord of 1868 and, moreover, that Mackenzie's strike abrogated provisions that each individual "be protected in his rights of property, person, and life" as specified in the draft agreement of 1876. Further, said Manypenny, in a reproach published later, "it was a grave offense, it was a crime, to attack this village, kill its inmates, and destroy their property. Such conduct should at all time be disavowed by the government, and such of its public servants as participate in it should be severely dealt with."[13]

In light of the sustained critique, Crook became defensive about his work and strove to highlight the Mackenzie attack as the signal accomplishment of his expedition. In truth, it was all he could do. And from a purely military standpoint, Mackenzie's victory over the Cheyennes merited special significance in ending the warfare by not only devastating that tribe physically, psychologically, and materially but also by extending through them a threat to the Lakotas that contributed to their own ultimate decision to submit. In sum, despite Crook's characteristic organizational disarray and his penchant for infuriating his superiors—especially Sheridan—by not carrying out their wishes to the letter, he nonetheless succeeded in doing to the Northern Cheyennes what Miles was accomplishing with the Lakotas. Together they effectually ruined the coalition of the Sioux on the one hand and the alliance between the Sioux and Cheyennes on the other. In later years Crook's relationship with Sheridan would fail altogether over the latter's disbelief in Crook's policy regarding Indian scouts and the former's repeated disregard of the instructions of higher authority.

To be sure, Miles's attack on the tribes at Wolf Mountains kept the pressure on through the winter. The two engagements, occurring almost in tandem scarcely one hundred miles apart, had an overall ruinous effect. In the weeks that followed, while the tribesmen in the Powder River country mulled over their fate, the army dealt with a number of local incidents in and around the Black Hills. In February, when the mayor of Deadwood pleaded for military help, Sheridan told Crook not to send cavalry relief because "there are four thousand . . . people in Deadwood [and] they ought to be able to defend themselves, especially as they are nearly all able bodied men."[14] On March 23, however, a company of the Third Cavalry under Second Lieutenant Joseph F. Cummings charged a Lakota camp of ten lodges along Crow Creek north of Deadwood, driving out the occupants and taking back assorted livestock previously captured from Black Hills citizens. For several weeks these and other troops ranged through the northern and eastern hills looking for Indians before returning to Camp Robinson in April.[15]

By this time, the Indian surrenders were imminent. In the north Colonel Miles had initiated contact with the tribes, while Crook had already sent out tribesmen from the Nebraska agencies to open negotiations. Hunts the Enemy (later known as George Sword), an Oglala, with thirty men had traversed the January snows to reach Crazy Horse, but his entreaties to the Indians to come in to the Red Cloud Agency had been politely rebuffed. In February Crazy Horse's uncle, Spotted Tail, the Brulé who the previous October had been designated by Crook as supreme chief of all the Sioux, journeyed to the Powder River country to induce his relative's submission with promises of an agency in the vicinity of the Black Hills and no removal of the tribesmen to Indian Territory. En route, Spotted Tail encountered other bands that listened to his words of peace and prosperity. Upon his return to Camp Sheridan on April 5, the chief told of the expected compliance of Crazy Horse and the others; they would indeed come in once the weather improved.[16]

As early as February 25, Minneconjou and Sans Arc Lakotas numbering 229 lodges delivered themselves over to authorities at Cheyenne River Agency in Dakota Territory. Among the Cheyennes, the decision to surrender was difficult. Some of the leaders had journeyed to the Tongue River Cantonment to consult with Miles, while Crazy Horse pulled his immediate followers away from the Cheyennes so that the Oglalas could decide their own course. The main Northern Cheyenne camp stood along Powder River, where Morning Star, Little Wolf, and the other leaders received a number of Cheyennes from the Red Cloud Agency who encouraged them to go in there. Eventually, the council decided that each could go in to Tongue River or to Red Cloud as he pleased. At that, the assemblage

divided, with Little Wolf; Morning Star; Standing Elk; Old
Bear; the hat keeper, Coal Bear; and most of the people opting
for Red Cloud, and a smaller contingent of 45 lodges (over three
hundred people), including Black Moccasin, deciding to go to
Tongue River. Box Elder, the blind holy visionary who had led
the people to safety during the encounter with Mackenzie, was
one of the latter. Some of the Cheyennes decided not to surrender and continued to stay afield in the Powder River region;
one of these was White Hawk, who joined his followers with
those of Lame Deer, the Minneconjou, who decided to hold
out. In May 1877 Miles's troops attacked Lame Deer's village
and destroyed it, driving the people away as refugees, who later
turned themselves in at the agencies.[17]

The larger number of Cheyennes under Morning Star and
Little Wolf began their journey toward Red Cloud Agency in
two groups. Those with Little Wolf led the way, moving rapidly
forward with only a few of the wounded from the army attack
in the Big Horns, though with many of the widows and orphans
of that encounter. The group with Morning Star passed along
more slowly because they transported the majority of the
wounded from the engagement. The column under Little Wolf
included Old Bear, Turkey Leg, and Black Wolf as well as the
Elkhorn Scraper and Crazy Dog leaders, who moved along in
the front and at the sides of the column, while a small number
of Dog Soldiers brought up the rear. All trailed the Sacred Buffalo Hat, which moved at the front of the column with the
mounted Coal Bear and his wife, who, walking, bore it on her
back. The trek took several weeks, and it was not until February
1877 when Little Wolf's party gained the agency and the chief
turned his weapons and ponies in to Mackenzie and Crook.
Smaller parties of Cheyennes continued to trickle in through
March, many accompanying Lakota tribesmen who were sur-
rendering at the same time. On March 13, for example, 133

Cheyennes turned themselves in at Red Cloud, followed the
next day by 130 Sioux. Camps of Arapahos also came in. By
April, 386 Northern Cheyennes had appeared. Many of Little
Wolf's followers, still incensed over the cool reception given
them by Crazy Horse after their attack by Mackenzie, volun-
teered to enlist and go forth with the soldiers to fight the Sioux.[18]

Finally, on April 21, Morning Star appeared with the balance of the people—524 of them—ending a journey of more
than three hundred miles that had been delayed by deep snows,
ice storms, extreme hunger, privation, and overall impoverish-
ment. Their clothing consisted of rags, and few owned blankets.
They had subsisted largely on horsemeat taken from their ema-
ciated mounts that they killed to survive, and many of the
women bore partly healed slash marks from their mourning over
relatives killed during Mackenzie's attack; others exhibited
wounds yet unhealed or flesh blackened from frostbite. Army
doctors would labor over horrendous wounds during the next
few days. Nonetheless, the people, arranged into four groups,
remained cheerful and sang as they approached the agency,
some men firing their weapons into the air. The column raised
a white flag as it came forward. Morning Star rode at the head,
with Standing Elk and other leaders by his side. Guided by Lieutenant Clark and Willis Rowland, these Cheyennes moved to a
place behind the agency and established their camp. Then the
leaders and men rode over to Camp Robinson to meet Crook
and Mackenzie. There Standing Elk, as designated spokesman,
told Crook: "We want to give up our guns today. We want to
shake hands and bury the hatchet." Altogether, Morning Star's
people turned in sixty-eight rifles and carbines, thirty-four pistols, and fourteen bows and arrows. After a meal at the camping place, they relinquished more than six hundred weakened
ponies to the troops.[19]

Within days, more of the Cheyennes came in to Camp Robinson and Red Cloud. A correspondent recorded their condition:

These people are entirely destitute, and haven't even the commonest accessories of life. Their village was destroyed by General Crook's cavalry in November last, under command of General Mackenzie, who was led in the canyon in which the Cheyennes were living by the company of Sioux and Arapahoes and friendly Cheyenne soldiers enlisted in the United States service. The Cheyennes say they suffered terribly in that engagement, their village of 200 lodges was burned to the ground, and everything they had in the world destroyed. Thirty of their warriors were killed and forty wounded, while next only to that in severity was the loss of nearly two-thirds of their herd of ponies, killed, wounded, and captured by the troops. As this happened in the latter part of November, and as the winters in Wyoming are exceptionally severe, the sufferings and privations of the Cheyennes may be imagined better than described.[20]

Scarcely two weeks after Morning Star's surrender, on May 6, with inducement from old Red Cloud himself, Crazy Horse led nearly nine hundred followers into Camp Robinson, providing, symbolically if not formally, an end to the Great Sioux War. His surrender prompted a discourse on the feasibility of punishing the leaders, "with the view of preventing any further trouble." Sheridan suggested sending them to Fort Marion, Florida, as had been done following the Red River War.[21] Ultimately, Crazy Horse's death on September 7—he was bayoneted by a sentry at the Camp Robinson guardhouse—ended any chance that the Lakotas would yet break away from the reservation and prolong the warfare. To further ensure against future outbreaks, that fall the Red Cloud and Spotted Tail people were ushered overland to new agencies established for them along the Missouri River. That move proved temporary, and in 1878 the Indians removed back to western Dakota, not far from the old Nebraska White River tracts, where they occupied new agencies at Pine Ridge and Rosebud.[22]

The Northern Cheyennes fared worse. Following the surrenders, the government decided to implement its old plan for removing them to the agency of their southern kinsmen in Indian Territory, a design that threatened their political unity. In late May, within but a few weeks of their surrender at Red Cloud Agency, almost one thousand Cheyennes started south under escort of Lieutenant Henry W. Lawton—one who had played an instrumental role for the army during the encounter in the Big Horns—and a small detachment of cavalry. The migration took seventy days, with wagons bearing along the sick, wounded, and elderly, accompanied by a herd of cattle providing sustenance. As before, the Sacred Buffalo Hat led the way, guiding the hurt and saddened people to the land of their relatives. On August 5, 1877, they reached Fort Reno, Indian Territory, overseeing the nearby Cheyenne and Arapaho Agency at Darlington, and over the following days the peoples of the north and south sought to rekindle their family ties as they feasted together.[23]

But from there the tragedy of the Northern Cheyennes only compounded. A year after their move, many of the people, afflicted with disease and languishing from near starvation in unfamiliar country, were desperate to return north. Forty-one had died from malaria and other sicknesses during the winter of 1877–78, and their existence at Darlington promised only continued futility. Together, Little Wolf and Morning Star plotted an escape, and under cover of darkness on the morning of September 10, 1878, as many as 353 Northern Cheyennes, including but a few dozen warriors, broke away toward Montana and the lands they loved. They passed through Kansas and Nebraska, fighting off army units sent to stop them, and mounted occasional attacks on settlements and ranches in search of food and resources as they proceeded. Beyond the Platte River in Nebraska, the people separated, the largest group continuing north into Montana with Little Wolf. In early April 1879 these people surrendered to troops near Fort Keogh along the Yellowstone River and ultimately were permitted to reside in the area. Morning Star's followers, meantime, en route to the site of the abandoned Red Cloud Agency, were arrested by soldiers in the Nebraska sand hills and taken as prisoners to Fort Robinson pending their return south. Incarcerated in an abandoned barracks without heat, food, and water after they refused to go back to Indian Territory, the freezing and famished people staged an escape during the night of January 9, 1879. Over the following weeks, troops from the post tracked down pockets of the refugees and killed many. Sixty-four Indians—men, women, and children—died in the various actions connected with the Fort Robinson Outbreak. Some were never found. Afterward, partly because of public opinion, Cheyenne survivors, including Morning Star, were moved to join Lakotas at the Pine Ridge Agency. In 1881 and 1883 the Northern Cheyennes still at Darlington who desired to do so were allowed to join their relatives at Pine Ridge. Four hundred forty-two did so; eventually, all Northern Cheyennes so inclined were permitted to remove from Dakota to Montana.[24]

As for the two principals who orchestrated the attack on the Northern Cheyennes in late November 1876, Brigadier General George Crook continued for thirteen years as a departmental commander with occasional field responsibilities. In 1883 he led troops into Mexico in pursuit of Apaches and three years later helped bring the Chiricahua leader Geronimo to bay in Arizona. That operation brought further difficulties with Sheridan over the use of Indian scouts, which forced Crook's reassignment.

After Sheridan's death, Crook won promotion to major general and command of the Division of the Missouri. He died in Chicago from a heart attack in March 1890 at age sixty-one. Colonel Ranald Mackenzie's fate was tragic. The mental problems evinced following his strike against Morning Star's people became more pronounced, possibly reflecting complications from a head injury he had sustained in 1875 in a fall from a wagon. Eventually, it compelled his retirement and treatment in an asylum. Mackenzie died in January 1889 in New York City at age forty-eight.[25]

More than one hundred years later, travelers to Lame Deer, Montana, seat of the Northern Cheyenne Reservation, occasionally visit the weathered cemetery near U.S. Highway 212 on the eastern edge of town where lie, side by side, the remains of Morning Star and Little Wolf. Morning Star died in 1883, Little Wolf in 1904.[26] In springtime, gentle breezes caress the barren mounds, while in winter blowing snows obscure them. At the graves, flowers and offerings of food and tobacco testify to the reverence accorded these two Old Man Chiefs by the Cheyennes today and how the relevance of their lives continues to inspire. For both Indians and whites, their presence signifies important moments in history, one of which occurred among the red-walled canyons of northern Wyoming when Mackenzie's soldiers stormed into the great conclave that bleak autumn morning, destroying lives and property and generating for the Northern Cheyennes the many tribulations that followed.

First Sergeant Thomas H. Forsyth, Company M, Fourth Cavalry, was the only person awarded a Medal of Honor for his performance in the attack on Morning Star's village, particularly for his service in protecting the fallen Lieutenant McKinney in the combat at the ravine. Forsyth was promoted to sergeant major of the regiment within months of the expedition and won the coveted medal fifteen years later on his own application. Courtesy Arizona Historical Society.

First Lieutenant Henry W. Lawton served with the Indiana volunteers during the Civil War. He commanded buffalo soldiers until his transfer to the Fourth Cavalry in 1871. Following service on the Powder River Expedition and his performance in the attack on the Northern Cheyennes along the Red Fork, he continued duty in the West and played a significant part in the Geronimo campaign of 1885–86. As a brigadier general of volunteers, Lawton was killed in battle at San Mateo, Philippine Islands, in December 1899. Courtesy National Archives.

Winter Attack on an Indian Village, by Frederic Remington, was used to illustrate an article in *Scribner's Magazine* in 1901, which used an alternate and perhaps inadvertently erroneous title, *The Defeat of Crazy Horse by Colonel Miles, January, 1877.* Because Colonel Nelson A. Miles's engagement with the Lakotas and Northern Cheyennes at Wolf Mountains, Montana Territory, on January 8, 1877, did not involve soldiers entering a village as depicted here, the scene more accurately reflects what happened in the direct aftermath of Mackenzie's assault on Morning Star's village, November 25, 1876, as troops searched the lodges following the initial attack. In this respect a 1904 publication of the picture in Cyrus Townsend Brady's *Indian Fights and Fighters* (opposite page 328) carries the title *Mackenzie's Men in Dull Knife's Village.* The original oil on canvas reposes in the Hogg Brothers Collection, Museum of Fine Arts, Houston.

John Augustine McKinney graduated from West Point a second lieutenant in 1871. An experienced officer in combat with Indians, the Memphis native won promotion to first lieutenant on May 17, 1876, scarcely six months before his death during Mackenzie's assault on Morning Star's village in the Big Horns, November 25. Courtesy U.S. Military Academy Library.

Second Lieutenant Joseph H. Dorst, Mackenzie's aide, as he appeared in 1877. Years later he wrote important accounts describing the action of the cavalry that he witnessed immediately following the shooting of Lieutenant McKinney. Dorst's varied military career eventually took him to Austria as military attaché at the U.S. Legation, to service in Cuba and the Philippines during the Spanish-American War and the Philippine Insurrection, and to becoming army superintendent of Sequoia National Park. Courtesy Richard W. Dorst.

Three Bears, an Oglala Lakota first sergeant who scouted for the army during the Powder River Expedition. Following the attack on Morning Star's camp, Three Bears evinced sympathy for the Northern Cheyennes. "I remember his coming into my tent one dismally cold night," wrote Lieutenant John Bourke. "Three Bears's eyes were moist, and he shook his head mournfully as he said, 'Cheyenne pappoose heap hung'y.'" Photograph by Daniel S. Mitchell. Courtesy Smithsonian Institution, National Anthropological Archives, NAA-3207-b.

Young Two Moon, son of Northern Cheyenne chief Two Moon, participated in the defense of Morning Star's village. Courtesy Smithsonian Institution, National Anthropological Archives.

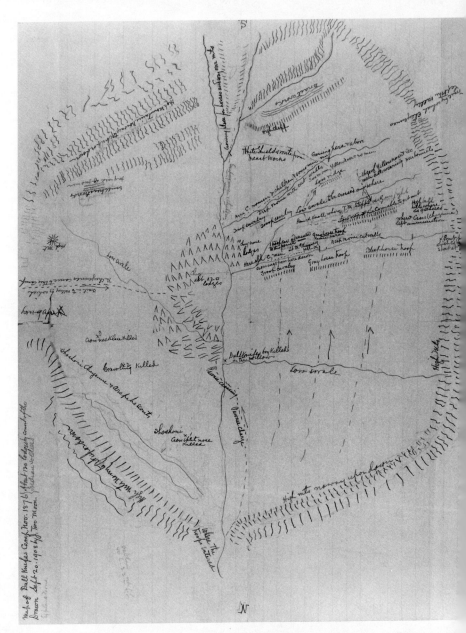

Young Two Moon's 1908 map of Mackenzie's attack on Morning Star's village is of particular importance in describing the actions of the Northern Cheyennes. But the north and south references should read east and west, and the place where Young Two Moon indicates McKinney was shot should be one ravine farther east. Courtesy Braun Research Library, Southwest Museum, Los Angeles.

In 1906 anthropologist James Mooney photographed Club Foot, Medicine Bear, and Coal Bear sitting before the tipi of *Esevone*, the Sacred Buffalo Hat. On the staff above the lodge is *Nimhoyoh*, the Turner. At the Red Fork in 1876, Medicine Bear waved the Turner to protect the women and children fleeing before Mackenzie's cavalrymen, while Coal Bear, keeper of the Sacred Buffalo Hat, and his wife managed to secure that vital object from capture by the troops. Courtesy Smithsonian Institution, National Anthropological Archives, NAA-55833.

"General Mackenzie's Fight with the Cheyennes, and Death of Lieut. McKinney," as drawn by Big Back, a Northern Cheyenne, and published in 1883. The accompanying text explained the events depicted: "Only prominent chiefs who were killed at this fight are represented on the Indian side, and the fatal wound of each is indicated by blood flowing from it, or—in some cases—from the mouth. The names of the chiefs thus shown in this picture are: (1) High Bull; (2) Walking Calf; (3) Whirlwind; (4) White Face Bull; (5) Bull Hump; (6) Old Bull. Short lines with a dot at one end represent flying bullets. The bullet passing through Lieut. McKinney's body (7) indicates the manner of his death." From Dodge, *Our Wild Indians*.

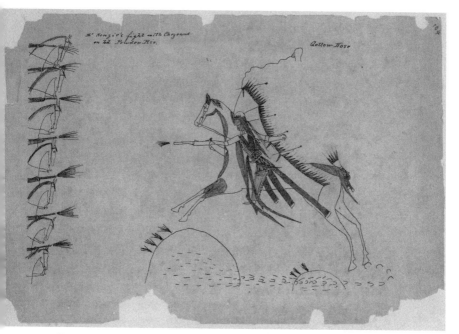

Yellow Nose's depiction of his role in the attempt of twenty-one war-bonneted warriors to rescue several men trapped behind a ridge (bottom foreground of pictograph) in front of Mackenzie's cavalry (pictured at left). Note the soldiers' bullets passing by Yellow Nose. Although the mission failed, the endangered warriors later managed to escape. Yellow Nose received a wound in later fighting. Courtesy Smithsonian Institution, National Anthropological Archives, Manuscript 490,978 (for other Northern Cheyenne ledger drawings of the attack on Morning Star's village, see Powell, *People of the Sacred mountain*, 2:982–91).

Marker erected in 1948 overlooking the field where Mackenzie's cavalry attacked the Northern Cheyennes and drove them from their village on November 25, 1876. Courtesy Paul L. Hedren.

9. "Report of the Commission Appointed to Obtain Certain Concessions from the Sioux," in *Report of the Commissioner of Indian Affairs, 1876*, 336.

10. For further details of the commission's work, see ibid., 330–47; Manypenny, *Our Indian Wards*, 324–25; Clow, "Sheridan's Legacy," 463–64; and Gray, *Centennial Campaign*, 260–64. An account of the negotiations at Spotted Tail Agency appears in *Cheyenne Daily Leader*, September 27, 1876. The 1876 Sioux Agreement appears in "Report of the Commission," 349–57; and in Kappler, *Indian Affairs*, 1:168–72. The "three-fourths" proviso constitutes article 12 of the 1868 treaty. Kappler, *Indian Affairs*, 2:1002.

11. Greene, *Slim Buttes*, 109–11; *Omaha Republican*, October 18, 1876. Quote is from Merritt to Crook, October 22, 1876, Box 45, Entry 3731, Department of the Platte, LR, RG 393.

12. *Outline Descriptions of the Posts in the Military Division of the Missouri*, 111, 112; Buecker, *Fort Robinson*, 32–34, 85.

13. Ibid., 46; Hedren, *Fort Laramie in 1876*, 147–49. Use of the term "rule of 1876" in reference to Sheridan's policy of disarmament and dismounting is extrapolated from period correspondence. See, for example, Terry to AG, Military Division of the Missouri, March 24, 1881, in Special Files of Headquarters, Division of the Missouri, Relating to Military Operations and Administration, 1862–85, RG 94, Records of the AGO, NA, M1495, Reel 5. See also Hedren, *Sitting Bull's Surrender*, 21.

14. First Lieutenant Morris C. Foote to AAG, District of the Black Hills, September 15, 1876, Sioux War Papers, Reel 279; Buecker, "Long Summer," 9–10; Gray, *Centennial Campaign*, 350; Hedren, *Fort Laramie in 1876*, 182–84. In the span of the three months from August to November 1876, the number of Indians at Red Cloud Agency, including Cheyennes, Arapahos, and Lakotas of various bands, fell by more than thirteen hundred. Major Julius W. Mason to AAG, Department of the Platte, November 14, 1876, Entry 3731, Box 45, Department of the Platte, LR, RG 393. See also Buecker and Paul, *Crazy Horse Surrender Ledger*, 6–7.

15. Hyde, *Spotted Tail's Folk*. Sheridan's quote is in his endorsement to Sherman, October 13, 1876, Sioux War Papers, Reel 279. Sherman's view is in Sherman to Secretary of War, October 17, 1876, Entry 3731, Box

45, Department of the Platte, LR, RG 393. For Spotted Tail's negative reaction to his visit to Indian Territory, see his two speeches as contained in Mason to AAG, Department of the Platte, December 21, 1876, Sioux War Papers, Reel 279.

16. Bruce, *Fighting Norths*, 41. Background history of the Pawnees scouts is in ibid.; Grinnell, *Two Great Scouts*; Danker, "Pawnee Scouts," 4–12; and various issues of *Motor Travel*, 1929–31. An act of 1866 authorized the president "to enlist and employ in the Territories and Indian country a force of Indians, not to exceed One Thousand, to act as scouts, who shall receive the pay and allowances of cavalry soldiers, and be discharged whenever the necessity for their further employment is abated, or at the discretion of the department commander." War Department General Orders No. 56, August 1, 1866, RG 94.

17. Wyoming's *Cheyenne Daily Leader* for November 25, 1876, reported in news from Indian Territory the Pawnees' concern over the role of the scouts. "The Sioux are to be the next door neighbors to the Pawnees presently, and it is feared that . . . the 'foolish and indiscreet action of a few irresponsible young men' may have unpleasant sequels."

18. Bruce, *Fighting Norths*, 41–43; "Pawnee Trails and Trailers," *Motor Travel* (July 1929): 7; (September 1929): 9–13; and (October 1929): 16–18; Luther North, "The Fighting Norths and Pawnee Scouts," *Motor Travel* (July 1931): 17; typescript comments on the Pawnee scouts, July 22, 1922, Item 283, George Bird Grinnell Collection, Braun Research Library, Southwest Museum, Los Angeles; Grinnell, *Two Great Scouts*, 248; Dunlay, *Wolves for the Blue Soldiers*, 161.

19. There is evidence that Sheridan planned, ultimately, to send the Norths and their Pawnees to support Miles's operations along the Yellowstone. Early in October, Dakota Department officials notified Miles that "one hundred Pawnee scouts . . . have been enlisted, and will be sent to you after a time." The colonel recruited a sufficient number of Crow scouts, however, and the Pawnees were never sent. AAG, Department of Dakota, to Miles, October 7, 1876, Item 3945, Records of the Military Division of the Missouri, RG 393.

Chapter 2

1. Sheridan to Sherman, October 26, 1876, containing Terry to Sheridan, telegram, October 25, 1876, Sioux War Papers, Reel 279; Major

Joseph G. Tilford, Seventh Cavalry, to AAG, Department of Dakota, September 21, 1877, in *Report of the Secretary of War, 1877*, 531–32; Clow, "Sheridan's Legacy," 464–67; Gray, *Centennial Campaign*, 266. For Sheridan's order respecting the dismounting and disarming of the tribesmen, see Hutton, *Phil Sheridan and His Army*, 322–23. A graphic personal account of the action at Standing Rock Agency is in Theodore Goldin, "A Winter Raid," n.d. Folder 16, Philip G. Cole Collection, The Gilcrease Institute, Tulsa, Okla. Disposition of the ponies is discussed in Garlington, *Narrative*, 15–26.

2. The standard treatments of Red Cloud are Hyde, *Red Cloud's Folk*; and Olson, *Red Cloud and the Sioux Problem*. A new addition to the literature is Larson, *Red Cloud*. For Red Leaf's background, see the indexed references in these books and Catherine Price, *The Oglala People, 1841–1879: A Political History* (Lincoln: University of Nebraska Press, 1996), 39–40, 60, 70–71, 136–37, 203–4.

3. Crook to Sheridan, October 30, 1876, Sioux War Papers, Reel 279; *New York Tribune*, October 25, 1876; Garnett, "Surround of Red Cloud and Red Leaf," 288–89 (reprinted in Paul, *Nebraska Indians Wars Reader*, 157–60). There are Lakota statements that suggest that the army had issued another warning to Red Cloud as late as the evening of October 21. See "Council at Sites of Surround," 281.

4. Crook to Sheridan, October 30, 1876, Sioux War Papers, Reel 279; *New York Tribune*, October 25, 1876; Buecker, *Fort Robinson*, 88.

5. Bruce, *Fighting Norths*, 45.

6. Wheeler, *Buffalo Days*, 116; Henry H. Bellas, "The Crook-Mackenzie Campaign and the Dull Knife Battle, November 25, 1876," in Greene, *Battles and Skirmishes of the Great Sioux War*, 170.

7. Greene, *Battles and Skirmishes of the Great Sioux War*, 170.

8. "Council at Sites of Surround," 285–86. Red Cloud's camp stood in the northwest quarter of Section 36, Township 33N, Range 49W. See "Detail Map of the Pine Ridge Country in the Middle Seventies," 16–17 (insert). Red Leaf's camp stood in Section 18, Township 32N, Range 48W. It was near the 1930s site of the Chadron reservoir. "Council at Sites of Surround," 280–81, 285.

9. Garnett, "Surround of Red Cloud and Red Leaf," 288; Grinnell, *Two Great Scouts*, 253. In 1932 the site of Red Cloud's camp was on a farm belonging to M. A. Gaffena along Chadron Creek. *Lincoln (Neb.)*

Sunday Journal and Star, October 2, 1932. This newspaper piece contains contemporary photos of the site.

10. George Bird Grinnell stated that during the capture of Red Cloud's camp, "a Sioux boy showed great courage in trying to run off a bunch of ponies, but left them after a few shots had been fired at him." *Fighting Cheyennes*, 361.

11. Ibid., 254–55; Wheeler, *Buffalo Days*, 116–17; Bellas, "Crook-Mackenzie Campaign," 170–72; Garnett, "Surround of Red Cloud and Red Leaf," 290 (which mentions the confusion regarding Gordon's command). The quote is from Red Cloud's daughter, Susie Kills Above, in "Council at Sites of Surround," 279.

12. But Lieutenant Homer Wheeler, Company L, Fifth Cavalry, remembered that one shot was fired accidentally, and "I was very much afraid that the shot might make trouble." *Buffalo Days*, 117. And Second Lieutenant Henry H. Bellas, Fourth Cavalry, speaking of both camps, later stated that there occurred "a rapid fusillade" followed by "a rush and a shout from the troops." "Crook-Mackenzie Campaign," 172. See other documents cited in note 16 below stating that no shooting occurred.

13. Crook reported that only seventy or eighty guns were taken. *New York Herald*, November 4, 1876. George E. Hyde, citing no particular authority, states that only fifty guns were delivered up by the Red Cloud and Red Leaf camps. *Red Cloud's Folk*, 285 n. 3. Mackenzie's initial report is in Mackenzie to Captain Azor Nickerson, October 22 [*sic*], 1876, Entry 3731, Box 45, Department of the Platte, LR, RG 393, Records of the U.S. Army Continental Command, NA. Crook's telegram announcing the action is in Sheridan to Sherman, October 24, 1876, Sioux War Papers, Reel 279.

14. Mackenzie's emissaries for this work were Red Dog and Big Crow. Mackenzie to Nickerson, October 22 [*sic*], 1876, Entry 3731, Box 45, Department of the Platte, LR, RG 393. Lieutenant Bellas recalled that, rather than walking the distance to the agency, the men rode, "2 being mounted on each pony," and that on reaching Camp Robinson, "the outfit, including Red Cloud and Red Leaf themselves, [were] safely secured in one of the warehouses of the post." "Crook-Mackenzie Campaign," 172.

15. *Omaha Herald*, November 3, 1876.

16. Beyond the sources cited, this account of the surrounding of Red Cloud and Red Leaf is based on Regimental Returns of the Fourth

Cavalry, October 1876, NA, M744, Reel 42; Regimental Returns of the Fifth Cavalry, October 1876, NA, M744, Reel 53 (which accounts for two soldier casualties in the operation); Grinnell, *Two Great Scouts*, 255; excerpt from Frank North's diary, in Bruce, *Fighting Norths*, 45; North, *Man of the Plains*, 201–4; Garnett, "Surround of Red Cloud and Red Leaf," 290–91; "Military Reports on the Red Cloud–Red Leaf Surround," 293; "Council at Sites of Surround," 283–84; Hyde, *Red Cloud's Folk*, 284–85; Hyde, *Spotted Tail's Folk*, 233–34 (both of Hyde's works have the events occurring a day later); Larson, *Red Cloud*, 207–8; and Buecker, *Fort Robinson*, 88–89. Reference to the approximate time of the returning Fourth Cavalry men with the Sioux men is in Smith, *Sagebrush Soldier*, 25. En route back to Camp Robinson, Red Cloud reportedly gathered his men and told them not to resist the soldiers but to "take this in good humor." Recollection of Susie Kills Above, in "Council at Sites of Surround," 280. Following their dispersal to the Pawnees, the remaining Sioux ponies from the Red Cloud and Red Leaf camps went on sale at Camp Sidney, Fort Laramie, and Cheyenne Depot. Despite initial stipulations to the contrary, proceeds from the sales were never used to purchase cattle for the Red Cloud Agency tribesmen, and the monies became unaccountable. Some redress was awarded descendants in 1944. Clow, "Sheridan's Legacy," 466, 474.

17. Sheridan to Sherman, October 24, 1876, containing Crook to Sheridan, October 23, 1876, Sioux War Papers, Reel 279.

18. Crook to Sheridan, October 30, 1876, Sioux War Papers, Reel 279. See Major Julius W. Mason to AAG, Division of the Missouri, November 16, 1876, Sioux War Papers, Reel 279. Mason attests to the quiet and obedient nature of the Red Cloud and Spotted Tail Agency Indians following the actions of October 23, writing, "I apprehend no trouble in keeping them in a proper state of subjugation."

19. Sheridan to Crook, October 25, 1876, Entry 3731, Box 44, Department of the Platte, LR, RG 393. Sheridan wired Sherman that Crook's "neglect to disarm and dismount other bands at that [Red Cloud] Agency is disapproved, and all . . . [Crook's] theories . . . seem to be given as a plea for not having performed what he promised and what was expected of him." Sheridan, first endorsement, November 6, 1876, of Crook to Sheridan, October 30, 1876, Sioux War Papers, Reel 279.

20. Crook to Sheridan, October 30, 1876, Sioux War Papers, Reel 279; *New York Tribune*, October 25, 1876; *Chicago Tribune*, November 4, 1876; *Omaha Herald*, November 3, 1876; *Army and Navy Journal*, October 28, 1876; Olson, *Red Cloud and the Sioux Problem*, 233; Larson, *Red Cloud*, 208–9. Quote is from Crook to Sheridan, October 24, 1876, in "Military Reports on the Red Cloud–Red Leaf Surround," 293–94.

21. *Chicago Tribune*, November 4, 1876.

22. Bruce, *Fighting Norths*, 46–47, citing *New York Herald*, November 4, 1876; excerpts from Frank North's diary, Bruce, *Fighting Norths*, 47. See also, Grinnell, *Two Great Scouts*, 255–56. Minor variances appear in North, *Man of the Plains*, 204.

23. Grinnell, *Two Great Scouts*, 257; Hedren, *Fort Laramie in 1876*, 195; Bruce, *Fighting Norths*, 47–48; Buecker, *Fort Robinson*, 89. Mackenzie was also desirous of using some of the captured stock to mount as scouts several Sioux prisoners who had been captured at Slim Buttes in September 1876. Mackenzie to Crook, October 28, 1876, Entry 3731, Box 45, Department of the Platte, LR, RG 393. Instead, 405 of the animals were auctioned at Fort Laramie on November 2 for an average of five dollars each. John G. Bourke, "Diary of John Gregory Bourke," November 2, 1876, vols. 14–15 (November–December 1876), U.S. Military Academy Library, West Point, N.Y., microfilm [hereafter cited as Bourke diary; all references are from volumes 14 and 15].

24. Crook to Sheridan, January 8, 1877, Sioux War Papers, Reel 280.

25. *Army and Navy Journal*, October 21, 1876.

26. Sheridan to Crook, October 30, 1876, Item 3526, Box 45, Entry 3731, Department of the Platte, LR, RG 393.

27. For biographical information about Crook, see Crook, *General George Crook: His Autobiography*; and Greene, "George Crook," 115–36. The most comprehensive treatment appears in Robinson, *General Crook and the Western Frontier*.

28. Regimental Returns of the Third Cavalry, October–November 1876, NA, Microfilm Publication M744, reel 31; Regimental Returns of the Fourth Cavalry, October–November 1876, ibid., Reel 42; Regimental Returns of the Fifth Cavalry, October–November 1876, ibid., reel 53; Regimental Returns of the Fourth Artillery, October–November 1876, NA, Microfilm Publication M727, Reel 30; Regimental Returns of the

Ninth Infantry, October–November 1876, NA, Microfilm Publication M665, Reel 104; Regimental Returns of the Fourteenth Infantry, October–November 1876, NA, Microfilm Publication M665, Reel 155; Regimental Returns of the Twenty-third Infantry, October–November 1876, NA, Microfilm Publication M665, Reel 237; *Roster of Troops Serving in the Department of the Platte*, 6–7; General Orders No. 6, Headquarters, District of the Black Hills, October 30, 1876, Entry 3743, Special Orders, District of the Black Hills, February–November 1876, RG 393; General Orders No. 7, Headquarters, Powder River Expedition, Fort Laramie, November 4, 1876, Entry 3936, General and Special Orders, Powder River Expedition, 1876, ibid.; Bourke, *On the Border with Crook*, 389; Wheeler, *Buffalo Days*, 124–27; "Pawnee Trails and Trailers," *Motor Travel* (January 1930): 21; Buecker, *Fort Robinson*, 87–88. For Lieutenant Colonel Dodge and his assignment, see Dodge, *Powder River Expedition Journals*, 9, 49, 50, 57.

29. *New York Herald*, January 14, 1877.

30. For Crook's rationale regarding Indian scouts, see Greene, "George Crook," 120–22; Dunlay, *Wolves for the Blue Soldiers*; and Easton, "Getting into Uniform," 40–42.

31. Mackenzie to Nickerson, October 28, 1876, Entry 3731, Item 3796, Box 45, Department of the Platte, LR, RG 393; Headquarters, District of the Black Hills, Special Orders No. 45, Camp Robinson, October 29, 1876, Entry 3743, Special Orders, District of the Black Hills, February–November 1876, ibid.; Bourke, *On the Border with Crook*, 390–92; Wheeler, *Buffalo Days*, 125–26; DeBarthe, *Life and Adventures of Frank Grouard*, 166; Taunton, *Sidelights of the Sioux Wars*, 38. Names of some of the Cheyenne, Lakota, and Arapaho scouts appear in Bourke, *On the Border with Crook*, 191–92; Powell, *Sweet Medicine*, 1:144; and Fowler, *Arapaho Politics*, 58–61.

32. Bourke, *On the Border with Crook*, 389–90; Wheeler, *Buffalo Days*, 125; Headquarters, District of the Black Hills, Special Orders No. 45, Camp Robinson, October 29, 1876, Entry 3743, Special Orders, District of the Black Hills, February–November 1876, RG 393; Surgeon Jonathan E. Summers to AAG, Department of the Platte, October 29, 1876, Entry 3731, Item 3521, Box 45, Department of the Platte, LR, RG 393; DeBarthe, *Life and Adventures of Frank Grouard*, 163–65.

33. For these seemingly miscellaneous, yet necessary, precampaign procedures, see Headquarters, District of the Black Hills, Special Orders No. 41, Camp Robinson, October 25, 1876; Headquarters, District of the Black Hills, Special Orders No. 42, Camp Robinson, October 26, 1876; Headquarters, District of the Black Hills, Special Orders No. 45, October 29, 1876; Headquarters, District of the Black Hills, Special Orders No. 46, Camp Robinson, October 30, 1876; and Headquarters, District of the Black Hills, Special Orders No. 47, Camp Robinson, October 31, 1876, all in Sioux War Papers, Reel 279.

34. Headquarters, District of the Black Hills, Special Orders No. 45, October 29, 1876, ibid.

35. Crook to AAG, Department of the Platte, October 28, 1876, Entry 3731, Item 3545, Box 45, Department of the Platte, LR, RG 393; penciled notes enclosed in Crook to AAG, Department of the Platte, November 8, 1876, Entry 3731, Item 3795, Box 45, Department of the Platte, LR, RG 393.

36. Headquarters, District of the Black Hills, General Orders No. 5, October 26, 1876, Entry 3743, Special Orders, District of the Black Hills, February–November 1876, RG 393; Mackenzie to AAG, Department of the Platte, October 23, 1876, Entry 3731, Item 3454, Box 44, Department of the Platte, LR, RG 393.

37. Headquarters, District of the Black Hills, General Orders No. 5, October 26, 1876, Entry 3743, Special Orders, District of the Black Hills, February–November 1876, RG 393; Mackenzie to Nickerson, October 30, 1876, Entry 3731, Item 3796, Box 45, Department of the Platte, LR, RG 393; First Lieutenant Walter S. Schuyler to Commanding Officer, Fort Laramie, October 31, 1876, Entry 3722, Letters Sent, Department of the Platte, vol. 4, 1874–76, p. 447, no. 844, RG 393; Special Orders No. 46, Headquarters, District of the Black Hills, Camp Robinson, October 30, 1876, Entry 3743, Special Orders, District of the Black Hills, February–November 1876, RG 393.

38. Pope to Crook, October 14, 1876, Entry 3731, Item 3460, Box 44, Department of the Platte, LR, RG 393; Sheridan to Pope, October 24, 1876, Entry 3731, Item 3461, ibid.; Captain Edwin Pollock to AAG, Department of the Platte, October 4, 1876, Entry 3731, Item 3307, ibid.

39. Headquarters, District of the Black Hills, General Orders No. 7, October 31, 1876, Entry 3743, Special Orders, District of the Black

Hills, February–November 1876, RG 393; Hanson, "A Forgotten Fur Trade Trail," 6–9; Robert Bruce, "The Fighting Norths and Pawnee Scouts: Historic Localities in the Old Northwest, Recalled for Motor Tourists," *Motor Travel* (November 1931): 17 (map).

40. "Diary of Sergeant James Byron Kincaid, Company B, 4th Cavalry—August 5th, 1876, to 1881," *Winners of the West*, July 1939. Kincaid's diary entries are one day behind the dates of the events. See also Frank North's diary, November 4, excerpted in Bruce, *Fighting Norths*, 48; *Tables of Distances and Itineraries of Routes*, 31. Private William Earl Smith, Company E, Fourth Cavalry, who served as Mackenzie's orderly, reported considerable trouble with the wagons, which were delayed crossing White River numerous times; several of the vehicles broke down during the march. Smith, *Sagebrush Soldier*, 27–28.

41. "Bi-monthly Inspection Report of Fort Laramie, W.T., made on the 2nd and 4th days of November 1876," Entry 3731, Box 46, Department of the Platte, LR, RG 393. For Fort Laramie, see *Outline Descriptions of the Posts in the Military Division of the Missouri*, 93–97; Circular No. 8, in Billings, *Report on the Hygiene of the United States Army*, 355–57; Hedren, *Fort Laramie in 1876*.

42. AAG Richard C. Drum to Crook, telegram, November 2, 1876, Entry 3731, Box 45, Department of the Platte, LR, RG 393. In fact, the attack on the Shoshones had come from Cheyennes, not Sioux. *Report of the Commissioner of Indian Affairs, 1877*, 209–10.

43. Bruce, *Fighting Norths*, 48.

44. Wheeler, *Buffalo Days*, 127. For a dissertation on the assorted winter clothing that accompanied Crook's earlier winter campaign, and which approximated that used on this one, see Bourke, *On the Border with Crook*, 252–53.

45. North quoted in Bruce, "Historic Localities in the Old Northwest," 21.

46. North, *Man of the Plains*, 207. Even Crook's aide did not know precisely when the departure would occur. On November 4 he wrote, "we get away to-morrow, I think." Bourke to Captain Azor Nickerson, November 4, 1876, Entry 3731, Box 45, Department of the Platte, LR, RG 393. Crook's direction of his Indian campaigns seems to have been his glaring weakness as a field commander. North further described Crook's "slipshod manner" of conducting the expedition, telling Walter M. Camp

that one day while the command traversed along the North Platte, "Crook selected a convenient camping place for himself and an escort of a company of cavalry. The others came along and marched on past 8 or 10 miles and camped where they pleased and the wagon train did not get up at all, coming along the next day without an escort. In the morning each part of the command moved pretty much as it pleased, without orders." Liddic and Harbaugh, *Camp on Custer*, 179. Similar criticism of Crook's management skills had surfaced during and following his earlier 1876 campaigns. See Greene, *Slim Buttes*, 12, 20–21, 68, 100, 112–13.

47. Both routes are delineated in "Annual Report of Capt. W. S. Stanton, Corps of Engineers, for the Fiscal Year ending June 30, 1878," in *Annual Report of the Chief of Engineers to the Secretary of War for the Year 1878*, pt. 2 (Washington, D.C.: Government Printing Office, 1878), 1725. See also the accompanying "Map of Reconnaissances of Routes in and Leading from the Department of the Platte by Captain W. S. Stanton, Corps of Engineers, 1875–76 & 1877."

48. Sheridan to Crook, telegram, November 5, 1876, Entry 3731, Box 45, Department of the Platte, LR, RG 393. This was Miles's fight with Sitting Bull at Cedar Creek, Montana. See Greene, *Yellowstone Command*, 92–113.

49. "Colonel Homer Wheeler's Account," George Bird Grinnell Collection, Item 91, Braun Research Library, Southwest Museum, Los Angeles, 2; North, *Man of the Plains*, 207; Bourke diary, November 7, 1876; Buecker, "Journals of James S. McClellan," 28; Flannery, *John Hunton's Diary*, 2:155. The distance is given in *Tables of Distances and Itineraries of Routes*, 18. A regional map showing period roads is in Flannery, *John Hunton's Diary*, 2:291. Private Smith recorded the distances marched thus: November 5, eighteen miles; November 6, eighteen miles; November 7, fifteen miles; November 8, fifteen miles; and November 9, eighteen miles. Smith, *Sagebrush Soldier*, 31–36.

50. Fort Fetterman was named for Captain William Judd Fetterman, killed in the Fort Phil Kearny "massacre," December 21, 1866. See Billings, *Report on the Hygiene of the United States Army*, 346–53; *Outline Descriptions of the Posts in the Military Division of the Missouri*, 97–101; Robrock, "History of Fort Fetterman," 5–76; Bourke, *Mackenzie's Last Fight*, 2–3. The routes between Fort Fetterman and Medicine Bow Station, and between Fort Fetterman and Fort D. A. Russell (at

Cheyenne), are delineated in "Annual Report of Capt. W. S. Stanton,"
1724, 1726; and accompanying "Map of Reconnaissances." Quotation is
from Captain Joseph R. Gibson to his mother, July 7, 1875, Gibson Personal Correspondence, 1875, 1883, Manuscripts Division, Army War College, U.S. Army Military History Institute, Carlisle, Pa.

51. "Bimonthly Inspection Report of Fort Fetterman, Wyo. Ty.,"
Entry 3731, Box 46, Department of the Platte, LR, RG 393; Robrock, "History of Fort Fetterman," 54–58; Flannery, *John Hunton's Diary*, 2:150–53.

52. North, *Man of the Plains*, 208; Buecker, "Journals of James S.
McClellan," 28; Headquarters, Artillery and Infantry Battalions, General
Orders Nos. 1, 2, and 3, November 10, 1876, Entry 3763, General and
Special Orders, Powder River Expedition, 1876, RG 393; Headquarters,
Artillery and Infantry Battalions, Special Orders No. 1, November 10,
1876, ibid.; Headquarters, Artillery and Infantry Battalions, Special Orders
No. 2, November 11, 1876, ibid.; Headquarters, Second Battalion, Powder
River Expedition, Special Orders No. 2, November 11, 1876, ibid.; Dodge,
Powder River Expedition Journals, 57–58.

53. *Cheyenne Daily Leader*, November 19, 1876; North, *Man of the
Plains*, 208–10; Bruce, *Fighting Norths*, 49. A somewhat different account
of this affair is given in Grinnell, *Two Great Scouts*, 258–61.

54. Bourke diary, November 8, 1876.

55. Ibid., November 10, 11, 1876; Dodge, *Powder River Expedition Journals*, 58.

56. Dodge, *Powder River Expedition Journals*, 59.

57. Headquarters, Artillery and Infantry Battalions, Powder River
Expedition, General Orders No. 4, November 13, 1876, Entry 3963,
General and Special Orders, Powder River Expedition, 1876, RG 393.

58. Bourke diary, November 10, 1876.

Chapter 3

1. North, *Man of the Plains*, 210; Flannery, *John Hunton's Diary*,
2:156; Bourke, *On the Border with Crook*, 390–91; Bourke, *Mackenzie's
Last Fight*, 7; Hill, "Bozeman and the Bozeman Trail," 212–14. The standard secondary work on the Bozeman Trail remains Hebard and Brininstool, *The Bozeman Trail*. For background on the trail and the warfare it
generated during the 1860s and 1870s, see Greene, "Warbonnets and Longknives"; and Hedren, "Beyond Red Cloud's War." For Captain William S.

Stanton's description of the same route and country as passed over the previous May and June, see "Annual Report of Captain W. S. Stanton, Corps of Engineers, for the Fiscal Year ending June 30, 1876," in *Annual Report of the Chief of Engineers to the Secretary of War for the Year 1876*, pt. 3 (Washington, D.C.: Government Printing Office, 1878), 707–8. The route is represented on "Map of Reconnaissances of Routes in and Leading from the Department of the Platte by Captain W. S. Stanton, Corps of Engineers, 1875–76 & 1877," in *Annual Report of the Chief of Engineers to the Secretary of War for the Year 1878*, pt. 2 (Washington, D.C.: Government Printing Office, 1878).

2. Bourke diary, November 14, 1876; Dodge, *Powder River Expedition Journals*, 61–62; Smith, *Sagebrush Soldier*, 46; Buecker, "Journals of James S. McClellan," 28.

3. Hyde, *Red Cloud's Folk*, 275; Hyde, *Spotted Tail's Folk*, 238; Utley, *Lance and the Shield*, 168–69; Vestal, *Sitting Bull*, 184; Colonel Nelson A. Miles to AAG, Department of Dakota, October 24, 1877, Records of the Military Division of the Missouri, Item 5074, RG 393, Records of the U.S. Army Continental Commands, NA; Miles, *Serving the Republic*, 147; Greene, *Yellowstone Command*, 66–67, 70–71, 115, 147, 152–53.

4. Bourke, *On the Border with Crook*, 256.

5. "Treaty with the Northern Cheyenne and Northern Arapaho," May 10, 1868 (proclaimed August 25, 1868), in Kappler, *Indian Affairs*, 2:1012–15.

6. For the Cheyennes' history and culture, see Powell, *Sweet Medicine*; John H. Moore, *The Cheyenne*; Moore, *Cheyenne Nation*; Berthrong, *Southern Cheyennes*; Grinnell, *Cheyenne Indians*; Stands in Timber and Liberty, *Cheyenne Memories*; Marquis, *Cheyennes of Montana*; and Powell, *People of the Sacred Mountain*. Population figures for the 1876 period are derived from Anderson, "Cheyennes at the Little Big Horn," 4–5.

7. Descriptions of Cheyenne society and political life are summarized from Powell, *Cheyennes*, 57–61, but see also, Berthrong, *Southern Cheyennes*, 27–75; Powell, *People of the Sacred Mountain*, vol. 1; Grinnell, *Cheyenne Indians*; Moore, *Cheyenne Nation*; Hoebel, *Cheyennes*; and Llewelleyn and Hoebel, *Cheyenne Way*.

8. For explication of these and other matters relative to the 1851 treaty, see McGinnis, *Counting Coup*, 85–88.

9. The Grattan Fight and Harney's campaign are explicated in Utley, *Frontiersmen in Blue*, 113–17. An important contribution to the literature on the Blue Water Battle is Hanson, *Little Chief's Gatherings*, 103–7. See also Mattison, "Harney Expedition against the Sioux," 89–130.

10. The most definitive presentation of the events leading to Sand Creek, together with graphic description and cogent analysis of the massacre, is Roberts, "Sand Creek." See also Hoig, *Sand Creek Massacre*. For context, see Josephy, *Civil War in the American West*, 292–316; and West, *Contested Plains*, 287–308. The only known comprehensive Cheyenne account of Sand Creek is in Hyde, *Life of George Bent*, 151–62. But see also Powell, *People of the Sacred Mountain*, 1:299–310. Government documents are reprinted in *The Sand Creek Massacre: A Documentary History*.

11. For early events along the Bozeman Trail, see Hebard and Brininstool, *The Bozeman Trail;* and Smith, "The Bozeman," 32–50. For the Platte Bridge fight, see Vaughn, *Battle of Platte Bridge*; and Grinnell, *Fighting Cheyennes*, 216–29. Connor's campaign is treated in Madsen, *Glory Hunter*, 137–54. Cheyenne accounts of the post–Sand Creek fighting in the northern plains appear in Hyde, *Life of George Bent*, 223–43; Grinnell, *Fighting Cheyennes*, 204–15; and Powell, *People of the Sacred Mountain*, 1:311–42.

12. The most complete account of the Fetterman affair and its collateral events remains Brown, *Fort Phil Kearny*, 173–90. But see also, Utley, *Frontier Regulars*, 93–110; and Grinnell, *Fighting Cheyennes*, 230–44. The most comprehensive Indian perspective is that presented in Powell, *People of the Sacred Mountain*, 1:451–61. For actions during the summer of 1867, see Greene, "Hayfield Fight," 30–43; Keenan, *Wagon Box Fight*; and Powell, *People of the Sacred Mountain*, 2:749–55.

13. For the southern plains campaigns, see Grinnell, *Fighting Cheyennes*, 245–328; Powell, *People of the Sacred Mountain*, 1:462–619, 2:846–94; Berthrong, *Southern Cheyennes*, 266–405; Leckie, *Military Conquest of the Southern Plains*; and Monnett, *Battle of Beecher Island*. The army's Washita campaign is treated in Hoig, *Battle of the Washita*. See also Monnett, *Massacre at Cheyenne Hole*.

14. Kappler, *Indian Affairs*, 2:1012–13, 1:169; Manypenny, *Our Indian Wards*, 322–24; Orlan J. Svingen, *Northern Cheyenne Indian Reservation*, 6–7. It is clear that most of the Cheyennes believed that Little Wolf,

Morning Star, and the other chiefs who signed the Fort Laramie Treaty of 1868 had in so doing misrepresented the interests of the Cheyennes as a whole, for the accord was never sanctioned by the Council of Forty-Four. For the roles of Little Wolf and Morning Star in the treaty negotiations, see Powell, *People of the Sacred Mountain*, 2:762–66. The first Red Cloud Agency stood in Wyoming Territory, thirty-three miles east of Fort Laramie. It was moved approximately seventy miles to White River near present Crawford, Nebraska, in 1873. Hyde, *Red Cloud's Folk*, 189n, 201–2.

15. Woodward, "Some Experiences with the Cheyennes," 188–91; Robrock, "History of Fort Fetterman," 22–23. George Bird Grinnell, who spent a lifetime studying the history and culture of the Cheyennes, called Little Wolf "the greatest Indian I have ever known." Grinnell to Robert S. Ellison, October 1, 1925, Robert S. Ellison Papers, Western History Department, Denver (Colo.) Public Library.

16. For background on Little Wolf and Morning Star, see Powell, *People of the Sacred Mountain*, 2:828–45; Moore, *Cheyenne Nation*, 201, 229–30; Roberts, "Shame of Little Wolf," 36–47; Hoig, *Peace Chiefs of the Cheyennes*, 123–30; and Eastman, *Indian Heroes and Great Chieftains*, 179–88, 213–24. For Morning Star, see Risingsun, "Chief Morning Star," 13; and Ted Risingsun, "Morning Star (Dull Knife)," in *Civilian, Military, and Native American Portraits of Fort Phil Kearny*, 240.

17. This view that the campaigning was directed against the Northern Cheyennes is advanced by Marquis *Cheyennes of Montana*, 258–60. See also Marquis, *Keep the Last Bullet for Yourself*, 74–78, 92. The argument has been refined by anthropologist Margot Liberty. For Northern Cheyenne perspectives relative to the encounters at Powder River, Rosebud, and Little Bighorn, see Grinnell, *Fighting Cheyennes*, 328–58; Powell, *Sweet Medicine*, 1:92–122; Powell, *People of the Sacred Mountain*, 2:937–1030; and Greene, *Lakota and Cheyenne*, 4–14, 21–30, 46–53, 61–72.

18. Powell, *Sweet Medicine*, 1:129–30; Powell, *People of the Sacred Mountain*, 2:1048–50; Marquis, *Cheyennes of Montana*, 258; Anderson, "Cheyennes at the Little Big Horn," 12. For more on the Warbonnet episode, see Hedren, *First Scalp*; Greene, *Lakota and Cheyenne*, 80–84; and Greene, *Battles and Skirmishes of the Great Sioux War*, 79–91. The Northern Cheyenne Buffalo Hump told Walter M. Camp in 1911 that

Morning Star "had always counseled peace, claiming that the whites were too numerous for the Inds [sic] to fight successfully," which was likely why he had stayed at Red Cloud Agency. Note in Folder FF1, Walter M. Camp Papers, Ellison Papers. Following the surrenders in 1877, Morning Star told Mackenzie that the colonel was the reason why the Cheyennes had broken away and gone over to the Big Horn country—"I was afraid of [you] when you came here [to Camp Robinson] last summer." Powell, *People of the Sacred Mountain*, 2:1146.

19. Lieutenant Colonel Jonathan P. Hatch to AAG, Department of the Missouri, September 24, 1876, Sioux War Papers, Reel 279; Mackenzie to Sheridan, October 29, 1876, Entry 3731, Box 45, Department of the Platte, LR, RG 393.

20. Bourke diary, November 15, 1876; Buecker, "Journals of James S. McClellan," 28; Dodge, *Powder River Expedition Journals*, 63–64.

21. Bourke diary, November 16, 1876.

22. Smith, *Sagebrush Soldier*, 47; Buecker, "Journals of James S. McClellan," 28.

23. Dodge, *Powder River Expedition Journals*, 65.

24. Ibid., 65–66.

25. Ibid., 66–67.

26. Bourke diary, November 17, 1876; Dodge, *Powder River Expedition Journals*, 67 and n. 47.

27. Bourke diary, November 17, 1876; Dodge, *Powder River Expedition Journals*, 68; Buecker, "Journals of James S. McClellan," 28–29.

28. Bourke diary, November 18, 1876; Dodge, *Powder River Expedition Journals*, 115; Smith, *Sagebrush Soldier*, 50; Buecker, "Journals of James S. McClellan," 29.

Chapter 4

1. Pollock to AAG, Department of Dakota, October 4, 1876, Entry 3731, Box 44, Department of the Platte, LR, RG 393, Records of the U.S. Army Continental Commands, NA; "Bi-Monthly Inspection Report of Cantonment Reno W.T.," December 31, 1876, Box 46, ibid.; first endorsement of First Lieutenant Wentz C. Miller to AAG, Department of Dakota, October 25, 1876, Box 44, ibid.; *Cheyenne Daily Leader*, November 21, 1876; Murray, *Military Posts in the Powder River Country*, 110–14; Murray, "Cantonment Reno/Fort McKinney No. 1," 275–79;

Robrock, "History of Fort Fetterman," 61. Second Lieutenant Homer Wheeler, Fifth Cavalry, remembered that at the time Crook's expedition showed up, "the officers and men . . . were living in dugouts." *Buffalo Days*, 128. And Bourke wrote that they were "living in holes excavated in the faces of clay-banks, or in make-shift quarters." *Mackenzie's Last Fight*, 8. The site of Cantonment Reno is on Bureau of Land Management property in Section 17, Township 44N, Range 78W, 6th Principal Meridian. In 1877 the name of the post was changed to Fort McKinney to honor First Lieutenant John A. McKinney, killed on November 25, 1876, during the attack on the Northern Cheyenne village. The post was largely abandoned in the summer of 1878 when Pollock's command removed to a new Fort McKinney along the Clear Fork of Powder River near the present community of Buffalo, Wyoming. Murray, *Military Posts in the Powder River Country*, 117.

2. Coates to AG, Department of the Platte, October 10, 1876, and first endorsement, October 12, 1876, Entry 3731, Box 44, Department of the Platte, LR, RG 393; *Cheyenne Daily Leader*, November 21, 23, 1876; Robrock, "History of Fort Fetterman," 62.

3. Bourke diary, November 18, 1876; *New York Herald*, December 11, 1876. William Garnett listed the names of several of the Sioux scouts as Red Shirt (sergeant), Six Feather, Little Bull, White Face, and Red Horse. William Garnett, interview, 1907, Tablet 2, Eli S. Ricker Collection, Manuscript Division, Nebraska State Historical Society, Lincoln, Reel 1 (hereafter cited as Garnett interview, 1907).

4. DeBarthe, *Life and Adventures of Frank Grouard*, 164–66; Garnett interview, 1907. Grouard's background reflected wide knowledge of Indian ways, and he reportedly had lived among the Sioux for several years before his scouting stint with the army in 1876. See DeBarthe, *Life and Adventures of Frank Grouard; and Gray*, "Frank Grouard," 57–59, 60–64. For Grouard's previous involvement in the 1876 campaigns under Crook, see Gray, *Centennial Campaign*; and Greene, *Slim Buttes*. A seemingly spurious account of Grouard's scouting activities immediately after joining Crook (and at odds with Grouard's autobiography as contained in DeBarthe) is affixed to the diary of Sergeant James Byron Kincaid, Company B, Fourth Cavalry, as published in *Winners of the West*, July 1939.

5. Headquarters, Artillery and Infantry Battalions, Powder River Expedition, Special Orders Nos. 8, 9, Camp near Cantonment Reno,

November 19, 20, 1876, Entry 3963, General and Special Orders, Powder River Expedition, 1876, RG 393.

6. Headquarters, Artillery and Infantry Battalions, Powder River Expedition, Circular No. 2, Camp near Cantonment Reno, November 21, 1876, ibid.

7. Pollock to Acting Assistant Surgeon E. P. LeCompte, November 23, 1876, Entry 3731, Box 46, Department of the Platte, LR, RG 393.

8. Frank M. Hopkins, Company E, Fourth Cavalry, to his brother, April 20, 1879, Indian Wars Miscellaneous Collection, Manuscript Division, Army War College, U.S. Army Military History Institute, Carlisle, Pa.; *Cheyenne Daily Leader*, November 26, 1876. See also Dodge, *Powder River Journals*, 75–76; and Bourke, *Mackenzie's Last Fight*, 10. Private William E. Smith noted in his diary that the casualty, a man from the Fifth Cavalry, got so inebriated "that he fell in to the crick and goot [got] wet and lad [laid] out on the bank. He frose to death and his company planted him in the after noon [of the twentieth]. *Sagebrush Soldier*, 58. Sergeant McClellan mentioned that two men had died, "one of Co. H 5 Cav and one of the arty [artillery]." Buecker, "Journals of James S. McClellan," 29.

9. Pollack to AAG, Department of the Platte, November 17, 1876, Entry 3731, Box 45, Department of the Platte, LR, RG 393; Trenholm and Carley, *Shoshonis*, 258–59; Bourke, *Mackenzie's Last Fight*, 9; *Cheyenne Daily Leader*, November 21, 24, 1876; Wheeler, *Buffalo Days*, 128–29; *Report of the Commissioner of Indian Affairs, 1877*, 209–10; "A Day with the 'Fighting Cheyennes': Stirring Scenes in the Old Northwest, Recalled for Motor Tourists of 1930," *Motor Travel* (May 1930): 17. The Shoshones brought with them twelve Sharpe's carbines, eleven Springfield rifles (.50 caliber), 5,150 cartridges, and one hundred lariats, all furnished by the U.S. Army. "Invoice of Ordnance and Ordnance Stores turned over . . . ," October 17, 1876, Entry 3731, Box 47, Department of the Platte, LR, RG 393.

10. Bourke diary, November 19, 1876; *Cheyenne Daily Leader*, November 26, 1876; Bourke, *On the Border with Crook*, 390; Taunton, *Sidelights of the Sioux Wars*, 38.

11. Bourke diary, November 19, 1876. All previous quoted material relative to Crook's council with the scouts is from the Bourke diary. See also Dodge, *Powder River Expedition Journals*, 72–74; Garnett interview, 1907; and Grinnell, *Two Great Scouts*, 262–63. Crook had earlier talked

with Frank North about the "distant" attitude of his Pawnees toward the others, reportedly saying that if they displayed friendliness, "I believe it would be better for all concerned." Quoted in Grinnell, *Two Great Scouts*, 261. Luther North summed up the meeting as follows: "After the General's speech some of the Indians made speeches, and finally Three Bears, the Sioux chief, walked across to our men and, speaking through an interpreter to one of our sergeants, gave him a horse and called him brother. Our men also made speeches and gave the Sioux some horses, and the council was dismissed." North, *Man of the Plains*, 211.

12. Grinnell, *Two Great Scouts*, 263.

13. Fowler, *Arapahoe Politics*, 63; Easton, "Getting into Uniform," 48.

14. Bourke diary, November 20, 1876; Dodge, *Powder River Expedition Journals*, 76–77; Smith, *Sagebrush Soldier*, 58; *New York Herald*, December 11, 1876; Wheeler, *Buffalo Days*, 129; Bourke, *Mackenzie's Last Fight*, 11 (quote).

15. Dodge, *Powder River Expedition Journals*, 77–78; Smith, *Sagebrush Soldier*, 58; Buecker, "Journals of James S. McClellan," 29; *Cheyenne Daily Leader*, November 28, 1876.

16. Garnett (whose interview remarks are hearsay) stated that the scouts were seated around campfires "warming and singing and exchanging jokes" when Many Beaver Dams approached. Red Shirt and the Arapahos told him "'Come up! The meal is on!'" "Red Shirt told him that these scouts had left the Agency to come to Sitting Bull and Crazy Horse's camps." After Many Beaver Dams had spoken freely to them, the Sioux and Arapahos took him prisoner, admonished him to "tell the General just what he had told themselves," and transported him on horseback to the cantonment. Garnett interview, 1907.

17. Crook to AAG, Division of the Missouri, January 8, 1877, Sioux War Papers, Reel 280; Dodge, *Powder River Expedition Journals*, 78; *New York Herald*, December 11, 1876; Powell, *Sweet Medicine*, 1:145; Bourke diary, November 21, 1876 (quote); Bourke, *Mackenzie's Last Fight*, 11. Bourke wrote that he further told Crook of the existence of "another Cheyenne village" in the Big Horns, although Bourke's diary, from which *Mackenzie's Last Fight* was drafted, does not contain this information. Presumably, Crook's scouts reported this fact as derived from Many Beaver Dams.

18. Bourke, *Mackenzie's Last Fight*, 12–13; map, "Line of March from Reno to Scene of Action with the Late Cheyenne Village on North Fork of Powder River," in John G. Bourke to Captain William S. Stanton, December 3, 1876, Letters, Reports, and Graphic Materials Received, Department of the Platte, RG 77, Records of Topographical Engineer Departments, Great Lakes Branch, NA, Chicago; Buecker, "Journals of James S. McClellan," 29; Dodge, *Powder River Expedition Journals*, 78–80; *New York Herald*, December 11, 1876; Bourke diary, November 22, 1876; Headquarters, Artillery and Infantry Battalions, Circular No. 3, Crazy Woman's Fork, November 22, 1876, Entry 3963, General and Special Orders, Powder River Expedition, 1876, RG 393.

19. Bourke diary, November 23, 1876; Smith, *Sagebrush Soldier*, 59–60; Garnett interview, 1907; Bourke, *Mackenzie's Last Fight*, 13–14; Dodge, *Powder River Expedition Journals*, 80–82 (quote); *New York Herald*, December 11, 1876; Dodge, *Our Wild Indians*, 494; DeBarthe, *Life and Adventures of Frank Grouard*, 166; Powell, *Sweet Medicine*, 1:145–46. Dodge, at least on the twenty-third, believed that the foot troops were to remain for a week at Crazy Woman Fork until Mackenzie returned, then the command would start for Crazy Horse, who presumably would be along the Rosebud. "We expect when McKenzie returns to march with our wagons to Goose Creek, then strike out with pack mules." If Crazy Horse should run, however, "our campaign will be a hard & unsuccessful one." *Powder River Expedition Journals*, 82–83.

20. Garnett interview, 1907.

21. Ibid.

22. Bourke, *Mackenzie's Last Fight*, 14.

23. Bourke diary, November 23, 1876 (quote); Dodge, *Powder River Expedition Journals*, 82; *New York Herald*, December 11, 1876; "Line of March from Reno to Scene of Action," in Bourke to Stanton, December 3, 1876; First Lieutenant Henry W. Lawton to "My Dear Carter," November 29, 1876, Manuscript Division, Center for the History of the American Indian, The Newberry Library, Chicago; Bourke, *Mackenzie's Last Fight*, 13, 14, 18; Smith, *Sagebrush Soldier*, 59–60. Another cartographic representation of Mackenzie's line of march on November 23 appears in Bourke's maps accompanying his diary, 14:1435–36. Sergeant McClellan recorded that the soldiers started their march at 9:00 A.M. He also countered Bourke, stating that "the ground was very wet

and uncomfortable . . . and not much wood for to make fires." Buecker, "Journals of James S. McClellan," 29.

24. North, *Man of the Plains*, 211; account of S. Millison, *The National Tribune*, May 17, 1923; Garnett interview, 1907. Garnett gave the names of three of the Sioux scouts as Kills a Hundred, Little Battle, and Skunk Head.

25. Bourke diary, November 24, 1876; Garnett interview, 1907; DeBarthe, *Life and Adventures of Frank Grouard*, 166–67; Mears, "Campaigning against Crazy Horse," 74; Lawton to Carter, November 29, 1876; Buecker, "Journals of James S. McClellan," 29; North, *Man of the Plains*, 211; account of S. Millison, *The National Tribune*, May 17, 1923; *New York Herald*, December 1, 11, 1876; Smith, *Sagebrush Soldier*, 61–64; Bourke, *Mackenzie's Last Fight*, 19–20. Sergeant McClellan learned that the village was "15 miles to the south west." Buecker, "Journals of James S. McClellan," 29.

26. Biographies of Mackenzie include Robinson, *Bad Hand*; and Pierce, *Most Promising Young Officer*. A brief treatment is Pate, "Ranald S. Mackenzie," 177–92. See also Heitman, *Historical Register*, 1:672; and Welsh, *Medical Histories of Union Generals*, 215–17. Welsh discusses Mackenzie's accumulating health problems.

Chapter 5

1. Powell, *Sweet Medicine*, 1:146–47; Garnett interview, 1907.

2. Young Two Moon, interview by George Bird Grinnell, September 19, 1908, Field Notebook 348, George Bird Grinnell Collection, Braun Research Library, Southwest Museum, Los Angeles. See also the detailed account in Grinnell, *Fighting Cheyennes*, 370–73.

3. Powell, *People of the Sacred Mountain*, 2:1049–50; Marquis, *A Warrior Who Fought Custer*, 282; Powell, "High Bull's Victory Roster," 15; Gray, *Centennial Campaign*, 350. I have used Harry H. Anderson's estimate, as well as his calculation of 7 people per lodge. Anderson judged each lodge to contain 1.29 warriors. Applying this figure to the 173 known tipis in Morning Star's village results in an estimated 223 warriors present in the camp. "Cheyennes at the Little Big Horn," 1–15. Under attack, however, young boys and older men might serve to defend the village in a warrior capacity; it is possible, therefore, that there were as many as 275–300 people who might be classified as "warriors."

Normally, the Sacred Arrows remained with the Southern Cheyennes. Black Hairy Dog's father, Stone Forehead, was the previous keeper, and he had brought the Sacred Arrows north to protect them following the Red River War of 1874–75. Stone Forehead's death early in 1876 meant that Black Hairy Dog succeeded as keeper, and he had arrived only recently from the south to assume his charge. Powell, *People of the Sacred Mountain*, 2:936, 1051. See also Chalfant, *Cheyennes at Dark Water Creek*, 58, 65, 172–73.

4. Field notes, Dull Knife battlefield, June 30, 1997, in author's possession; Luther H. North, "The Fighting Norths and Pawnee Scouts," *Motor Travel* (March 1931): 19; Moore, *Cheyenne Nation*, 178; Liddic and Harbaugh, *Camp on Custer*, 178; U.S. Geological Survey, Quadrangle Map "Fraker Mountain, Wyo.," 1984.

5. Young Two Moon interview, September 19, 1908; Jack Keegan, "They Fought Crook and Custer," n.d., Miscellaneous Articles File, WPA Collection, Wyoming Historical Department, Cheyenne; Grinnell, *Fighting Cheyennes*, 373–75; Powell, *People of the Sacred Mountain*, 2:1056–71; Powell, *Sweet Medicine*, 1:152–55; Stands in Timber and Liberty, *Cheyenne Memories*, 215–16; Powell, "High Bull's Victory Roster," 14–15; Dunlay, *Wolves for the Blue Soldiers*, 82–83. It is evident from the various sources that the precise chronology of warnings from Sits in the Night, Box Elder, and Crow Split Nose is not clear. The precipitate action of Last Bull in countering Crow Split Nose caused lingering and grudging resentment toward him and eventually contributed to his downfall and ousting by his own society. Llewelleyn and Hoebel, *Cheyenne Way*, 120–21.

6. James S. McClellan, "A Day with the 'Fighting Cheyennes,'" *Motor Travel* (February 1931): 19–20; Smith, *Sagebrush Soldier*, frontispiece photo of Private William Earl Smith. For descriptions of clothing and equipment of the Indian wars soldier of the 1870s, see McChristian, *U.S. Army in the West*.

7. The "total war" concept as used against Indians is discussed at length in Utley, *Frontier Regulars*, 50–52; and Wooster, *The Military and United States Indian Policy*, 135–42. See also Greene, *Yellowstone Command*, 10–12.

8. *New York Herald*, December 11, 1876.

9. Smith, *Sagebrush Soldier*, 64–65; *New York Herald*, December 11, 1876; First Lieutenant Henry Lawton to "My Dear Carter," November

29, 1876, Manuscripts Division, Center for the History of the American Indian, The Newberry Library, Chicago; Buecker, "Journals of James S. McClellan," 29; account of S. Millison, *The National Tribune*, May 17, 1923.

10. According to Private Smith, the shot was fired by a trooper dispatching his worn-out horse. *Sagebrush Soldier*, 65.

11. North, *Man of the Plains*, 211–12.

12. Bourke diary, November 24, 1876.

13. Most of Mackenzie's exact route from the head of the Crazy Woman Fork to the east entrance of the Red Fork canyon where the Northern Cheyenne village stood is not known with certainty. Reasoned conjecture, together with pieces of physical evidence collected by local settlers over the years, nonetheless permits an estimate of the cavalry column's course on November 24 and through the mountains the night of November 24–25. This suggests that the troops and scouts arrived somewhere in the vicinity of modern Horn Creek Reservoir by midday on Friday the twenty-fourth, remaining there until late afternoon, when they began their forced march to Morning Star's village. From there they surmounted high country, moving southwestwardly en route to the North Fork of Powder River, which they forded probably in the vicinity of present Mayoworth, and then continued south along the east side of EK Mountain, a relatively level area that is perhaps the "racecourse" mentioned in the accounts. From there the column followed the narrow and difficult Red Canyon for four miles (army canteens and equipment have reportedly been found in this area) before meeting the Red Fork, which they followed northwest for five miles until gaining the entrance to the canyon below the Cheyenne camp. The march totaled about fifteen miles. This tentative route conforms generally, though not precisely, with the map, "Line of March from Reno to Scene of Action with the Late Cheyenne Village on North Fork of Powder River," in Bourke to Stanton, December 3, 1876, Letters, Reports, and Graphic Materials Received, Department of the Platte, RG 77, Records of Topographical Engineer Departments, Great Lakes Branch, NA, Chicago. See also Bourke's maps accompanying his diary, 14:1435–36, especially for the halting place of November 24 relative to the Crazy Woman Fork tributaries. For local views and place names, see Condit, "Hole in the Wall," 32–33; and U.S. Geological Survey, Quadrangle Map "Kaycee, Wyoming," 1978.

14. Bourke, *Mackenzie's Last Fight*, 21. This account of the advance on Morning Star's village is drawn from the sources cited above as well as the following: account of S. Millison, *The National Tribune*, May 17, 1928; Lawton to "My Dear Carter," November 29, 1876; Garnett interview, 1907; Frank M. Hopkins to brother (Taylor Hill Hopkins), April 20, 1879, Indian Wars Miscellaneous Collection, Manuscript Division, Army War College, U.S. Army Military History Institute, Carlisle, Pa.; statement of William L. Judkins, December 7, 1905, Folder 11, Box 19, Eli S. Ricker Collection, Nebraska State Historical Society, Lincoln, Reel 7; DeBarthe, *Life and Adventures of Frank Grouard*, 167; Henry H. Bellas, "The Crook-Mackenzie Campaign and the Dull Knife Battle, November 25, 1876," in Greene, *Battles and Skirmishes of the Great Sioux War*, 176, Grinnell, *Two Great Scouts*, 264–65.

15. North referred to Mackenzie by his brevet rank of major general. *Man of the Plains*, 212. Lieutenant Lawton wrote as to Mackenzie's plan: "It was our intention to charge through the village with a portion of the command and take possession of the upper end of the gorge, holding the lower end thus having the Indians between us [and] compel their surrender." Lawton to "My Dear Carter," November 29, 1876. During the stop, Luther North nearly missed the assault, having wandered a short distance from the trail and dozed off, awakening at the last possible moment to join in the attack. *Man of the Plains*, 212–13; "Pawnee Trails and Trailers: An Important Chapter in the Geography and History of the Old West," *Motor Travel* (July 1929): 7.

16. Private William L. Judkins told Walter M. Camp that the placement of the scouts was based upon their perceived trustworthiness as determined by past history. Thus, the Lakota scouts were in the van, followed by the Cheyennes, then the Shoshones who had served Crook the previous summer, and finally Captain North's Pawnees, whose loyalty was never an issue. Judkins told Camp that because "the use of Indians as soldiers under white commanders was an uncertain experiment, this fact received consideration in the formation of the troops for the assault." statement of William L. Judkins, December 7, 1905. But this arrangement is not borne out in other accounts, which clearly put the Pawnees in front.

17. Forsyth to Captain Joseph H. Dorst, April 6, 1891, Entry 3369, LR, 1891, RG 94, Records of the AGO, NA.

18. Garnett interview, 1907.

19. Ibid.

20. This account of the final preparations of Mackenzie's command constitutes an amalgam of information drawn from the following primary accounts: *New York Herald*, December 1, 11, 1876; Smith, *Sagebrush Soldier*, 65–66; account of S. Millison, *The National Tribune*, May 17, 1923; Garnett interview, 1907; Bourke diary, November 24, 25, 1876; Bourke, *Mackenzie's Last Fight*, 21–22; Grinnell, *Two Great Scouts*, 265–66; DeBarthe, *Life and Adventures of Frank Grouard*, 167; Bellas, "Crook-Mackenzie Campaign," 177; North, *Man of the Plains*, 212–13; statement of William L. Judkins, December 7, 1905; Lawton to "My Dear Carter," November 29, 1876.

Chapter 6

1. Garnett interview, 1907. Garnett recollected that some of the Cheyennes' horses "had buffalo shoes to protect their feet from the rasping stones which covered that country and had made their feet sore. These shoes were pieces of raw buffalo hide wrapped about the hoof and drawn up to the fetlock and fastened by a string." Lieutenant Lawton later criticized the scouts: "From the impetuosity of our Indians, the alarm was given before the cavalry had come up, the path being such that they had to come in single file, and the Indians [Cheyennes] had time to get into the ravines." First Lieutenant Henry Lawton to "My Dear Carter," November 29, 1876, Manuscripts Division, Center for the History of the American Indian, The Newberry Library, Chicago.

2. North, *Man of the Plains*, 214; Grinnell, *Two Great Scouts*, 269–70. It is not known whether the movement of the Shoshones up the hill was in accordance with any plan or orders. As subsequent events proved, however, the position assumed by these scouts for the most part benefited Mackenzie's success.

3. *New York Herald*, December 1, 1876. Days later Colonel Dodge wrote in his journal that he had learned that the advance had been impeded by "deep ravines [that] cut the valley with deep & narrow canons—(gullies). These delayed the advance very greatly as the snow covered sides were soon slippery as ice." *Powder River Expedition Journals*, 93. All indications are that the companies were stretched out in the advance. Adjutant Joseph Dorst remembered that "all were delayed so long in reaching the village by having to cross a very boggy stream and

then pick their way through a wide growth of high and almost impenetrable brush, that the head of the column was engaged for some time before the rear troops could come into action. They had to advance about half a mile after getting clear of the brush." Dorst to AG, U.S. Army, May 10, 1891, Entry 3369, LR, 1891, RG 94, Records of the AGO, NA.

4. Grinnell stated that Mackenzie ordered his trumpeter to sound the charge, but if the colonel still hoped to surprise the Indians, this seems doubtful. *Two Great Scouts*, 269. No known participant account of the engagement mentions such a trumpet call.

5. According to Roche, "Lieutenant Clark found himself alone with Lieutenant DeLany, just beyond the village, a few minutes before the cavalry column entered, and had sharp work for the time being to save himself from the bullets of the fleeing hostiles. His position, however, enabled him to give General Mackenzie, when he entered, some valuable information, respecting the situation, and he did so." *New York Herald*, January 14, 1877.

6. Garnett stated that as he, Scraper, Fast Thunder, and Pourier mounted the Red Butte trying to keep the Cheyenne warriors in check, they found themselves caught in a crossfire between Cheyennes occupying the high ground southwest of the village and the onrushing cavalrymen, who, seeing the scouts on the butte and believing they were Cheyennes, fired on them, causing them to take cover. Garnett interview, 1907.

7. Garnett and Louis Shangrau viewed this man after the fight, apparently where he fell south of the Red Fork and southwest of the core village area. Garnett recognized him as Morning Star's son, having seen him at Red Cloud Agency, and described him as wearing a half-red, half-blue blanket "doubled and suspended from his waist. Around him was a belt, holding to his body a gun of the pattern then in use in the army, pointing diagonally across his body." Garnett and Shangrau touched coup on the corpse, and Shangrau took his gun and moccasins. Garnett learned later that the body had been scalped. Ibid. George Bent, the mixed-blood Southern Cheyenne, identified the youth as Young Bird. Interview notes, Folder 15, Walter L. Camp Papers, Robert S. Ellison Collection, Western History Department, Denver (Colo.) Public Library. See also Red Bird's account in Williams, *Soul of the Red Man*, 244. Young Two Moon's map placed this incident just north of the Red Fork at the northeast extremity of the camp.

8. "When the troops at the head of the column rushed through the village, the Indians fled in all directions, and many ran up into the ravines for shelter and followed them up to get under the cover of the rocks and trees on the [north] side of the canyon." Dorst to AG, U.S. Army, May 10, 1891, Entry 3369, LR, 1891, RG 94.

9. Luther North described this significant landform: "The ravine was of course irregular, both in width and depth; but I should say that where Lt. McKinney [fell] . . . it was on an average 20 feet wide and perhaps 10 feet deep. The banks there were probably about 20 feet high and more than that wide; down near the Red Butte it was more likely 50 feet wide, but with lower banks." North, "The Fighting Norths and Pawnee Scouts," *Motor Travel* (April 1931): 18.

10. Years later, Second Lieutenant Homer W. Wheeler, Company L, Fifth Cavalry, maintained that McKinney's company was serving as support to the attacking column, "but instead of doing as he was ordered he went in with us and was killed." The statement is significant in placing McKinney in a support position, likely from which Mackenzie later directed the lieutenant's advance on the warriors in the ravine. Wheeler, *Buffalo Days*, 131. More likely, however, McKinney's and Davis's companies were simply bringing up the rear of Gordon's battalion and had been slowed in their advance by the difficult terrain. Dorst recalled that Mackenzie had sent him to the rear with instructions, probably for Mauck's battalion far back, and en route was passed by McKinney's company moving forward at a gallop. Dorst to AG, U.S. Army, May 10, 1891, Entry 3369, LR, 1891, RG 94.

11. Dorst recalled that Otis had started away from the ravine on McKinney's yelled order to withdraw, "not noticing that Lieut. McKinney was hurt." Dorst to AG, U.S. Army, May 10, 1891, Entry 3369, LR, 1891, RG 94.

12. On November 29 Lieutenant Lawton wrote that McKinney had come "upon a ravine, through which a party of Indians were making their escape, and at a range of not more than ten feet, they poured a volley into the front of his company which carried him down with a bullet through his head, one through his body, and one through the leg, and his horse . . . shot through the head and neck, and six men . . . wounded, and six horses killed." Lawton to "My Dear Carter," November 29, 1876. Adjutant Dorst wrote almost fifteen years later that the lieutenant had *not* been aware of

the ravine but, spying it on his approach, decided to turn his column to the right "evidently to go around its head. The column was within eight or ten feet of the ravine, and just as the column turned, the Indians fired. . . . As the Indians fired, Lieut. McKinney called 'Fall back' and fell from his horse." Under this interpretation, McKinney had called out to his men and started to the right *before* the Indians opened fire. Dorst to AG, U.S. Army, May 10, 1891, Entry 3369, LR, 1891, RG 94. There are other accounts of the action that suggest that McKinney's men charged ahead without knowledge of a ravine in their front, a proposition that is contrary to at least some of the documentary evidence indicating that McKinney had been directed by Mackenzie to halt the flow of Indians by that route. See, for example, DeBarthe, *Life and Adventures of Frank Grouard*, 168. Despite his rank, McKinney by 1876 was a veteran officer whose frontier duty included stints at Victoria and Fort Richardson, Texas, in 1871–72 and combat against Comanches at McClellan Creek, Texas, on September 29, 1872. Through 1873 and 1874, he performed scouting duty with other units of the Fourth Cavalry and, during the latter year, took part in the Red River War in Indian Territory. McKinney was stationed at Forts Sill and Reno, Indian Territory, until August 1876, when he came north to campaign with the Powder River Expedition. Cullum, *Biographical Register*, 3:173–74. William Garnett said that "McKenny died with a sword in his hand. From Fetterman to the time of his fall he had been boasting his intention, if he got in reach of an Indian on the campaign, to dispatch him with his sword." Garnett interview, 1907.

13. McClellan, "A Day with the 'Fighting Cheyennes,'" *Motor Travel* (November 1930): 15.

14. Buecker, "Journals of James S. McClellan," 29.

15. Beyond the quoted sources, this reconstruction of the attack on Morning Star's village and the McKinney affair and its immediate aftermath is drawn from information contained in *New York Herald*, November 29, December 1, 11, 1876; recommendation of Sergeant Major Thomas H. Forsyth to the Secretary of War, January 1880, Entry 3369, LR, 1891, RG 94; Forsyth to Dorst, April 6, 1891, ibid.; Dorst to AG, U.S. Army, May 10, 1891, ibid.; Smith, *Sagebrush Soldier*, 72–73; accounts of James S. McClellan and others, *Motor Travel* (March, April, August, October, and November 1930; January and February 1931); Bourke diary, map "Scene of Action, Nov. 25, 1876"; Bourke, *Mackenzie's Last*

Fight, 23–24; Garnett interview, 1907; Grinnell, *Two Great Scouts,* 270–71; Wheeler, *Buffalo Days,* 131–33. See also Lieutenant Otis to Mackenzie, November 30, 1876, in McClellan, "A Day with the 'Fighting Cheyennes,'" *Motor Travel* (July 1930): 16; McChristian, "A Soldier's Best and Noblest Remembrance," 27–31. Otis cited the heroism of Forsyth, Linn, and Murray. Inexplicably, Private Ryan was omitted in the citation. Forsyth recalled of Ryan that after his own (Forsyth's) wounding, "all credit is due him, as had he not acted as he did, the Indians would, in all probability, either [have] killed me or driven me back." Dorst to AG, U.S. Army, May 10, 1891.

16. "Pawnee Trails and Trailers," *Motor Travel* (March 1930): 20. McClellan described his trophies, "a Sharps carbine, and also a cartridge belt full of .50 caliber cartridges," in some detail: "On this belt was a silver belt plate, with the name Little Wolf stamped thereon; also in an old-fashioned army cap box studded with brass nails, was a steel used for striking fire and a flint stone." Ibid., 19. The items eventually landed in the collection of Guthrie Y. Barber in New York City. The warrior Bull Head was later scalped by one of the white scouts. See also Buecker, "Journals of James S. McClellan," 29; McClellan, "A Day with the Fighting Cheyennes," *Motor Travel* (September 1930): 10–11; and *The National Tribune,* September 29, 1927.

17. Dorst to AG, U.S. Army, March 12, 1894, Joseph H. Dorst Papers, Special Collections, U.S. Military Academy Library, West Point, N.Y. Luther North later confirmed the near rout of the soldiers. He told Walter Camp that "when McKinney charged on the gully and was killed [*sic*—McKinney died later in the field hospital], the soldiers all ran back but Ralph Weeks, one of our Pawnees who was educated and spoke good English, . . . rode up in front of them and cried out: 'What are you running for? There are only six or seven Indians in there.' In this way the soldiers turned again and attacked the Indians in the gully and followed them up." Camp, *Camp on Custer,* 177–78.

18. In another document Dorst stated, "the speedy success of these men [returning to the ravine] was due to Lieut. . . . Lawton, who noticed the disorder in the troop, at once assumed command of it, rallied it, and took it back to the place it had fled from." Dorst to AG, U.S. Army, May 10, 1891, Entry 3369, LR, 1891, RG 94. At any rate, Lawton did not mention his role in his missive four days later describing the action, simply

saying: "The company turned, but a few men remained, and saved the body [McKinney's body] from the Indians." Lawton to "My Dear Carter," November 29, 1876.

19. Remarks of Dr. LaGarde at the annual dinner meeting of the Order of Indian Wars, March 6, 1915, L-2, Order of Indian Wars Files, Manuscripts Division, Army War College, U.S. Army Military History Institute, Carlisle, Pa. A contemporary account stated that McKinney exclaimed "Oh! My poor mother! Tell her! Tell her!" before he died. *New York Herald*, December 1, 1876. Garnett recounted the following story: "When the dead [*sic*—wounded at the ravine] were being gathered up, someone undertook to raise the soldier lying near McKenny, and the man asked if the Indians were gone and when told that they were, he announced that he was not hurt and immediately arose." Garnett interview, 1907.

20. Cartridge evidence indicates that the Shoshones were primarily firing .50/70, .45/70 (or .45/55), and .44 Henry/Winchester cartridges. Gene Galloway to Paul L. Hedren, September 20, 1975, copy in author's possession.

21. McClellan, "A Day with the 'Fighting Cheyennes,'" *Motor Travel* (October 1930): 18–19.

22. These movements are described further in *New York Herald*, December 11, 1876; and Bourke, *Mackenzie's Last Fight*, 24.

23. This man was identified by Lieutenant Wheeler as Private McFarland, who had been a Civil War veteran. *Buffalo Days*, 133.

24. It might have been the events connected with the aftermath of McKinney's fall that prompted the Sioux scout, Sergeant Three Bears, to go with Garnett to speak with Mackenzie. Three Bears told the colonel to "let the soldiers fight as Indians do. If you don't, we are all going to leave you; and if we do, you will all be killed as Long Hair [Custer] was." Garnett maintained that Mackenzie followed Three Bear's advice and from then on "different results followed." Garnett interview, 1907.

25. North, *Man of the Plains*, 215. Frank Grouard claimed to have shot and killed the Cheyenne chief Little Wolf from this position. DeBarthe, *Life and Adventures of Frank Grouard*, 168–69. William Garnett also claimed to have shot and wounded Little Wolf during the fighting. Months later, Garnett talked with Little Wolf, who said he had received six flesh wounds in the Red Fork encounter. Walter M. Camp,

interview by William Garnett, n.d., Camp interview notes, Walter Mason Camp Collection, L. Tom Perry Special Collections, Harold B. Lee Library, Brigham Young University, Provo, Utah, microfilm, Reel 2.

26. Years later Lieutenant Schuyler, who had remained on the bluff with the Shoshones, reported, "when I returned from that campaign I threw away my Winchester and got the longest range Sharps sporting rifle on the market." "A Day with the 'Fighting Cheyennes,'" *Motor Travel* (August 1930): 18.

27. Bourke diary, November 25, 1876.

28. North, *Man of the Plains*, 215.

29. Bourke, *Mackenzie's Last Fight*, 25.

30. Bourke diary, November 25, 1876. Luther North recollected Mackenzie riding "across the open ground to the Red Butte alone, his horse just jogging along on a little trot. There was no officer of his staff, or even a bugler, with the ranking officer on the field. At the time I wondered why he did it, because by coming down the ravine he would have been under cover all the way; but, so far as I can learn, Mackenzie never seemed to do anything to protect himself, and his example was a great inspiration to his men. Passing over the open ground west of the dry gulch, the Colonel crossed it right at the foot of the Red Butte." "The Fighting Norths and Pawnee Scouts," *Motor Travel* (March 1931): 20. The packer Millison maintained that Mackenzie's horse was slightly wounded passing over the field. Account of S. Millison, *The National Tribune*, May 17, 1923. Undoubtedly, Lieutenants Lawton and Dorst felt the need to emulate Mackenzie in their own movements on the field. Dorst remembered "the most uncomfortable duty I had to perform was to ride along this line twice while the Indians on our flanks and to our front concentrated their fire on me for the whole distance—about three-eighths of a mile. I was kept at this kind of work until about the middle of the afternoon." Dorst to AG, U.S. Army, March 12, 1894, Dorst Papers.

31. Bourke diary, November 25, 1876.

32. *New York Herald*, December 11, 1876.

33. This juxtapositioning of Davis's movement with the loss of Private Sullivan is something of a supposition, for Sullivan was apparently killed in this area around this time and his remains could not be retrieved until the next morning. See Ordnance Sergeant Joseph Sudsburger to Colonel J. H. Dorst, January 11, 1908, enclosing sketch map, Special Col-

lections, U.S. Military Academy Library, West Point, N.Y.; former first sergeant Benjamin F. Graves to "Whom It May Concern," December 5, 1907, ibid.; and Lieutenant Colonel Henry W. Lawton to AG, U.S. Army, March 11, 1891, ibid. All three pertain to the killing of an Indian by Sudsburger.

34. This incident occurred on the extreme right of the line, the warriors occupying a deep draw constituting an extension into the mountainside of the ravine along which most of the troops were deployed. Cheyenne informants told Grinnell that six warriors died there. Field Notebook 354, George Bird Grinnell Collection, Braun Research Library, Southwest Museum, Los Angeles.

35. Frank Grouard stated that at one juncture two unarmed warriors emerged from their cover and walked back and forth only twenty paces from the soldiers' line, this to draw their fire while many of the women and children made their way out of the canyon. Neither man was hit during their action. DeBarthe, *Life and Adventures of Frank Grouard*, 169.

36. *New York Herald*, December 11, 1876.

37. This incident, which Luther North described as occurring "south of the Cheyenne village" in "an opening in the mountains," possibly occurred in the area of the Barnum road, leading in to the present ranch from the south. See North's detailed account in Bruce, Fighting Norths, 58–59. See also Grinnell, *The Fighting Cheyennes*, 368–69. A version of the incident at considerable variance with North's appears in account of S. Millison, *The National Tribune*, May 17, 1923. See also Gatchell, "Battle on the Red Fork," 36 (this article is reprinted in Hanson, *Powder River Country*).

38. Luther North identified the area where this happened. See "The Fighting Norths and Pawnee Scouts," *Motor Travel*, (March 1931): 20. As a principal interpreter, Willis Rowland figured prominently in this incident. About age fifty-two in 1876, he had lived with the Northern Cheyennes since the early 1840s and served the army several times during the Sioux-Cheyenne campaigns. McClellan, "A Day with the 'Fighting Cheyennes,'" *Motor Travel* (June 1930): 17. A variation of the verbal exchange is in Smith, *Sagebrush Soldier*, 79–80. Others who accompanied this party included Hard Robe, a seventeen-year-old Cheyenne scout and brother-in-law to Rowland. Hard Robe maintained that Grouard also went along, although the scout's reminiscence does not mention his

involvement. See Gatchell, "Battle on the Red Fork," 35. Hard Robe also stated that the men approached the Cheyennes via a gulch running north from the Red Fork and that they spoke with Little Wolf, not Morning Star. Gatchell said that Hard Robe claimed that when he started to speak, an Indian fired at him, "the bullet coming so close to his cheek that he thought his entire face had been shot away." Ibid., 35–36.

39. DeBarthe, *Life and Adventures of Frank Grouard*, 169. William Garnett claimed that "Sergeant Red Shirt and Charging Bear (and possibly others) were given this mission." Garnett interview, 1907.

40. Luther North stated that "as one of the enemy went down, the Pawnees would give a shout of triumph, *Ki-de-de-de!*, which might be compared with our *Hip, Hip, Hurrah!*" North, "The Fighting Norths and Pawnee Scouts," *Motor Travel* (May 1931): 23. He elsewhere quoted Mackenzie as telling his brother, "Major, take your men into the village and destroy it!" See "Fighting Norths and Pawnee Scouts," *Motor Travel* (March 1931): 20.

41. Garnett interview, 1907. Garnett indicated that some of the Shoshones also descended from the bluff during the afternoon.

42. Account of S. Millison, *The National Tribune*, May 17, 1923.

43. Remarks of Dr. LaGarde at the annual dinner meeting of the Order of Indian Wars, March 6, 1915, Order of Indian Wars Files, No. L-2. The hospital was moved to a point southeast of the Red Butte. McClellan, "A Day with the 'Fighting Cheyennes,'" *Motor Travel* (November 1930): 17.

44. Smith, *Sagebrush Soldier*, 81, 88; Luther North, "The Fighting Norths and Pawnee Scouts," *Motor Travel* (April 1931): 16. In addition to the quoted and explanatory material cited above, this description of the phase of the engagement following McKinney's fall has been reconstructed from the following sources: *New York Herald*, December 1, 11, 1876, January 14, 1877; Mackenzie to Acting AAG, Powder River Expedition, November 26, 1876, Sioux War Papers, Reel 280; *Bozeman Times*, February 2, 1877 (containing an interview with J. S. McKenzie, participant in the engagement); Smith, *Sagebrush Soldier*, 77–81; Bourke, *Mackenzie's Last Fight*, 24–28; *Motor Travel* issues for March 1930, February 1931 (especially former sergeant McClellan's map on p. 21), March 1931, April 1931, and May 1931; Frank North's diary, November 25, 1876, in Bruce, *Fighting Norths*, 49; Bourke diary, November 25, 1876,

and map, "Scene of Action, Nov. 25th, 1876"; Buecker, "Journals of James S. McClellan," 29, 31 (map); Dorst to AG, U.S. Army, March 12, 1894, Dorst Papers; Grinnell, *Two Great Scouts*, 270–74; Bruce, *Fighting Norths*, 51–52, 58–59; North, *Man of the Plains*, 214–17; account of S. *Millison, The National Tribune*, May 17, 1923; Garnett interview, 1907; DeBarthe, *Life and Adventures of Frank Grouard*, 168–69; Henry H. Bellas, "The Crook-Mackenzie Campaign and the Dull Knife Battle, November 25, 1876," in Greene, *Battles and Skirmishes of the Great Sioux War*, 179–80; and Wheeler, *Buffalo Days*, 132–36.

45. *New York Herald*, December 11, 1876.

46. Ibid.; Bourke, *Mackenzie's Last Fight*, 25; Wheeler, *Buffalo Days*, 135.

47. Bourke, *Mackenzie's Last Fight*, 26. See also Wheeler, *Buffalo Days*, 133–34. Luther North offered a less romanticized version of the event in Bruce, *Fighting Norths*, 52–53. The point where this action occurred is described in North, "The Fighting Norths and Pawnee Scouts," *Motor Travel* (August 1931): 18.

48. Male survivors of the engagement told Grinnell that the warrior, Crow Split Nose, shouted out a warning that soldiers were coming; women told Grinnell that the man's name was Meat. Field Notebook 354 (1916), Grinnell Collection. Grinnell stated that Black Hairy Dog cried: "Get your guns. The camp is charged. They are coming." *Fighting Cheyennes*, 375. This composite account by Northern Cheyennes appears in Greene, *Lakota and Cheyenne*, 114–19. For an account of Red Bird (Lone Wolf), later known as Stacey Riggs, see Williams, *Soul of the Red Man*, 241–42.

49. Account of Iron Teeth, excerpted from Marquis, "Red Ripe's Squaw," quoted in Greene, *Lakota and Cheyenne*, 114. See also Iron Teeth's extended account in Marquis and Limbaugh, *Cheyenne and Sioux*, 18.

50. Williams, *Soul of the Red Man*, 243.

51. Ibid.

52. Powell, *People of the Sacred Mountain*, 2:1060; Powell, *Sweet Medicine*, 1:155–56; Grinnell, *Fighting Cheyennes*, 364–65, 375, 380; Buffalo Wallow Woman, interview by George Bird Grinnell, September 20, 1908, Field Notebook 348, Grinnell Collection; account of Black White Man, Item 91, "Mackenzie's Fight and Cheyenne War Miscellany," Grinnell Collection (reprinted in Greene, *Lakota and Cheyenne*, 121–24); Young Two Moon, interview by George Bird Grinnell, September 19,

1908, Field Notebook 348, Grinnell Collection; account of Beaver Heart, in Keenan, "They Fought Crook and Custer," 9–10 (excerpted in Greene, *Lakota and Cheyenne*, 119–21). Buffalo Wallow Woman recalled that when the bullets struck the lodges, the ponies tied near them, breaking free, would run from that sound and toward the distant sound of the shooting. The wounding of Limpy's wife is chronicled in a pictographic drawing executed by Limpy in 1930 and presently reposing in the collections of Little Bighorn Battlefield National Monument. See Greene, *Lakota and Cheyenne*, 122–23. The routes of the noncombatants fleeing the village lay up the Red Fork to its north branch, then along that until they reached the westernmost ridges overlooking the battlefield to the east. Others ascended the westernmost gully nearest the west end of the village, following it north and northwest toward the high ground and north mountain face. J(ohn) Two Moon (Young Two Moon), "Map of Dull Knife's Camp, Nov. 1876," September 20, 1908, Grinnell Collection (hereafter cited as Young Two Moon's map).

53. The warrior Weasel Bear, who was fifteen years old during the encounter, recollected that firearms were at a premium because so many had been left in the village with most of the ammunition. "We boys had bows and arrows. There was not enough rifles—only for the men." Edward Burnett, "Dull Knife Battle," in Hanson, *Powder River Country*, 104.

54. Powell, *Sweet Medicine*, 1:156; Powell, *People of the Sacred Mountain*, 2:1063–64.

55. Powell, *People of the Sacred Mountain*, 2:1064; Buffalo Wallow Woman interview, September 20, 1908; Grinnell, *Fighting Cheyennes*, 380.

56. Williams, *Soul of the Red Man*, 244; Powell, *Sweet Medicine*, 1:158–59; Powell, *People of the Sacred Mountain*, 2:1064–65; Stands in Timber and Liberty, *Cheyenne Memories*, 217. The Sacred Arrows ceremony was also directed at the Cheyenne army scouts and reportedly was instrumental in their individually dying off in later years. Ibid.

57. Powell, *People of the Sacred Mountain*, 2:1059, 1061. Grinnell names the individuals killed in the ravine as Tall Bull, Walking Whirlwind, Burns Red (in the Sun), Walking Calf, Hawks Visit, and Four Spirits. The wounded were Scabby, who died two days later; Curly; and Two Bulls. *Fighting Cheyennes*, 365, 376. Young Two Moon stated that nine Cheyenne men were killed in the gorge. Young Two Moon interview, September

19, 1908. He erroneously placed McKinney's fall and the subsequent troop positions along the next ravine west of the actual site. Young Two Moon's map. Grinnell used this map for the basis of his own map of the encounter as published in the original edition of *The Fighting Cheyennes* (New York: Charles Scribner's Sons, 1915), opposite 352. On that rendering, the directions are confused, and north should be east. When Grinnell discovered the directional error, he was mortified, for his book had been published the previous year. "I [had] showed [the] map to Schuyler, Wheeler, North, and [Young] Two Moon [(all participants)] and asked specifically about compass points, but no one could tell about them. Who is responsible for the blunder[?]" Field Notebook 354 (1916), Grinnell Collection. The error was not corrected in the University of Oklahoma edition, published in 1956 (see p. 366).

58. Account of Young Two Moon, Field Notebook 354 (1916), Grinnell Collection.

59. Account of Bull Hump, Field Notebook 348 (1908), Grinnell Collection; Grinnell, *Fighting Cheyennes*, 379; Powell, *People of the Sacred Mountain*, 2:1061. Grinnell mentioned that one man who died in the fighting was a Dog Soldier who, as was their custom, tethered himself to a pin stuck in the ground and fought until he was killed. Field Notebook 334 (1901), Grinnell Collection. The exact place where this warrior fought and died is not known.

60. Young Two Moon interview, September 19, 1908; Field Notebook 354 (1916), Grinnell Collection; Grinnell, *Fighting Cheyennes*, 376, 379–80; Powell, *People of the Sacred Mountain*, 2:1059–62; Stands in Timber and Liberty, *Cheyenne Memories*, 217. According to Young Two Moon, the women-raised breastworks stood east of the north branch of the Red Fork along a north-south running ridge or cliff, probably in the area of the eastern half of Section 20. He also indicated that a lesser breastwork existed to the southeast, on the ridge overlooking the confluence of the north and south branches of the Red Fork, at a point immediately west of the village. These latter works apparently straddled the line between Sections 20 and 29. See Young Two Moon's map; U.S. Geological Survey, Quadrangle Map "Fraker Mountain, Wyo.," 1984.

61. Young Two Moon interview, September 19, 1908; Young Two Moon's map; Grinnell, *Fighting Cheyennes*, 376–79; Powell, *People of the Sacred Mountain*, 2:1068–69. Regarding Many Beaver Dams, Roche

reported on his escape, noting that "he was only missed some hours after the fight, so we do not know whether he was killed or fled to the enemy, nor has any one troubled himself to find out." *New York Herald*, January 14, 1877.

62. Young Two Moon interview, September 19, 1908; Young Two Moon, interview by George Bird Grinnell, September 20, 1908, Field Notebook 348, Grinnell Collection; Grinnell, *Fighting Cheyennes*, 380, 381; Stands in Timber and Liberty, *Cheyenne Memories*, 217; Powell, *People of the Sacred Mountain*, 2:1063, 1065, 1069–70. Old Crow later maintained that after the Cheyennes surrendered and many of them had enlisted as scouts themselves, the young men refused to listen to him because of his betrayal at the Red Fork. Powell, *People of the Sacred Mountain*, 2:1179; Easton, "Getting into Uniform," 51–52; Buffalo Wallow Woman interview, September 20, 1908; accounts of Young Two Moon, Hairy Hand, et al., Field Notebook 354 (1916), Grinnell Collection; Greene, *Lakota and Cheyenne*, 114–19; Powell, *People of the Sacred Mountain*, 2:1069–70. In other accounts, Young Two Moon mentioned having visited the lodges unaccompanied. Young Two Moon interview, September 19, 1908; account of Beaver Heart, in Keenan, "They Fought Crook and Custer," 10 (excerpted in Greene, *Lakota and Cheyenne*, 119–21). He placed the casualties of Crow Necklace, Crawling (erroneously noted as killed), and Crow Split Nose as occurring in the southeast quadrant of the canyon, locations that are most unlikely given the reported attempted rescues by their tribesmen, for this part of the field was firmly in the control of Mackenzie's force. Young Two Moon's map. Red Bird stated that Crow Necklace was killed at the southwest end of the village, and that Crow Split Nose was killed in front of his lodge in the village. Williams, *Soul of the Red Man*, 244.

63. Bourke, *Mackenzie's Last Fight*, 28.

64. *New York Herald*, December 11, 1876.

65. Bourke, *Mackenzie's Last Fight*, 29 (quote); Bourke diary, November 26, 1876; Garnett interview, 1907; Grinnell, *Two Great Scouts*, 274; Powell, *Sweet Medicine*, 1:165. In later years many of the metal objects destroyed in the camp could be found on the ground. See J. Elmer Brock, "Observations," in Hanson, *Powder River Country*, 88.

66. Lawton to "My Dear Carter," November 29, 1876; *New York Herald*, December 11, 1876.

67. Bourke, *Mackenzie's Last Fight*, 28, 31–32; Garnett interview, 1907; Powell, *People of the Sacred Mountain*, 2:1069; Porter, *Paper Medicine Man*, 56. This necklace, along with another like it, had been found by Baptiste Pourier. One was buried, apparently on the field. Bourke, *On the Border with Crook*, 403. Jerry Roche reported that three such necklaces were found, one with seven fingers, one with eight, and one with ten. *New York Herald*, December 11, 1876. A detailed description of each appears in Bourke, "Medicine Men of the Apaches," 480–83. The remains of one, perhaps that buried, were reportedly found on the site many years later. See Brock, "Observations," 106. Years later Mackenzie's former adjutant, Joseph H. Dorst, stated that all but twelve lodges were destroyed. Dorst to AG, U.S. Army, March 12, 1894, Dorst Papers. He did not explain why the lodges were spared, but they perhaps served as shelters for the wounded men, an action that was customarily employed following army destruction of other villages during the Indian campaigns. See, for example, Greene, *Slim Buttes*, 71.

68. Bourke, *Mackenzie's Last Fight*, 29.

69. Ibid., 30–31; Bourke diary, November 26, 1876; Bourke, *On the Border with Crook*, 393; *New York Herald*, December 11, 1876; Garnett interview, 1907; Vaughn, *With Crook at the Rosebud*, 207 (roster, Company I, Third Cavalry).

70. Bourke, *Mackenzie's Last Fight*, 30; Powell, "High Bull's Victory Roster," 17–18, 18–21; George Bird Grinnell, "Double Trophy Roster," n.d., Item 415, Grinnell Collection. The roster book, captured by High Bull in the Custer fight, passed from Sergeant Turpin to Lieutenant Wheeler, who eventually deposited it with the museum of the Military Service Institution of the United States on Governor's Island in New York Harbor. Somehow a New York City dealer acquired it and sold it to John J. White, a friend of Grinnell, who borrowed it in 1898 and brought it west. When Grinnell showed it to some of the older Northern Cheyennes, they recognized it and helped him identify the artists. High Bull was himself killed during Mackenzie's attack. The morocco leather–bound roster book presently reposes in the Museum of the American Indian, Smithsonian Institution, temporarily quartered in New York City. Grinnell, *Fighting Cheyennes*, 367; Powell, "High Bull's Victory Roster," 22. See also Wheeler, *Buffalo Days*, 146–47.

71. Bourke, *Mackenzie's Last Fight*, 31, 32. See also Bourke diary, November 26, 1876; Garnett interview, 1907; and Powell, *Sweet Medicine*, 1:166.

72. Besides McKinney, the other dead were Corporal Patrick F. Ryan, Company D, Fourth Cavalry; Private James Baird, Company D, Fourth Cavalry; Private John Sullivan, Company B, Fourth Cavalry; Private Alexander Keller, Company E, Fourth Cavalry; Private John Menges, Company H, Fifth Cavalry; and Private Alexander McFarland, Company L, Fifth Cavalry (who died of wounds on November 27). Of the wounded, Companies I and M of the Fourth Cavalry suffered most, losing five and six men, respectively. Other Fourth Cavalry company losses were as follows: B, 3; D, 1; E, 2; and F, 2. Company H, Third Cavalry, lost three men wounded, while Company H, Fifth Cavalry, lost two to wounds. "Return of Killed, Wounded, and Missing of the Cavalry Battalion, Powder River Expedition, in Action with Hostile Indians on the North Fork of Powder River, November 25th 1876, Wyoming Territory," enclosed in Crook to AG, U.S. Army, December 1, 1876, Division of the Missouri, Item 9119, RG 393, Records of the U.S. Army Continental Commands, NA (also found as Entry 3731, Box 46, Department of the Platte, LR, RG 393; and in Sioux War Papers, Reel 279). This document does not provide information as to the nature of wounds for those men killed. See also Regimental Returns of the Fourth Cavalry, November 1876, M744, NA, Reel 42; Regimental Returns of the Fifth Cavalry, November 1876, ibid., Reel 53; and *New York Herald*, December 11, 1876.

73. Mackenzie to Assistant AAG, Powder River Expedition, November 26, 1876, Sioux War Papers, Reel 280; Crook report, January 8, 1877, Sioux War Papers, Reel 280; Bourke, *Mackenzie's Last Fight*, 27. Following discussions with participants in the action four days later, however, Colonel Dodge reported that "it is believed about 50 [Cheyennes] were killed & 100 wounded." *Powder River Expedition Journals*, 96.

74. Buecker, "Journals of James S. McClellan," 29. One very specific figure for Indian losses was that given by Lieutenant Clark, who stated that the soldiers "killed fourteen bucks and two squaws[;] wounded many more." Clark, who was present during the encounter, did not reveal his source for this information. Buecker, "Lt. William Philo Clark's Sioux War Report," 19. Also, Sioux emissaries sent from Cheyenne River Agency in December to locate the Indians and induce their surrender visited

Crazy Horse's camp. They later reported of the battle with the Cheyennes that "fifteen were killed and a number wounded, some of whom died afterwards." Colonel William H. Wood, Eleventh Infantry, to AAG, Department of Dakota, January 24, 1877, Entry 3731, Box 47, Department of the Platte, LR, RG 393.

75. Dorst to AG, U.S. Army, March 12, 1894, Dorst Papers (reprinted, in part, in *The Dull Knife Symposium* [Sheridan, Wyo.: Fort Phil Kearny/Bozeman Trail Association, 1989], 33). In support of this view that Mackenzie did not report all Indian casualties, Lieutenant Lawton wrote, "The Gen'l would only report 28 Indians killed, although I am positive there were more than twice that number [killed]." Lawton to "My Dear Carter," November 29, 1876.

76. Bourke, *Mackenzie's Last Fight*, 27–28; *Chicago Tribune*, May 2, 1877.

77. Edward Burnett, "Dull Knife," unpublished ms. ca. 1935, affixed to Roger W. Toll to Burnett, November 4, 1935, John D. McDermott Personal Collection, Rapid City, S.Dak., copy. About 1936, the Cheyenne participant Stacey Riggs, earlier known as Red Bird and Lone Wolf, named twelve individuals killed as a result of the army attack: Four Spirits (son of Morning Star), Young Bird (son of Morning Star), Tall Bull, Walking Whirlwind, Hawk's Visit, Walking Calf, Burns Red, Crow Necklace, Crow Split Nose, Mrs. White Thunder, Spotted Turtle, and the unidentified daughter of White Face Bull, who perished later from her injuries. Williams, *Soul of the Red Man*, 244.

Chapter 7

1. The burial of Private Baird on the field is mentioned in "Return of Killed, Wounded, and Missing of the Cavalry Battalion, Powder River Expedition, in Action with Hostile Indians on the North Fork of Powder River, November 25th 1876, Wyoming Territory," enclosed in Crook to AG, U.S. Army, December 1, 1876, Division of the Missouri, 9119, RG 393, Records of the U.S. Army Continental Commands, NA. Surviving participant Thomas B. Garrett indicated the site where Baird was buried near the field hospital during a visit to the scene in 1929. James McClellan, "A Day with the 'Fighting Cheyennes,'" *Motor Travel* (September 1930): 17. The reason why Baird alone was buried at this place was not officially explained, although McClellan, writing sixty-four years after the

fact, stated that the burial occurred "by mistake." "Snow soon covered the grave, and it is unlikely that its location was ever discovered." Ibid., 10. Wheeler stated that two of the dead were so interred. *Buffalo Days*, 137.

2. Account of S. Millison, *The National Tribune*, May 17, 1923. McClellan recalled that each "dead man was thrown across the back of the mule like a saddle, and strapped stomach down." "A Day with the 'Fighting Cheyennes,'" 9.

3. Bourke, *Mackenzie's Last Fight*, 33.

4. Details of the preparation and use of the travois following the Red Fork engagement appear in Wheeler, *Buffalo Days*, 137–41. According to the lieutenant: "I assigned two men to each mule that carried the bodies and four men to each travois, one to lead the mule, two to dismount and ease the travois over rough places, and the fourth to hold their horses. . . . Great care had to be exercised that the dead should not be disfigured by a mule running away or brushing against objects which might break a leg or arm." Ibid., 138.

5. Bourke, *Mackenzie's Last Fight*, 33.

6. Account of S. Millison, *The National Tribune*, May 17, 1923.

7. Bourke diary, November 26, 1876; Buecker, "Journals of James S. McClellan," 29, 33–34; Garnett interview, 1907; Smith, *Sagebrush Soldier*, 94; excerpt from Frank North's diary, in Bruce, *Fighting Norths*, 49. See also North, "Fighting Norths and Pawnee Scouts," *Motor Travel* (March 1931): 16.

8. "The trail we took was in fact almost identical with our outgoing line of march." Bourke diary, November 29, 1876. See also McClellan, "A Day with the 'Fighting Cheyennes,'" *Motor Travel* (September 1930): 9.

9. Buecker, "Journals of James S. McClellan," 29. See also McClellan, "A Day with the 'Fighting Cheyennes,'" *Motor Travel* (September 1930): 9–10.

10. Buecker, "Journals of James S. McClellan," 29. That the troops were on the backtrack of their route into the Cheyenne camp is confirmed by the discovery in the 1890s near EK Mountain of the skeletal remains of numerous horses, evidently those played-out beasts killed in 1876. They had been shot, and the skeletons still wore the specially fitted horseshoes, filed for use on icy terrain, as called for in the official correspondence. Condit, "Hole in the Wall," 37; J. Elmer Brock, "Observations," in Hanson, *Powder River Country*, 106.

11. McClellan, "A Day with the 'Fighting Cheyennes,'" *Motor Travel* (September 1930): 10.

12. Buecker, "Journals of James S. McClellan," 29; Smith, *Sagebrush Soldier*, 94; McClellan, "A Day with the 'Fighting Cheyennes,'" *Motor Travel* (September 1930): 10.

13. On the twenty-fourth, skirmish drill proceeded with the admonition that particular attention be "directed to the deployment forward, [wherein] the habit of crowding in sets of fours should be corrected." Headquarters, Second Battalion, Circular No. 2, Crazy Woman's Fork, November 24, 1876, Entry 3963, General and Special Orders, Powder River Expedition, 1876, RG 393.

14. Crook to Sheridan, November 26, 1876, contained in AAG, Division of the Missouri, to Sherman, telegram, November 28, 1876, Sioux War Papers, Reel 279. See also Bourke diary, November 29, 1876.

15. Dodge, *Powder River Expedition Journals*, 86.

16. Ibid., 92.

17. Buecker, "Journals of James S. McClellan," 29.

18. Bourke, *Mackenzie's Last Fight*, 32–33; Wheeler, *Buffalo Days*, 140–41.

19. First Lieutenant Henry W. Lawton to "My Dear Carter," November 29, 1876, Manuscript Division, Center for the History of the American Indian, The Newberry Library, Chicago. Nearly a month later Lawton wrote, "We all regret very deeply the loss of McKinney and a number of our best men." Lawton to "My Dear Sergeant," December 21, 1876, Archives Ms. 20191, State Historical Society of North Dakota, Bismarck.

20. Luther North recalled that Crook wanted "to send a scouting party over to Clear Creek to see if the Cheyennes had come out of the mountains there. It was a thirty mile ride, and the weather was very cold, but there was a full moon." The men returned to the Crazy Woman the next day. North, *Man of the Plains*, 218–19.

21. "Return of Killed, Wounded, and Missing of the Cavalry Battalion, Powder River Expedition"; Buecker, "Journals of James S. McClellan," 30; Dodge, *Powder River Expedition Journals*, 91–92, 97; North, Man of the Plains, 218–19; North, "The Fighting Norths and Pawnee Scouts," *Motor Travel* (September 1931): 15; McClellan, "A Day with the 'Fighting Cheyennes,'" *Motor Travel* (September 1930): 10. According to William Garnett, the ponies were dealt as follows:

The eight Sioux and Arapaho scouts who discovered the village were given pref-erence of choice of the whole number, taking one apiece; next choice fell to the Sioux and Arapaho scouts who went out from Fort [Cantonment] Reno and cap-tured the Cheyenne Indian who came to their camp, each taking one; the third choice fell to the Snake and Pawnees scouts who had the skirmish and had returned the day before [sic—on the twenty-sixth], these taking one each. Garnett was now told by Mackenzie to go in and get . . . [two horses]; the next party to select were Red Shirt and his party who had been sent back to Crook while the bat-tle was going on (these had come out from Crazy Woman to meet the soldiers); then one scout from each tribe was sent to take a horse; for instance, a Sioux, then an Arapahoe, next a Snake, then a Pawnee, and so on around these scouts till each one had a horse. After this he began again at the head of the list and repeated the selection till the herd was reduced to about seventy (70) head. There not being enough to go around again, . . . Mackenzie told them to go and take the rest as they were minded; but only a few cared to have any more and quite a number, sup-posed to be upwards of 40, were left; and it is understood that some camp follow-ers picked them up.

Garnett interview, 1907. See also Frank North's diary, November 28, 1876, in Bruce, *Fighting Norths*, 49. Frank North recorded that the scouts were sent out on the evening of November 30. McClellan recalled the standby status of his comrades as they awaited word from the scouts: "After the Dull Knife fight, it was rumored around the camps that at the time of the battle, White Antelope and a bunch of his braves had been absent from the main village on a hunt; later it was reported that he had assembled a lot of followers and set out to take revenge on our column. . . . Provision was . . . made to have 25 picked men and horses from each troop in readi-ness to make the dash and take the measure of that chief." "A Day with the 'Fighting Cheyennes,'" *Motor Travel* (January 1931): 22.

22. Headquarters, Cavalry Battalions, Powder River Expedition, General Field Orders No. 4, November 30, 1876, Entry 3963, General and Special Orders, Powder River Expedition, 1876, RG 393; AAG to Crook, telegram, November 29, 1876 (enclosing request of McKinney's father), Entry 3726, vol. 397, ibid.; Headquarters, Fourth U.S. Cavalry, Powder River Expedition, General Orders No. 21, Camp on Belle Fourche River, December 21, 1876, Joseph H. Dorst Papers, Special Collections, U.S. Mil-itary Academy Library, West Point, N.Y.; Bourke diary, December 3, 1876; Buecker, "Journals of James S. McClellan," 30; Bourke, *Mackenzie's Last*

Fight, 35; Henry H. Bellas, "The Crook-Mackenzie Campaign and the Dull Knife Battle, November 25, 1876," in Greene, *Battles and Skirmishes of the Great Sioux War*, 183. See also McClellan, "A Day with the 'Fighting Cheyennes,'" *Motor Travel* (September 1930): 10. Mackenzie's General Field Order No. 4 respecting the funeral, appears in Bourke diary, November 30, 1876. Grinnell erroneously stated that the dead, including McKinney, were buried at Cantonment Reno. Two Great Scouts, 275–76. McKinney's remains were laid to rest in Elmwood Cemetery near Memphis on Christmas Eve. *Memphis Daily Appeal*, December 26, 1876.

23. Wheeler, *Buffalo Days*, 143. A teamster named Sam Stringer reported that the men "were buried by caving banks off onto them" and that they were reinterred the following spring at Cantonment Reno. Brock, "Observations," 107. Private Smith, who served as a pallbearer, jotted in his diary: "I would never like to bee left in the ground in this wild cuntry whear no white man would ever see the place a gane. The way they berrey in this cuntry they take and sow a man up in a Blanket and dont have no coffin." *Sagebrush Soldier*, 102. It is likely that the remains were disinterred for reburial at Fort McKinney (near present Buffalo, Wyoming) in 1879–80 after Cantonment Reno was abandoned. In 1895, following the abandonment of Fort McKinney, the post cemetery interments were removed to Custer Battlefield National Cemetery, Montana, where they repose today.

24. Dodge, *Powder River Expedition Journals*, 98; Bourke, *Mackenzie's Last Fight*, 35; Robinson, *Bad Hand*, 223–24.

25. Young Two Moon, interview by George Bird Grinnell, September 19, 1908, Field Notebook 348, Grinnell Collection, Braun Research Library, Southwest Museum, Los Angeles; accounts of Young Two Moon, Hairy Hand, et al., Field Notebook 354 (1916), ibid.; Grinnell, *Fighting Cheyennes*, 381; Powell, *People of the Sacred Mountain*, 2:1070; Powell, *Sweet Medicine*, 1:167–68. In making their escape, the people likely passed within the eastern third of Sections 8 and 17, Township 44N, Range 84W. See U.S. Geological Survey, Quadrangle Map "Fraker Mountain, Wyo.," 1984.

26. Young Two Moon interview, September 19, 1908; accounts of Young Two Moon, Hairy Hand, et al. (1916); Buffalo Wallow Woman, interview by George Bird Grinnell, September 20, 1908, ibid.; Grinnell, *Fighting Cheyennes*, 381–82; Powell, *People of the Sacred Mountain*, 2:1070; Stands

in Timber and Liberty, *Cheyenne Memories*, 217–18. The course of the people was likely diagonally northwest through Section 5 to Arch Creek. U.S. Geological Survey, Quadrangle Map "Fraker Mountain, Wyo.," 1984. Regarding the Cheyenne's route through this area, during the 1930s or 1940s, local rancher J. Elmer Brock wrote the following:

> *On the crest of the ridge are fortifications which could protect the high point on the mountain as well as provide a most excellent observation point. There are also old stumps of small trees there which are evidently cut with tomahawks [axes?]. Farther north along the Arch Creek Ridge there were at one time two miles of shelter built up under the rock rim. They were made of slabs of rotten logs and small trees. These undoubtedly sheltered the women and children. From the Arch Creek Slip to the south these shelters were all destroyed in a grass fire about 1894. . . . From the Arch Creek Slip west these shelters are still in evidence in a few places. Where Arch Creek turns sharply to the southwest before entering Bear Trap [Creek] there are numerous evidences of this Indian retreat in the form of fortifications and barricaded caves. The caves are just below the [geological formation known as the] Arch, while above the Arch are fortifications and shelters which were still bullet proof a few years ago.*

"Observations," 107. For a nearly identical quote, see Condit, "Hole in the Wall," 37–38.

27. Young Two Moon interview, September 19, 1908; Grinnell, *Fighting Cheyennes*, 382; Powell, *People of the Sacred Mountain*, 2:1071; Grinnell, *Two Great Scouts*, 275; Gatchell, "Battle on the Red Fork," 35; Stands in Timber and Liberty, *Cheyenne Memories*, 218.

28. Young Two Moon interview, September 19, 1908; account of Beaver Heart, in Keenan, "They Fought Crook and Custer," 10–11 (excerpted in Greene, *Lakota and Cheyenne*, 121); Grinnell, *Fighting Cheyennes*, 382; Powell, *People of the Sacred Mountain*, 2:1071; Powell, *Sweet Medicine*, 1:168–69; Dodge, *Our Wild Indians*, 499–500; Bourke, *On the Border with Crook*, 394; Stands in Timber and Liberty, *Cheyenne Memories*, 218; Hyde, *Spotted Tail's Folk*, 239. Wooden Leg gave no indication that the Oglalas were suffering from lack of game when the Cheyennes arrived. Marquis, *Wooden Leg*, 287–88.

29. For the Wolf Mountains action, see Greene, *Yellowstone Command*, 165–78.

30. Major Julius W. Mason to AAG, Division of the Missouri, November 16, 1876, Sioux War Papers, Reel 279.

31. Bourke diary, December 20, 1876; Mason to AAG, Division of the Missouri, December 3, 1876, Sioux War Papers, Reel 279; Commissary General of Subsistence Robert MacFeeley to Acting Commissioner of Indian Affairs, October 13, 1876, ibid.; MacFeeley to Secretary of War, October 13, 1876, ibid.; AAG to Sheridan, October 17, 1876, ibid.; Captain Thomas F. Tobey, Fourteenth Infantry, Indian agent at Red Cloud, to Commissioner of Indian Affairs, December 9, 1876, ibid.

32. See *New York Herald*, November 29, December 1, 11, 1876. A brief notice of the action, evidently drawn from army dispatches sent from Crook's command on November 26 or from their couriers, appeared in the *Cheyenne Daily Leader* on November 29, four days after the engagement, with more details from Roche's various dispatches appearing in the editions of November 30 and December 6.

33. Sheridan to Sherman, November 28, 1876, enclosing Crook's telegram of November 26, Sioux War Papers, Reel 279; Sheridan to Sherman, December 1, 1876, enclosing Crook's telegram of November 28 and Mackenzie's report of November 26, Sioux War Papers, Reel 279.

34. Sheridan to Crook, December 3, 1876, Entry 3963, General and Special Orders, Powder River Expedition, RG 393. See also Sherman to Sheridan, December 2, 1876, Sioux War Papers, Reel 279; and *New York Herald*, February 5, 1877. The congratulatory messages reached the command via telegraph on December 5. Dodge, *Powder River Expedition Journals*, 106.

35. Bourke diary, December 1, 1876; Bourke, *Mackenzie's Last Fight*, 35; Dodge, *Powder River Expedition Journals*, 105–6; *New York Herald*, January 14, 1877; Headquarters, Artillery and Infantry Battalions, Powder River Expedition, General Orders No. 8, Camp on Dry Fork Powder River, December 4, 1876, Entry 3963, General and Special Orders, Powder River Expedition, 1876, RG 393; Garnett interview, 1907. The sergeant killed was George W. Patterson. Bourke, *Mackenzie's Last Fight*, 35. Private Smith reported that the man was buried on December 4. *Sagebrush Soldier*, 110.

36. Bourke diary, December 8, 1876; Buecker, "Journals of James S. McClellan," 30; Garnett interview, 1907; Pollock to AG, Department of

the Platte, November 28, 1876, Entry 3731, Box 45, Department of the Platte, LR, RG 393; Crook to Commanding Officer, Fort Fetterman, November 27, 1876, Entry 3726, vol. 386, RG 393; AAG to AG, Department of the Platte, December 7, 1876, Entry 3731, Box 46, Department of the Platte, LR, RG 393; Captain Gilbert S. Carpenter, Fourteenth Infantry, to AAG, Department of the Platte, November 23, 1876, Entry 3731, Box 45, ibid.; Major Caleb H. Carlton, Third Cavalry, to AAG, December 13, 1876, Entry 3731, Box 46, ibid.; Dodge, *Powder River Expedition Journals*, 102–3; Robrock, "History of Fort Fetterman," 62–63.

37. Crook to Sheridan, November 30 and December 1, 1876, Powder River Expedition Order Book, John Gregory Bourke Papers, Special Collections, U.S. Military Academy Library, West Point, N.Y.; Headquarters, Artillery and Infantry Battalions, Powder River Expedition, Special Orders No. 16, Camp on Dry Fork Powder River, December 3, 1876, Entry 3963, General and Special Orders, Powder River Expedition, 1876, RG 393; Headquarters, Artillery and Infantry Battalions, Powder River Expedition, General Orders No. 9, Camp at Guard Springs, December 6, 1876, ibid.; Dodge, *Powder River Expedition Journals*, 103.

38. Crook to John Mise, December 2, 1876, Powder River Expedition Order Book, Bourke Papers; Bourke diary, December 1, 3, 4, 1876; Bourke, *Mackenzie's Last Fight*, 35; Smith, *Sagebrush Soldier*, 110; *New York Herald*, February 5, 1877; Dodge, *Powder River Expedition Journals*, 103–4, 105.

39. Dodge, *Powder River Expedition Journals*, 106. Luther North commented on Crook's delinquency on this occasion. "That night was very cold, the thermometer showing thirty below zero in the morning. After breakfast we saw that McKenzie's command were taking down their tents and saddling their horses, and we did likewise, and then waited for General Crook to make a move. We waited until noon, then we saw General McKenzie ride down toward General Crook's camp. When he returned he came through our camp and told us we were not going to move camp that day, so we unpacked our wagons and went into camp again. The same thing happened the next day, and on the third day we waited until we saw General Crook pulling out of camp before we took down our tents; then we followed him." *Man of the Plains*, 220. Frank North grumbled to his diary: "I never saw such an outfit in my life. Nobody knows five minutes beforehand what is to be done." Ibid., 220 n. 18.

40. Bourke diary, December 4, 1876; Buecker, "Journals of James S. McClellan," 30; Flannery, *John Hunton's Diary*, 2:162; Robrock, "History of Fort Fetterman," 64. The sick included six men from the Ninth and Twenty-third Infantry and the Fourth Artillery. Headquarters, Artillery and Infantry Battalions, Powder River Expedition, Special Orders No. 16, December 3, 1876, Camp on Dry Fork, Powder River, Entry 3963, General and Special Orders, Powder River Expedition, 1876, RG 393; Smith, *Sagebrush Soldier*, 110.

41. Smith, *Sagebrush Soldier*, 111; Dodge, *Powder River Expedition Journals,* 107–9. Correspondent Roche succinctly reported Crook's rationale: "General Crook judged that Crazy Horse, on hearing of our fight, would leave the Rosebud and move toward the bad lands at the head of the Little Missouri. . . . The best approach to these fastnesses was that selected for the expedition, but our advance was necessarily controlled by the elements, by the quantity of supplies on hand and capable of being forwarded, and the effectiveness of scouts sent out to determine the exact location of the hostile camp." *New York Herald*, January 14, 1877. An identical scenario is outlined in Bourke diary, December 4, 1876. William Garnett stated that the scouts from Red Cloud Agency were supposed to meet Crook on the Belle Fourche at the point "where the regular Indian trail from Red Cloud Agency crossed to go to the Powder River country." Garnett interview, 1907.

42. Bourke diary, December 4, 7, 1876; Buecker, "Journals of James S. McClellan," 30; Dodge, *Powder River Expedition Journals*, 110–14, 119; *New York Herald*, February 7, 1877; Garnett interview, 1907.

43. North, "The Fighting Norths and Pawnee Scouts," *Motor Travel* (June 1931): 21.

44. Special Orders No. 8, Powder River Expedition Order Book, Bourke Papers; Headquarters, Second Battalion (Infantry), Powder River Expedition, General Field Orders No. 9, Camp on Belle Fourche, December 8, 1876, Entry 3963, General and Special Orders, Powder River Expedition, 1876, RG 393; Bourke diary, December 8, 1876; Dodge, *Powder River Expedition Journals*, 115–16; *New York Herald*, February 5, 1877; Smith, *Sagebrush Soldier*, 112.

45. Dodge, *Powder River Expedition Journals*, 117; Bourke diary, December 9, 1876; First Lieutenant Charles H. Rockwell to Major Caleb Carlton, December 5, 1876, Powder River Expedition Order Book,

Bourke Papers; Crook to Carlton, December 9, 1876, ibid.; *New York Herald*, February 5, 1877.

46. Garnett interview, 1907. Roche referred to a body of miners who were hangers-on to Crook's expedition, apparently having followed it into the Big Horns at the time of the encounter with Morning Star's people and later following it north to the Belle Fourche country. "These fellows become a perfect pest to a command operating against Indians in this region. Winter and summer they follow in its wake, picking and stealing, begging and borrowing everything they need or can dispose of for cash at the first settlement they come upon." *New York Herald*, February 5, 1877.

47. Bourke diary, December 11, 1876; Buecker, "Journals of James S. McClellan," 30; McClellan, "A Day with the 'Fighting Cheyennes,'" *Motor Travel* (January 1931): 22; Dodge, *Powder River Expedition Journals*, 117–18; Grinnell, *Two Great Scouts*, 276. Private Smith's diary is at variance with Dodge's journal, placing the passing of the miners on the seventh rather than the tenth and having them en route to rather than from the Black Hills. Smith, *Sagebrush Soldier*, 111. McClellan did not mention the passage of the miners but alluded to them in his entry for December 11 (Buecker, "Journals of James S. McClellan,", 30).

48. Dodge, *Powder River Expedition Journals*, 118–20; North, *Man of the Plains*, 221–22; Frank North's diary, December 11, 1876, in Bruce, *Fighting Norths*, 50; Bourke diary, December 11, 1876; *New York Herald*, February 5, 1877. George Bird Grinnell stated, without indicating authority, that the Indians were Lakotas. *Fighting Cheyennes*, 169. He elsewhere identified them only as "Indians." *Two Great Scouts*, 276–77. Six of the miners, Michael Nolan, M. A. Malone, James Lewis, D. Hunsdon, J. C. Smith, and Frederick Ferdinand, received blankets and rations from the command. Powder River Expedition Order Book, Bourke Papers.

49. Bourke, *Mackenzie's Last Fight*, 36.

50. *New York Herald*, January 14, 1877; Bourke diary, December 4, 8, 1876; Bourke, *Mackenzie's Last Fight*, 36–37; Dodge, *Powder River Expedition Journals*, 123; Smith, *Sagebrush Soldier*, 112, 113.

51. Dodge, *Powder River Expedition Journals*, 123–24; Buecker, "Journals of James S. McClellan," 30; McClellan, "A Day with the 'Fighting Cheyennes,'" *Motor Travel* (January 1931): 22; Bourke diary, December 12, 13, 14, 1876.

52. McClellan claimed that another sutler—"a wildcat trader"—"hung around on our flank, and sold inferior whiskey for 75 cents a drink; but Col. Mackenzie soon put him out of business." "A Day with the 'Fighting Cheyennes,'" *Motor Travel* (January 1931): 22.

53. Rumors swirled that Randall and his Crows had been wiped out by Indians. Sheridan to Sherman, telegram, December 22, 1876, Sioux War Papers, Reel 279. Regarding the enlistment of the Crows, see McClellan, "A Day with the 'Fighting Cheyennes,'" *Motor Travel* (September 1930): 8. Roche offered the following account of Randall's time with the Crows:

From the first he was surrounded with difficulties not easy to surmount. The Crows had been frightened a good deal in the Rosebud fight and were not very eager for another contest with the Sioux. He had some trouble, therefore, in persuading them to join him for a winter campaign, and expected no less than a general desertion as he proceeded on his way toward us. There were a great many impediments, too, in the way of his successful progress in the direction he was obliged to take. The snow was very deep on the mountains, and his supplies being limited, he was obliged to operate "long" on experience and "short" on provisions. Fortunately he had had some Indian experience, and was ready to devour his share of raw buffalo meat, hot, too—blood hot—when the animal was killed, and hunger taught him to scramble for first cut of uncooked liver, &c. Reviewing such an experience as [Brevet] Major Randall has had one is very glad to be alive, and is ready even to jest on past trials, however rough, though he may not crave to live over again the life just past. Marching through snow from one to five feet deep is not pleasant, no matter how bright the sun, if you are hungry and there does not happen to be a supply depot within 100 miles of you. Nor does a bivouac at night with scant wood beside a frozen stream help one much. To keep warm you must herd closely then, and Major Randall did herd very closely.

New York Herald, January 14, 1877. Randall's route from the Crow Agency had taken him and the Crows down the Yellowstone to Clark's Fork River, up that stream to the head of the Greybull (or Stinking Water), down the Bighorn River and across the Big Horn Mountains to the head of Tongue River, then to the Bozeman Trail and on to Cantonment Reno. Bourke diary, December 25, 1876.

54. Buecker, "Journals of James S. McClellan," 32; Dodge, *Powder River Expedition Journals,* 124–33; Headquarters, Artillery and Infantry Battalions, Powder River Expedition, Special Orders No. 21, Camp on

Belle Fourche, December 15, 1876, Entry 3963, General and Special Orders, Powder River Expedition, 1876, RG 393; Headquarters, Artillery and Infantry Battalions, Powder River Expedition, Special Orders No. 22, Fourth Camp on Belle Fourche River, December 16, 1876, ibid.; Lawton to "My Dear Sergeant," December 21, 1876; Buecker, "Journals of James S. McClellan," 30; Bourke diary, December 15, 16, 17, 18, 19, 1876; *New York Herald*, February 5, 1877; Smith, *Sagebrush Soldier*, 113, 117. The presence of alcohol brought on at least one confrontation on the eighteenth, between a private and a first sergeant, that escalated to the point that one (private) pulled his gun on the other (sergeant) and tried to shoot him. The pistol misfired three times, and the man was subdued before anyone was badly hurt. Smith, *Sagebrush Soldier*, 118.

55. Bourke diary, December 21, 1876 (containing the draft of the telegram to Sheridan); Powder River Expedition Order Book, Bourke Papers, 91–92. Although Crook had apparently reached his decision to close the expedition before he met with his scouts, they offered him counsel that must have ratified his decision. Among other things, they promised to work to influence the "hostiles" to come in to the agencies the following spring. The Sioux scouts Three Bears and Fast Thunder and the Arapaho Sharp Nose were prominent in this discourse to convince Crook to close his operation. Garnett interview, 1907. Garnett and Willis Rowland accompanied the Sioux, Arapahos, and Cheyennes back to the agencies. En route they met Richard, Shangrau, and several hundred scouts enlisted at Red Cloud and Spotted Tail and directed them to turn back. Richard and Shangrau then cut across country to rejoin the expedition. Ibid. See also Bourke diary, December 26, 1876.

56. Dodge, *Powder River Expedition Journals*, 134–36; Frank North's diary, December 20, 21, 1876, in Bruce, *Fighting Norths*, 50; Bourke, *Mackenzie's Last Fight*, 37–38; Smith, *Sagebrush Soldier*, 121. Regarding the weather, Garnett, who was raised in these climes, related: "The months of January and February—the worst of winter—were yet to come and be endured. The soldiers were less inured to these rigors than the Indians and less likely to hold out—their animals were not so hardy as the Indian ponies and would give out under the strain of work and the assaults of wind and frost and want of forage and shelter." Garnett interview, 1907.

Chapter 8

1. Dodge, *Powder River Expedition Journals*, 136, 137.

2. Ibid., 138–39.

3. Dodge, *Powder River Expedition Journals*, 146–49; Bourke diary, December 22, 23, 24, 25, 26, 1876; *New York Herald*, January 14, 1877; Frank North's diary, in Bruce, *Fighting Norths*, 50; Buecker, "Journals of James S. McClellan," 32; Bourke, *Mackenzie's Last Fight*, 42.

4. Dodge, *Powder River Expedition Journals*, 149–57; Bourke diary, December 26, 27, 28, 1876; Frank North's diary, in Bruce, *Fighting Norths*, 50; North, *Man of the Plains*, 224. For more events of the march, see also Wheeler, *Buffalo Days*, 149–51. For the Reynolds and Moore courts-martial, see Vaughn, *Reynolds Campaign*, 166–90.

5. Bourke diary, December 29, 1876; Headquarters, Artillery and Infantry Battalions, Powder River Expedition, General Orders No. 12, December 30, 1876, Entry 3963, General and Special Orders, Powder River Expedition, 1876, RG 393, Records of the U.S. Army Continental Command, NA; Headquarters, Second Battalion (Infantry), Powder River Expedition, Orders No. 10, December 30, 1876, ibid.; Dodge, *Powder River Expedition Journals*, 160–69; Bourke diary, December 31, 1876; Frank North's diary, in Bruce, *Fighting Norths*, 50; AAG to Crook, January 6, 1877, Entry 3731, Box 47, Department of the Platte, LR, RG 393; Robinson, *Bad Hand*, 232.

6. Regimental Returns of the Third Cavalry, January 1877, M744, NA; Regimental Returns of the Fourth Cavalry, January 1877, ibid., Reel 42; Headquarters, Artillery and Infantry Battalions, Powder River Expedition, Orders No. 12, January 6, 1877, Entry 3963, General and Special Orders, Powder River Expedition, 1876, RG 393; Crook to Sheridan, telegram, April 16, 1877, Sioux War Papers, Reel 281; Headquarters Department of the Platte, Special Orders No. 5, January 12, 1877, ibid., Reel 279; Frank North's diary, in Bruce, *Fighting Norths*, 50–51; Buecker, "Journals of James S. McClellan," 32; North, *Man of the Plains*, 224–25, 228–29; Wheeler, *Buffalo Days*, 152; North, "The Fighting Norths and Pawnee Scouts," in *Motor Travel* (March 1931): 22; and (October 1931): 18; Grinnell, *Two Great Scouts*, 279–81. See also comments by Luther North in Buecker, "Journals of James S. McClellan," 60.

7. *Cheyenne Daily Leader*, November 30, 1876; *Bozeman Times*, February 1, 1877; *Life and Adventures of Frank Grouard*, 169; Trenholm and Carley, *Shoshonis*, 260.

8. Reproduced in McClellan, "A Day with the 'Fighting Cheyennes,'" *Motor Travel* (July 1930): 16. An original copy reposes with the Commissary Sergeant Thomas Hall Forsyth Collection, Manuscripts Library, Arizona Historical Society, Tucson.

9. Submittal of name of Private Thomas Ryan, January 8, 1880, Item 3369, LR, AGO 1880, RG 94, Records of the AGO, NA; Forsyth to Dorst, April 6, 1891, LR, AGO 1891, ibid.; *U.S. Army Gallantry and Meritorious Conduct*, 68; *Medal of Honor of the United States Army*, 229; McChristian, "A Soldier's Best and Noblest Remembrance," 31. For Dorst's protest over the brevet appointments, see Dorst to AG, U.S. Army, March 12, 1894, Joseph H. Dorst Papers, Special Collections, U.S. Military Academy Library, West Point, N.Y.

10. Headquarters, Powder River Expedition, General Orders No. 10, January 8, 1877, Sioux War Papers, Reel 280; *New York Herald*, January 14, 1877.

11. Crook to AAG, Military Division of the Missouri, January 8, 1877, with endorsements from Sheridan and Sherman, Sioux War Papers, Reel 280.

12. Quoted without attribution in Athearn, *Sherman and the Settlement of the West*, 314. See also Miles to Sherman, March 29, April 8, 1877, William T. Sherman Papers, Library of Congress, microfilm, Reel 23.

13. Manypenny, *Our Indian Wards*, 329.

14. For scouting activities in the area of Camp Robinson, see Second Lieutenant James Simpson, Third Cavalry, to Post Adjutant, Camp Robinson, January 1, 1877, Entry 3731, Box 47, Department of the Platte, LR, RG 393. For the Deadwood matter, see Sheridan to Crook, February 15, 1877, Entry 3731, Box 48, ibid.; and Sheridan to Crook, February 18, 1877 (quote), ibid.

15. Post Adjutant, Fort Laramie, to AG, Department of the Platte, March 6, 1877, enclosing Cummings's report of February 26, 1877, Entry 3731, Box 48, Department of the Platte, LR, RG 393; Buecker, *Fort Robinson*, 90–91; Schubert, *Outpost of the Sioux Wars*, 15. As a precaution, the patrols into and around the Black Hills continued through the

summer of 1877 on direction of Mackenzie's successor, Lieutenant Colonel Luther P. Bradley.

16. "Report of Brigadier General Crook," August 1, 1877, in *Report of the Secretary of War, 1877*, 85; Sheridan to Sherman, April 8, 1877, Sioux War Papers, Reel 280; "Report of First Lieutenant Jesse M. Lee, Spotted Tail Agency," August 10, 1877, in *Report of the Commissioner of Indian Affairs, 1877*, 66; Greene, *Yellowstone Command*, 187–92. Spotted Tail did not meet with Crazy Horse but with the chief's father. Olson, *Red Cloud and the Sioux Problem*, 237.

17. "Report of Lieutenant General P. H. Sheridan," October 25, 1877, in *Report of the Secretary of War, 1877*, 55; Powell, *People of the Sacred Mountain*, 2:1124–26. There appears to have been much distress manifested over the condition of the women and children, and this concern became a prime motivation for the Cheyennes to yield. Risingsun, "Chief Morning Star," 14. The Lame Deer Fight is described in Greene, *Yellowstone Command*, 205–14.

18. Powell, *People of the Sacred Mountain*, 2:1128, 1141–44; Schubert, *Outpost of the Sioux Wars*, 15; Bourke, *Mackenzie's Last Fight*, 43; Bourke, *On the Border with Crook*, 394; *New York Herald*, May 11, 1877; Sheridan to Sherman, March 23, 1877, Sioux War Papers, Reel 280. The Sioux surrenders at Red Cloud and Spotted Tail Agencies began in February and lasted into May. See Clark to Bourke, March 3, 1877, Sioux War Papers, Reel 280; First Lieutenant Jesse M. Lee to Assistant AAG, Department of the Platte, March 6, 1877; and Clark to Bourke, March 8, 1877; and accompanying papers, Entry 3731, Box 48, Department of the Platte, LR, RG 393. On March 19 Sheridan informed Sherman, confirming "the breaking up of the hostiles. A number of scattering lodges have already surrendered with arms and ponies at Red Cloud and Spotted-tail's, and quite a considerable number are on the way in between the Belle Fourche and Red Cloud Agency." Sheridan to Sherman, March 19, 1877, Sioux War Papers, Reel 280. Sheridan reported that more than 2,200 Indians—Lakotas and Cheyennes—came in to Spotted Tail and Red Cloud Agencies March 1–21. Another 303 Northern Cheyennes turned themselves in to Miles on April 22. "Report of Lieutenant General P. H. Sheridan," October 25, 1877. Other Cheyennes journeyed through the Big Horn Mountains to join relatives in Indian Territory, while a number traveled into Wyoming to live with the Shoshones and Arapahos at Wind River.

Greene, *Yellowstone Command*, 197; Svingen, *Northern Cheyenne Indian Reservation*, 12–13.

19. Powell, *People of the Sacred Mountain*, 2:1144–45; Buecker, *Fort Robinson*, 93. For the list of names of heads of families who surrendered, see Buecker and Paul, *Crazy Horse Surrender Ledger*, 105–6, 114.

20. *New York Herald*, May 11, 1877. Some later Cheyenne arrivals are discussed in Crook to AAG, Division of the Missouri, May 17, 1877, Sioux War Papers, Reel 281.

21. Sheridan to Sherman, May 7, 1876, Sioux War Papers, Reel 281. Concerning punishment, Sherman wrote: "If some of the worst Indians could be executed I doubt [but?] as the result would be good." Commissioner of Indian Affairs John Q. Smith to the Secretary of the Interior, May 23, 1877, with endorsement by Sherman, June 1, 1877, ibid.

22. Sheridan to Sherman, April 23, 1877, ibid.; Hyde, *Red Cloud's Folk*, 299–303.

23. Sheridan to Sherman, May 15, 1877, Sioux War Papers, Reel 281; Smith to Sheridan, May 18, 1877, ibid.; Sheridan to Smith, May 21, 1877, ibid. The Northern Cheyennes who went south with Lawton numbered approximately 980 people. First Lieutenant Charles A. Johnson, Fourteenth Infantry, to Commissioner Smith, June 4, 1877, LR by the Office of Indian Affairs, 1824–81, Red Cloud Agency, 1871–80, NA Microfilm Publication M234, Reel 720; Powell, *People of the Sacred Mountain*, 2:1149–54.

24. For the odyssey of the Northern Cheyennes from Indian Territory north, including the Fort Robinson Outbreak, see Powell, *People of the Sacred Mountain*, 2:1155–1261; and (most recently) Monnett, *Tell Them We Are Going Home*.

25. Robinson, *General Crook*, 308; Robinson, *Bad Hand*, 313–29; Welsh, *Medical Histories of Union Generals*, 85, 216.

26. Llewelleyn and Hoebel, *Cheyenne Way*, 215. For Little Wolf's last years, see Roberts, "Shame of Little Wolf." For Dull Knife and his descendents, see Starita, *Dull Knifes of Pine Ridge*.

Bibliography

Archival Materials

Arizona Historical Society, Tucson. Manuscripts Library. Commissary Sergeant Thomas Hall Forsyth Collection.

Brigham Young University, Provo, Utah. Harold B. Lee Library. L. Tom Perry Special Collections. Walter Mason Camp Collection.

Denver (Colo.) Public Library. Western History Department. Robert S. Ellison Papers.

The Gilcrease Institute, Tulsa, Okla. Philip G. Cole Collection.

Great Lakes Branch, National Archives, Chicago. Record Group 77, Records of the Office of the Chief of Engineers.

John D. McDermott Personal Collection, Rapid City, S.Dak. Edward Burnett, "Dull Knife." Unpublished manuscript, ca. 1935.

Library of Congress, Washington, D.C. William T. Sherman Papers. Microfilm.

National Archives, Washington, D.C. Regimental Returns of the Fourth Artillery, 1876–77. Microfilm Publication M727.

———. Regimental Returns of the Ninth Infantry, Fourteenth Infantry, and Twenty-third Infantry, 1876–77. Microfilm Publication M665.

———. Regimental Returns of the Third Cavalry, Fourth Cavalry, and Fifth Cavalry, 1876–77. Microfilm Publication M744.

———. Record Group 94. Records of the Adjutant General's Office.

———. Record Group 393. Records of the U.S. Army Continental Commands.

———. Sioux War Papers. Microfilm Publication M666. Reels 279–81.

Nebraska State Historical Society, Lincoln. Manuscript Division. Eli S. Ricker Collection.

The Newberry Library, Chicago. Center for the History of the American Indian. Manuscripts Division. First Lieutenant Henry Lawton to "My Dear Carter," November 29, 1876.

Southwest Museum, Los Angeles. Braun Research Library. George Bird Grinnell Collection.

State Historical Society of North Dakota, Bismarck. Manuscripts Division. First Lieutenant Henry Lawton to "My Dear Sergeant," December 21, 1876. Archives Ms. 20191.

U.S. Army Military History Institute, Carlisle, Pa. Army War College. Manuscripts Division. (Joseph R.) Gibson Personal Correspondence, 1875, 1883.

———. Indian Wars Miscellaneous Collection.

———. Order of Indian Wars Files.

U.S. Military Academy Library, West Point, N.Y. Special Collections. John Gregory Bourke Papers.

———. Joseph H. Dorst Papers.

Wyoming Historical Department, Cheyenne. Manuscript Division. WPA Collection.

Government Publications

Billings, John S. *Report on the Hygiene of the United States Army with Descriptions of Military Posts*. Circular No. 8. Washington, D.C.: War Department, Surgeon General's Office, 1875.

Heitman, Francis B. *Historical Register and Dictionary of the United States Army, from Its Organization, September 29, 1789, to March 2, 1903*. 2 vols. Washington, D.C.: Government Printing Office, 1903.

Kappler, Charles J. *Indian Affairs. Laws and Treaties*. 2 vols. Washington, D.C.: Government Printing Office, 1904.

The Medal of Honor of the United States Army. Washington, D.C.: Government Printing Office, 1948.

Outline Descriptions of the Posts in the Military Division of the Missouri, Commanded by Lieutenant General P. H. Sheridan. Chicago: Military Division of the Missouri, 1876. Reprint, Fort Collins, Colo.: Old Army Press, 1972.

Report of the Commissioner of Indian Affairs, 1876. Washington, D.C.: Government Printing Office, 1876.

Report of the Commissioner of Indian Affairs, 1877. Washington, D.C.: Government Printing Office, 1877.

Report of the Secretary of War, 1876. Washington, D.C.: Government Printing Office, 1876.

Report of the Secretary of War, 1877. Washington, D.C.: Government Printing Office, 1877.

Roster of Troops Serving in the Department of the Platte, Commanded by Brigadier General George Crook. Omaha: Headquarters, Department of the Platte, November 1876.

Tables of Distances and Itineraries of Routes between the Military Posts in, and to Certain Points Contiguous to, the Department of the Platte. Omaha: Engineers Office, Headquarters Department of the Platte, 1877.

Thian, Raphael P. *Notes Illustrating the Military Geography of the United States, 1813–1880.* Washington: Government Printing Office, 1881. Reprint, Austin: University of Texas Press, 1979.

U.S. Geological Survey. Quadrangle Map "Fraker Mountain, Wyo.," 1984.

———. Quadrangle Map "Kaycee, Wyoming," 1978.

Newspapers

Army and Navy Journal, 1876.

Bozeman Times, 1877.

Cheyenne Daily Leader, 1876.

Chicago Tribune, 1876.

Lincoln (Neb.) Sunday Journal and Star, 1932.

Memphis Daily Appeal, 1876.

The National Tribune, 1923, 1927–28.

The New York Daily Graphic, 1876.

New York Herald, 1876–77.

New York Tribune, 1876.

Omaha Republican, 1876.

Winners of the West, 1939.

Books

Athearn, Robert G. *William Tecumseh Sherman and the Settlement of the West.* Norman: University of Oklahoma Press, 1956.

Berthrong, Donald J. *The Southern Cheyennes*. Norman: University of Oklahoma Press, 1963.

Bourke, John G. *Mackenzie's Last Fight with the Cheyennes: A Winter Campaign in Wyoming and Montana*. Governor's Island, N.Y.: Military Service Institution, 1890. Reprint, Bellevue, Neb.: Old Army Press, 1970.

———. *On the Border with Crook*. New York: Charles Scribners's Sons, 1891.

Brady, Cyrus Townsend. *Indian Fights and Fighters*. New York: Doubleday, Page, 1904.

Brown, Dee. *Fort Phil Kearny: An American Saga*. New York: G. P. Putnam's Sons, 1962.

Bruce, Robert. *The Fighting Norths and Pawnee Scouts: Narratives and Reminiscences of Military Service on the Old Frontier*. New York: Privately printed, 1932.

Buecker, Thomas R. *Fort Robinson and the American West, 1874–1899*. Lincoln: Nebraska State Historical Society, 1999.

Buecker, Thomas R., and R. Eli Paul, eds. *The Crazy Horse Surrender Ledger*. Lincoln: Nebraska State Historical Society, 1994.

Chalfant, William Y. *The Cheyennes at Dark Water Creek: The Last Fight of the Red River War*. Norman: University of Oklahoma Press, 1997.

Crook, George. *General George Crook: His Autobiography*. Edited by Martin F. Schmitt. Norman: University of Oklahoma Press, 1960.

Cullum, George W., ed. *Biographical Register of the Officers and Graduates of the U.S. Military Academy at West Point, N.Y., from Its Establishment, in 1802, to 1890*. Vol. 3. Boston: Houghton Mifflin, 1891.

DeBarthe, Joe. *Life and Adventures of Frank Grouard*. Edited by Edgar I. Stewart. Norman: University of Oklahoma Press, 1958.

Dodge, Richard Irving. *Our Wild Indians: Thirty-three Years Personal Experience among the Red Men of the Great West*. Hartford, Conn.: A. D. Worthington, 1883.

———. *The Powder River Expedition Journals of Colonel Richard Irving Dodge*. Edited by Wayne R. Kime. Norman: University of Oklahoma Press, 1997.

Dunlay, Thomas W. *Wolves for the Blue Soldiers: Indian Scouts and Aux-iliaries with the United States Army, 1860–90.* Lincoln: University of Nebraska Press, 1982.

Eastman, Charles A. *Indian Heroes and Great Chieftains.* Boston: Little, Brown, 1929.

Flannery, L. G., ed. *John Hunton's Diary.* 5 vols. Lingle, Wyo.: Privately printed, 1958.

Fowler, Loretta. *Arapaho Politics, 1851–1978: Symbols in Crises of Author-ity.* Lincoln: University of Nebraska Press, 1982.

Fox, Richard Allan, Jr. *Archaeology, History, and Custer's Last Battle: The Little Big Horn Reexamined.* Norman: University of Oklahoma Press, 1993.

Garlington, Ernest A. *The Lieutenant E. A. Garlington Narrative: Part 1.* Edited by John M. Carroll. Bryan, Tex.: Privately printed, 1978.

Gray, John S. *Centennial Campaign: The Sioux War of 1876.* Fort Collins, Colo.: Old Army Press, 1976.

———. *Custer's Last Campaign: Mitch Boyer and the Little Bighorn Reconstructed.* Lincoln: University of Nebraska Press, 1991.

Greene, Jerome A. *Slim Buttes, 1876: An Episode of the Great Sioux War.* Norman: University of Oklahoma Press, 1982.

———. *Yellowstone Command: Colonel Nelson A. Miles and the Great Sioux War, 1876–1877.* Lincoln: University of Nebraska Press, 1991.

———, comp., ed. *Battles and Skirmishes of the Great Sioux War, 1876–1877: The Military View.* Norman: University of Oklahoma Press, 1993.

———, comp., ed. *Lakota and Cheyenne: Indian Views of the Great Sioux War, 1876–1877.* Norman: University of Oklahoma Press, 1994.

Grinnell, George Bird. *The Cheyenne Indians.* 2 vols. New York: Cooper Square, 1923.

———. *The Fighting Cheyennes.* Norman: University of Oklahoma Press, 1956.

———. *Two Great Scouts and Their Pawnee Battalion: The Experiences of Frank J. North and Luther H. North, Pioneers in the Great West, 1856–1882, and Their Defence [sic] of the Building of the Union Pacific Railroad.* Cleveland: Arthur H. Clark, 1928.

Hanson, James A. *Little Chief's Gatherings: The Smithsonian Institution's G. K. Warren 1855–1856 Plains Indian Collection and the New York State Library's 1855–1857 Warren Expedition Journals*. Crawford, Neb.: Fur Press, 1996.

Hanson, Margaret Brock, ed. *Powder River Country: The Papers of J. Elmer Brock*. Cheyenne: Frontier, 1981.

Hassrick, Royal B. *The Sioux: Life and Customs of a Warrior Society*. Norman: University of Oklahoma Press, 1964.

Hebard, Grace Raymond, and Earl A. Brininstool. *The Bozeman Trail*. 2 vols. Cleveland: Arthur H. Clark, 1922. Reprint, Glendale, Calif.: Arthur H. Clark, 1960.

Hedren, Paul L. *First Scalp for Custer: The Skirmish at Warbonnet Creek, Nebraska, July 17, 1876*. Glendale, Calif.: Arthur H. Clark, 1980.

———. *Fort Laramie in 1876: Chronicle of a Frontier Post at War*. Lincoln: University of Nebraska Press, 1988.

———. *Sitting Bull's Surrender at Fort Buford: An Episode in American History*. Williston, N.Dak.: Fort Union Association, 1997.

Hoebel, E. Adamson. *The Cheyennes, Indians of the Great Plains*. New York: Holt, Rinehart, and Winston, 1960.

Hoig, Stan. *The Battle of the Washita*. Lincoln: University of Nebraska Press, 1979.

———. *The Peace Chiefs of the Cheyennes*. Norman: University of Oklahoma Press, 1980.

———. *The Sand Creek Massacre*. Norman: University of Oklahoma Press, 1961.

Hutton, Paul A. *Phil Sheridan and His Army*. Lincoln: University of Nebraska Press, 1985.

Hyde, George E. *Life of George Bent Written from His Letters*. Edited by Savoie Lottinville. Norman: University of Oklahoma Press, 1968.

———. *Red Cloud's Folk: A History of the Oglala Sioux Indians*. Norman: University of Oklahoma Press, 1936.

———. *Spotted Tail's Folk: A History of the Brule Sioux*. Norman: University of Oklahoma Press, 1961.

Jackson, Donald. *Custer's Gold*. New Haven: Yale University Press, 1966.

Josephy, Alvin M. *The Civil War in the American West*. New York: Alfred A. Knopf, 1991.

Keenan, Jerry. *The Wagon Box Fight*. Boulder, Colo.: Lightning Tree, 1992.

Larson, Robert W. *Red Cloud, Warrior-Statesman of the Lakota Sioux*. Norman: University of Oklahoma Press, 1997.

Leckie, William H. *The Military Conquest of the Southern Plains*. Norman: University of Oklahoma Press, 1963.

Liddic, Bruce R., and Paul Harbaugh, eds. *Camp on Custer: Transcribing the Custer Myth*. Spokane, Wash.: Arthur H. Clark, 1995.

Llewelleyn, K. N., and E. Adamson Hoebel. *The Cheyenne Way: Conflict and Case Law in Primitive Jurisprudence*. Norman: University of Oklahoma Press, 1941.

Madsen, Brigham D. *Glory Hunter: A Biography of Patrick Edward Connor*. Salt Lake City: University of Utah Press, 1990.

Mangum, Neil C. *Battle of the Rosebud: Prelude to the Little Bighorn*. El Segundo, Calif.: Upton and Sons, 1987.

Manypenny, George W. *Our Indian Wards*. Cincinnati: Robert Clark, 1880. Reprint, New York: Da Capo, 1972.

Marquis, Thomas. *The Cheyennes of Montana*. Edited by Thomas D. West. Algonac, Mich.: Reference Publications, 1978.

———. *Keep the Last Bullet for Yourself: The True Story of Custer's Last Stand*. New York: Two Continents, 1976.

———. *A Warrior Who Fought Custer*. Minneapolis: Midwest, 1931.

Marquis, Thomas, comp., and Ronald H. Limbaugh, ed. *Cheyenne and Sioux: The Reminiscences of Four Indians and a White Soldier*. Stockton, Calif.: Pacific Center for Western Historical Studies, University of the Pacific, 1973.

McChristian, Douglas C. *The U.S. Army in the West, 1870–1880: Uniforms, Weapons, and Equipment*. Norman: University of Oklahoma Press, 1995.

McGinnis, Anthony. *Counting Coup and Cutting Horses*. Evergreen, Colo.: Cordillera, 1990.

Miles, Nelson A. *Serving the Republic: Memoirs of the Civil and Military Life of Nelson A. Miles, Lieutenant General, United States Army*. New York: Harper and Brothers, 1911.

Monnett, John H. *The Battle of Beecher Island and the Indian War of 1867–1869*. Niwot: University Press of Colorado, 1992.

———. *Massacre at Cheyenne Hole: Lieutenant Austin Henely and the Sappa Creek Controversy*. Niwot: University Press of Colorado, 1999.

————. *Tell Them We Are Going Home: The Odyssey of the Northern Cheyenne*. Norman: University of Oklahoma Press, 2001.

Moore, John H. *The Cheyenne*. Cambridge, Mass.: Blackwell, 1996.

————. *The Cheyenne Nation*. Lincoln: University of Nebraska Press, 1987.

Murray, Robert A. *Military Posts in the Powder River Country of Wyoming, 1865–1894*. Lincoln: University of Nebraska Press, 1968.

Neff, Emily Ballew, with Wynne H. Phelan. *Frederic Remington: The Hogg Brothers Collection of the Museum of Fine Arts, Houston*. Princeton, N.J.: Princeton University Press in Association with the Museum of Fine Arts, Houston, 2000.

North, Luther. *Man of the Plains: Recollections of Luther North, 1856–1882*. Edited by Donald F. Danker. Lincoln: University of Nebraska Press, 1961.

Olson, James C. *Red Cloud and the Sioux Problem*. Lincoln: University of Nebraska Press, 1965.

Paul, R. Eli, ed. *The Nebraska Indian Wars Reader, 1865–1877*. Lincoln: University of Nebraska Press, 1998.

Pierce, Michael D. *The Most Promising Young Officer: A Life of Ranald Slidell Mackenzie*. Norman: University of Oklahoma Press, 1993.

Porter, Joseph C. *Paper Medicine Man: John Gregory Bourke and His American West*. Norman: University of Oklahoma Press, 1986.

Powell, Peter J. *The Cheyennes, Ma'heo'o's People: A Critical Bibliography*. Bloomington: Indiana University Press, 1980.

————. *People of the Sacred Mountain: A History of the Northern Cheyenne Chiefs and Warrior Societies, 1830–1879, with an Epilogue, 1969–1974*. 2 vols. San Francisco: Harper and Row, 1981.

————. *Sweet Medicine: The Continuing Role of the Sacred Arrows, the Sun Dance, and the Sacred Buffalo Hat in Northern Cheyenne History*. 2 vols. Norman: University of Oklahoma Press, 1969.

Robinson, Charles M., III. *Bad Hand: A Biography of General Ranald S. Mackenzie*. Austin: State House, 1993.

————. *General Crook and the Western Frontier*. Norman: University of Oklahoma Press, 2001.

————. *A Good Year to Die: The Story of the Great Sioux War*. New York: Random House, 1995.

Schubert, Frank N. *Outpost of the Sioux Wars: A History of Fort Robinson*. Lincoln: University of Nebraska Press, 1993.

Smith, Sherry L. *Sagebrush Soldier: Private William Earl Smith's View of the Sioux War of 1876*. Norman: University of Oklahoma Press, 1989.

Stands in Timber, John, and Margot Liberty. *Cheyenne Memories*. New Haven: Yale University Press, 1967.

Starita, Joe. *The Dull Knifes of Pine Ridge: A Lakota Odyssey*. New York: G. P. Putnam's Sons, 1995.

Stewart, Edgar I. *Custer's Luck*. Norman: University of Oklahoma Press, 1955.

Svingen, Orlan J. *The Northern Cheyenne Indian Reservation, 1877–1900*. Niwot: University Press of Colorado, 1993.

Taunton, Francis A., ed. *Sidelights of the Sioux Wars*. London: English Westerners' Society, 1967.

Trenholm, Virginia Cole, and Maurine Carley. *The Shoshonis, Sentinels of the Rockies*. Norman: University of Oklahoma Press, 1964.

U.S. Army Gallantry and Meritorious Conduct, 1866–1891. Alexandria, Va.: Planchet, 1986.

Utley, Robert M. *Frontier Regulars: The United States Army and the Indian, 1866–1890*. New York: Macmillan, 1973.

———. *Frontiersmen in Blue: The United States Army and the Indian, 1848–1865*. New York: Macmillan, 1967.

———. *The Lance and the Shield: The Life and Times of Sitting Bull*. New York: Random House, 1993.

Vaughn, J. W. *The Battle of Platte Bridge*. Norman: University of Oklahoma Press, 1963.

———. *The Reynolds Campaign on Powder River*. Norman: University of Oklahoma Press, 1961.

———. *With Crook at the Rosebud*. Harrisburg, Pa.: Stackpole, 1956.

Vestal, Stanley. *Sitting Bull: Champion of the Sioux*. Norman: University of Oklahoma Press, 1957.

Welsh, Jack D. *Medical Histories of Union Generals*. Kent, Ohio: Kent State University Press, 1996.

Werner, Fred. *The Dull Knife Battle: "Doomsday for the Northern Cheyennes."* Greeley, Colo.: Werner, 1981.

West, Elliott. *The Contested Plains: Indians, Goldseekers, and the Rush to Colorado*. Lawrence: University Press of Kansas, 1998.

Wheeler, Homer W. *Buffalo Days*. Indianapolis: Bobbs-Merrill, 1923.

Williams, Thomas Benton. *The Soul of the Red Man*. Privately printed, 1937.

Wooster, Robert. *The Military and United States Indian Policy, 1865–1903*. New Haven: Yale University Press, 1988.

Articles

Anderson, Harry H. "Cheyennes at the Little Big Horn—A Study of Statistics." *North Dakota History* 27 (spring, 1960): 3–15.

Bourke, John G. "The Medicine Men of the Apaches." In *Ninth Annual Report of the Bureau of Ethnology*, 480–83. Washington, D.C.: Government Printing Office, 1892.

Buecker, Thomas R. "The Journals of James S. McClellan, 1st Sgt., Company H, 3rd Cavalry." *Annals of Wyoming* 57 (spring 1985): 21–34.

———. "The Long Summer: Red Cloud Agency and Camp Robinson in 1876." *Papers of the Seventh Little Big Horn Symposium* (1993), 1–12.

———. "Lt. William Philo Clark's Sioux War Report and Little Big Horn Map." *Greasy Grass* 7 (May 1991): 11–21.

Clow, Richmond. "General Philip Sheridan's Legacy: The Sioux Pony Campaign of 1876." *Nebraska History* 57 (winter 1976): 461–77.

Condit, Thelma Gatchell. "The Hole in the Wall." *Annals of Wyoming* 28 (April 1956): 41–65.

"Council at Sites of Surround." *Nebraska History Magazine* 15 (October–December 1944): 279–87.

Daniel, Forest W. "Dismounting the Sioux." *North Dakota History* 41 (summer 1974): 8–13.

Danker, Donald F. "The Pawnee Scouts and the North Brothers." *The Trail Guide* 11 (March 1966): 1–13.

"Detail Map of the Pine Ridge Country in the Middle Seventies." *Nebraska History* 22 (January–February 1941): 16–17 (insert).

Garnett, William. "The Surround of Red Cloud and Red Leaf." Interview by Judge Eli S. Ricker, January 10, 1907. *Nebraska History Magazine* 15 (October–December 1934): 288–91.

Gatchell, T. J. "The Battle on the Red Fork." *Old Travois Trails* 3 (July–August 1942): 29–36, 45.

Gray, John S. "Frank Grouard: Kanaka Scout or Mulatto Renegade?" *Chicago Westerners Brandbook* 16 (October 1959): 57–59, 60–64.

Greene, Francis V. "The United States Army," *Scribner's Magazine* 30 (November 1901): 593–613.

Greene, Jerome A. "George Crook." In *Soldiers West: Biographies from the Military Frontier*, edited by Paul A. Hutton, 115–36. Lincoln: University of Nebraska Press, 1987.

————. "The Hayfield Fight: A Reappraisal of a Neglected Action." *Montana, the Magazine of Western History* 22 (autumn 1972): 30–43.

————, ed. "Chasing Sitting Bull and Crazy Horse: Two Fourteenth U.S. Infantry Diaries of the Great Sioux War." *Nebraska History* 78 (winter 1997): 187–201.

————. ed. "Conflict in Dakota Territory: Episodes of the Great Sioux War." *South Dakota History* 23 (spring 1993): 1–47.

Hanson, James A. "A Forgotten Fur Trade Trail." *Nebraska History* 68 (spring 1987): 2–9.

Hill, Burton S. "Bozeman and the Bozeman Trail." *Annals of Wyoming* 36 (October 1964): 204–33.

Marquis, Thomas B. "Red Ripe's Squaw." *Century Magazine* 118 (June 1929): 201–9.

Mattison, Ray H., ed. "The Harney Expedition against the Sioux: The Journal of Capt. John B. S. Todd." *Nebraska History* 43 (June 1962): 89–130.

McChristian, Douglas C. "A Soldier's Best and Noblest Remembrance: First Sergeant Thomas H. Forsyth in the Dull Knife Fight— November 25, 1876." In *The Dull Knife Symposium*, 27–31. Sheridan, Wyo.: Fort Phil Kearny/Bozeman Trail Association, 1989.

Mears, David. "Campaigning against Crazy Horse." *Proceedings and Collections of the Nebraska State Historical Society* 15 (1907): 68–77.

"Military Reports on the Red Cloud–Red Leaf Surround." *Nebraska History Magazine* 15 (October–December 1934): 291–95.

Motor Travel. The series of articles that appeared in this periodical between 1929 and 1931 defies easy classification because of confusing similarities or variations in titles, subtitles, and authors (some of whom have not been identified). Articles entitled "Pawnee Trails and Trailers" appeared in the issues of June 1929 (8–11), July 1929 (5–7), September 1929 (9–13), October 1929 (9–13), January 1930 (20–21), February 1930 (17–20), March 1930 (17–20), and May

1931 (20–23). Those entitled "A Day with the Fighting Cheyennes" appeared in April 1930 (17–20), May 1930 (15–19), June 1930 (15–18), July 1930 (15–18), August 1930 (15–18), September 1930 (7–11), October 1930 (18–20), November 1930 (15–17), January 1931 (20–22), and February 1931 (19–22). Those entitled "The Fighting Norths and Pawnee Scouts" appeared in the issues of March 1931 (19–22), April 1931 (16–19), June 1931 (18–21), July 1931 (17–19), August 1931 (17–19), September 1931 (15–17), October 1931 (16–18), November 1931 (16–18), and December 1931 (18–20).

Murray, Robert A. "Cantonment Reno/Fort McKinney No. 1—New Views of an Old Wyoming Army Post." *Annals of Wyoming* 48 (fall 1976): 275–79.

Pate, J'Nell. "Ranald S. Mackenzie." In *Soldiers West: Biographies from the Military Frontier*, edited by Paul A. Hutton, 177–92. Lincoln: University of Nebraska Press, 1987.

Powell, Peter J. "High Bull's Victory Roster." *Montana, the Magazine of Western History* 25 (January 1975): 14–21.

Risingsun, Ted. "Chief Morning Star: Cheyenne Man of the Plains." In *The Dull Knife Symposium*, 13–19. Sheridan, Wyo.: Fort Phil Kearny/Bozeman Trail Association, 1989.

Roberts, Gary L. "The Shame of Little Wolf." *Montana, the Magazine of Western History* 28 (July 1978): 36–47.

Robrock, David P. "A History of Fort Fetterman, Wyoming, 1867–1882." *Annals of Wyoming* 48 (spring 1976): 5–76.

Smith, Sherry L. "The Bozeman—Trail to Death and Glory." *Annals of Wyoming* 55 (spring 1983): 32–50.

Wade, Arthur P. "The Military Command Structure: The Great Plains, 1853–1891." *Journal of the West* 15 (July 1976): 5–22.

Woodward, George A. "Some Experiences with the Cheyennes." *The United Service* 1 (April 1879): 184–95.

Unpublished Works

Easton, Karen M. "Getting into Uniform: Northern Cheyenne Scouts in the United States Army, 1876–81." Master's thesis, University of Wyoming, Laramie, 1985.

Greene, Jerome A. "Warbonnets and Longknives: Military Use of the Bozeman Trail in the 1860s." Paper delivered at the Bozeman Trail Symposium, Bozeman, Mont., July 28–30, 1999.

Hedren, Paul L. "Beyond Red Cloud's War: The Bozeman Trail in the 1870s." Paper delivered at the Bozeman Trail Symposium, Bozeman, Mont., July 28–30, 1999.

Roberts, Gary L. "Sand Creek: Tragedy and Symbol." Ph.D. diss., University of Oklahoma, 1984.

Index